Traffic

Traffic

Genius, Rivalry, and Delusion in the
Billion-Dollar Race to Go Viral

Ben Smith

Penguin Press • New York • 2023

PENGUIN PRESS
An imprint of Penguin Random House LLC
penguinrandomhouse.com

LIBRARY OF CONGRESS CATALOGING-IN-PUBLICATION DATA

Names: Smith, Ben (Journalist), author.
Title: Traffic : genius, rivalry, and delusion in the billion-dollar race
   to go viral / Ben Smith.
Description: New York : Penguin Press, 2023. | Includes bibliographical
   references and index.
Identifiers: LCCN 2022028861 | ISBN 9780593299753 (hardcover) |
   ISBN 9780593299760 (ebook)
Subjects: LCSH: Peretti, Jonah. | Denton, Nicholas. | News Web
   sites—United States. | Digital media—Economic aspects—United States.
   | Internet industry—United States.
Classification: LCC PN4867.2 .S65 2023 | DDC 070.4/30973—dc23/eng/20220927
LC record available at https://lccn.loc.gov/2022028861

Printed in the United States of America
1st Printing

BOOK DESIGN BY LUCIA BERNARD

For Liena

Contents

1

....

The Bet

Jonah Peretti and his best friend at grad school, Cameron Marlow, bet on everything. The sum was always two dollars. They'd bet on the winner of a basketball game, or whether Jonah could jump up on top of a chest-high wall in Cambridge, Massachusetts. Their patter was objectively kind of annoying, these two skinny graduate students with their floppy brown hair, marching around the campus of the Massachusetts Institute of Technology, where they'd met in the fall of 1999, trying to one-up each other. Cameron, fresh out of college at twenty-two, was one of the youngest in the new class at the MIT Media Lab, and he wore that chip on his shoulder. Jonah was twenty-five. His left-wing politics and laughing California calm failed to conceal his intense competitiveness.

So it made sense that when Jonah went viral, truly viral, for the first time, on January 5, 2001, his friend and rival wouldn't let him bask in his glory. Cameron said it was a fluke. The internet was too random, culture too unpredictable, to pull something like that off again. "Two-dollar bet," Jonah suggested automatically. He'd spend the next twenty years trying to win that bet.

January 5, 2001, was a Friday, a freezing day in Cambridge. It was the last year of the American Century, when public intellectuals were spending their time worrying about the ennui at the end of history. The question was what young Americans, having conquered the Soviet Union and dominated the world, were supposed to do next. Jonah, whose lean height and bouncy gait gave you the sense that he was about to take flight, had turned twenty-seven on New Year's Day. He and Cameron were charting the digital future from their offices looking into the Cube, the glass box at the center of the Media Lab. Cameron was working on turning old issues of *Time* magazine into digital visualizations. In the next office, Jonah was supposed to be completing the research project on education that had gotten him admitted to MIT from his position running a high school computer lab in New Orleans. But, in fact, Jonah was on nike.com, looking at sneakers.

The company was letting shoppers customize shoes. Jonah chose a pair of size 10 Zoom XC USA running shoes and typed "fuck" into the white box where you could put a word of your choice. The site blocked it. To test how sophisticated the system was, he tried a different word: "sweatshop." It went through, so he charged the fifty dollars to his credit card and waited for his sneakers.

Instead, he got an email from Nike. His submission violated their policies—in particular, one against "inappropriate slang."

Jonah wrote back, noting that "sweatshop" "is in fact part of standard English," defined by Webster's dictionary as a "factory in which workers are employed for long hours at low wages and under unhealthy conditions."

He received another polite rejection. He didn't mind being a little annoying, obviously, and kept writing back. And after seven emails from Nike, Jonah made one final request: "Could you please send me a color snapshot of the ten-year-old Vietnamese girl who makes my shoes?"

That was the end of his correspondence with polite Nike customer service representatives. Jonah was pleased with his prank and, in particular, the line about the Vietnamese girl, so he put all the emails in order and submitted the exchange to *Harper's Magazine*, hoping he could reach what was then the pinnacle of success and attention for something like that: the *Harper's* Readings section, a monthly—print!—compilation of odd and timely documents. The magazine declined, so on January 15, he forwarded the email to ten friends. Some forwarded it from there—it was the kind of slacker anti-corporate joke that hit at the complacent end of the Clinton era. On January 17, Jonah's old roommate from New Orleans, Tim Shey, put the text of the exchange on his personal website, something people were starting to call a blog. Then bigger websites, like *MetaFilter* and *Slashdot*, picked it up. Over the next few weeks, the email traveled from inbox to inbox, a catchy little corporate protest. Pretty soon Jonah was getting emails from newspaper reporters and, then, a booker for the biggest morning television program in America, the *Today* show.

On February 28, 2001, just six weeks after he forwarded that first email, Jonah was sitting nervously on a gray couch in Rockefeller Center in a gray wool Calvin Klein jacket that was too big at the shoulders and not quite long enough for his long arms. He had no real idea where to look or what to say, but told Katie Couric that he'd read some bad things in the newspapers about Nike's labor practices. That was really all he had—he didn't know much about sweatshops and was winging it. He thought Couric could sense his weakness. So she did his work for him, reading his line about Vietnamese child labor to a Nike spokesman who had joined them over video link from Phoenix. The spokesman, too, was trying to make the best of it, defending his company's labor practices—while thanking Jonah for calling attention to Nike's foray onto the internet.

"Traffic and contact between Nike and consumers is up 75 percent in some categories and 100 percent in others," the spokesman, a Nike Swoosh on his tight black T-shirt, defiantly told Couric. "There's certainly more awareness of the fact that we personalize shoes."

Couric thanked her guests and moved on to the next segment, an interview with *Spin City* star Heather Locklear. Jonah walked off the set feeling like an imposter. He wasn't studying economics or international relations or labor at MIT. He didn't know anything about sweatshops. What he was studying was the same thing the Nike spokesman had fixated on: he knew about traffic. As it turned out, Jonah would devote his career to collecting it and quantifying it, immersing himself in its patterns and in its power, which could equally hold Nike to account over its labor practices, or just sell sneakers.

Traffic was, literally, just the record of the request your desktop computer made of the computer hosting the article you were reading. When one of Katie Couric's producers visited Tim Shey's blog, that visit counted as one view, the elemental unit of traffic. But traffic, Jonah was among the first to discover, wasn't merely mechanical. Traffic was human emotion, human psychology, desire and curiosity and humor. It was easiest to see this sort of pattern when you felt like an outsider, an alien. Jonah sometimes looked at behavior the way the linguist Noam Chomsky, an MIT professor, looked at language. Chomsky wrote about how a Martian anthropologist would look at humans, and how simple and uniform our speech would look through alien eyes.

Jonah had been making a study of humans since kindergarten, when his mother, Della, had enrolled him in the Oakland public school system. He was a happy, gregarious little kid, the kind who babbled away to puzzled friends about the polar ice caps. The first day of kindergarten, his dad moved out. And as that year went on, Della noticed that something seemed a little wrong: this kid, so interested in ideas, had no interest at all in symbols—in particular, in letters. Soon, Jonah was diagnosed with dyslexia and enrolled in special ed, and his mother, getting her graduate degree in education, was losing sleep worrying about the dire fate of smart, angry kids who never learned to read.

Jonah felt trapped in school, isolated among strange children who could look at the blackboard and understand it. He looked forward to Saturdays, when he took a pottery class. The clay absorbed his anger, his desire for freedom, and his intelligence: he realized he could make long spindly legs, and that if he built a giant monster around the finished legs, the clay would contract and make the structure surprisingly secure, standing half as tall as him. Finally, in fourth grade, he began to read, painstakingly, recognizing words rather than sounding them out, and he gave up on the monsters.

In seventh grade, he left his neighborhood school for Claremont Middle School, where he was even more obviously an outsider, the gangly white boy in a class that was mostly Black, mixed in with the children of Cambodian refugees. Della got a job teaching there, and taught him one class she knew he'd never survive on his own—French. She passed him by ignoring the errors that fell within the scope of the school's accommodations for his dyslexia.

Della used money she'd inherited from her father to pull Jonah out of public school for high school, sending him to the College Preparatory School, a small private high school whose progressive philosophy was belied by its intense focus on getting students into Harvard and Stanford. His classmates recalled a sweet-natured student whose competitive edge came out mostly through sports. He was the star of the volleyball team and trained obsessively until he could dunk a basketball. Della edited every paper he turned in, ironing out the typos.

Nobody thought he was a particularly brilliant student until the junior year philosophy class, a sort of Nietzsche for Dummies, where it became clear that the kind of slow, deep reading that philosophy requires matched both Jonah's disabilities and what his friend Romesh Ratnesar recognized as his "extreme gifts." Romesh went on, like many of their classmates, to the bosom of the establishment, Stanford and *Time* magazine. Jonah applied to only one college, the University of California, Santa Cruz, the unconventional, cross-disciplinary school that the Grateful Dead's surviving members would later choose as the right "seat of neo-Bohemian culture" to house their archive.

Jonah had been steeped in Berkeley's leftist politics, and had spent high school reading anti-corporate tracts and theories of anarchism, along with translations of the Tao Te Ching and other works of Eastern philosophy that were ubiquitous at local bookstores. He began to feel the limits of those politics at Santa Cruz, where he majored in environmental studies but sometimes bridled at what he felt was the discipline's antihuman thrust and its tendency to choose nostalgia over technology, and gravitated toward the more abstract spaces of Santa Cruz's famous History of Consciousness program. Jonah loved theory; the more unskimmably dense the subject, the more his painfully slow reading could be an advantage. He read Marx and Kant and Freud, and was one of a small number of male teaching assistants in an Introduction to Women's Studies class, where college students wrestled with the lines between sex and rape, and grappled in sometimes comical ways with America's various histories of oppression. After the class's Black teaching assistants walked out in protest once, the professor convened a healing session in which the teaching assistants passed around a crystal. During the heartfelt discussion of race that ensued, one teaching assistant took the crystal and turned the discussion to the millennia of oppression of her own minority:

Wiccans. Jonah stifled his laughter, and emerged with a resistance to a certain kind of performative ideology.

Jonah's favorite professor at Santa Cruz was Donna Haraway, a creator of what was then called cyberfeminism and the author of the famous "Cyborg Manifesto," an argument that the new technologies and modes of communication had overtaken old arguments about men and women, nature and nurture. He was a star undergrad, the kind who published dense articles in scholarly journals about the way pop culture shaped new kinds of identities in "late capitalism." Jonah struck Haraway as a deep reader, curious and open to criticism. She wasn't surprised that he became a "generative and also controversial figure in technoculture and culture at large."

Jonah struggled to merge his playful interest in media with loftier ideas about late-stage capitalism. Soon after he graduated in 1996, he published a dense article in the philosophical journal *Negations* about the links between capitalism, media, and the formation of identity in an already disorienting media age. When he came home from college, Jonah put some of what he'd absorbed about capitalism and media into practice. There was a new set of billboards around town that was driving him nuts: a drink called Tejava was marketing itself with images of smiling Javanese women and the loaded (at least to a young academic) slogan "The purest expression of tea." Late one summer night, he climbed up the outside of a building onto the roof to spray-paint, in six-foot-tall letters, a new word over the slogan, so it read "The purest expression of exploitation."

There was a straight line from those graffitied billboards to the Nike email, both in their hazily leftist politics and in Jonah's preference for a kind of individual, unfettered action. He would note later that the internet was a far better outlet than graffiti for spreading a message, with "more impact and leverage with less legal risk!"

Jonah took a detour after college, teaching computer science at a private school in New Orleans while he applied to the MIT Media Lab, which sat at the intersection of all the ideas and technologies that captivated him. He was rejected the first time, and taught another year before he was admitted. Arriving in Cambridge, he loved MIT's nerd paradise as much as he'd hated elementary school. He was "finally out on the playground with the other kids," he'd later write.

To be at the heart of a big viral moment like the Nike email, and follow the vertiginous path from your bedroom in Cambridge to Katie Couric's couch, and back, to have all that traffic—that is, attention—rain down on you, is to have your life redirected. Some people react to experiences like this by embracing the cause they stumbled upon. Others spend their lives trying to replicate the fleeting moment of celebrity. But Jonah found the camera's gaze personally uncomfortable. He also cared too much about the medium to fully embrace the message, and turned down an opportunity to endorse a union-made line of golf T-shirts because, he thought, he'd never wear that stuff. So Jonah went back to Cambridge to measure the same substance the hapless Nike spokesman had touted: traffic.

Jonah made a pair of charts, which both followed the now familiar curve of an internet phenomenon: the exponential rise in traffic, the spike, the gradual decay. One chart showed the number of emails he'd gotten about the prank, which rose to a peak of more than 300 a day on February 23 and 24, and then gradually declined, ending with a total of 3,655. Even the *Today* show interview could produce only a second, smaller, spike. The other chart was of the traffic to Shey's website, which exploded to more than 2,500 visitors one day in late January and ultimately reached about 70,000 people—more views than on an established website like *The Village Voice*. You could just watch the tides of human attention move, and Cameron, looking over Jonah's shoulder, thought you might be able to map this engagement in real time. Cameron switched the focus of his research to something he called Blogdex, a new kind of measurement tool that could turn internet conversations into math—tracking, measuring, and mapping them.

The numbers were still, by the standards of today's internet, quite small. But they'd been a spark, Jonah realized, for a fire that scorched a giant corporation's multimillion-dollar marketing campaign. That spring, he drafted an analysis of the "sweatshop" episode and played around with words for what had happened: "culture jamming" and "micromedia" were favorite terms of the moment. Later, we'd call it "social media."

"A broad social and technical transformation is creating new possibilities for political participation and direct action," he wrote in a guide for activists, reflecting on this new power. "Although the future is always uncertain, it is clear that there are exciting opportunities for participation right now."

Jonah sought to draw broader lessons from his experience. Cameron was skeptical. Jonah had just gotten lucky, he insisted. Cameron saw a profound randomness to the power of these new digital social networks and thought it would be impossible to rig them or control them, to replicate your past success. The substance of the challenge was clear to them both. Cameron bet Jonah that he could never do it again, that he could never control the power he'd glimpsed. Jonah leapt to take the bet, to show that he could re-create his success, systematize it, bottle it up.

He knew where he needed to go to try his luck. Back in 2001, the young men at MIT knew that they needed to go not west, but south. The place to prove yourself in the nascent, experimental new media scene was downtown Manhattan.

2

···

Traffic Control

J onah moved to New York in the summer of 2001, the last few months of American innocence. His profession, well, that wasn't so clear—technology? media? comedy?—but fortunately he'd found a job that didn't make him decide, even if it was a bit hard to explain. He'd been hired by John Johnson, an inquisitive, soft-spoken heir to the Johnson & Johnson pharmaceutical fortune, to serve as head of "research and development" for Johnson's art-and-tech not-for-profit, called Eyebeam. Jonah rented a sixth-floor walk-up over a hipster Cuban restaurant on the corner of Houston and Elizabeth in SoHo, and began work, which is to say he began trying to figure out his next viral prank.

Cameron's ticket to New York arrived the next spring, in the form of the man who would soon become the central figure of a new downtown New York scene, and would also be Jonah's nemesis, his archrival, and his polar opposite—Nick Denton. While Jonah struggled to understand what the sort of traffic his Nike prank had garnered should be *for*—activism, politics, business, or simply fun—Nick set out on a relentless project of garnering thousands, then tens of thousands, then hundreds of thousands of page views for his blogs. The most famous would be Gawker. All of Nick's offerings promised their audiences a faster, truer version of reality than you'd find in the tired and fusty mainstream media.

Nick had spotted Cameron across the room at the media-and-tech conference in Austin, South by Southwest, in the spring of 2002, and walked over to him to talk about Blogdex. Nick made a formidable impression on young techies: he was ten years older than they, better dressed, his big head inclined at an angle, his enthusiasm for the new world expressed in a posh British accent. Cameron knew him vaguely as a tech entrepreneur who had made money in the first boom. Nick told the younger man of his plans to build a new kind of company in New York that summer, one that would merge the insights of technology with the social connections of media, all in the service of getting at that elusive commodity, the truth. The new thing was blogs, which, Nick told him, would deeply disrupt the clunky media world—they were "shorter, faster, younger."

Blogdex initially operated from a server underneath Cameron's desk in the Cube, jacked directly into MIT's internet backbone. The software crawled every blog it could find for links, and then produced a ranking of those links—showing, for the first time, what was actually traveling around the internet, and perhaps spotting the next Nike email. It was perhaps the first automated index of internet relevance, of what was hot. It turned the social substance of media into data. Nick offered Cameron $2,000 a month and a rent-free apartment on Sullivan Street to spend the summer helping him build a "large-scale blogging aggregation platform," a system that would give individual bloggers the capacity to link to and feed one another. Cameron, who grew up in tiny Yreka in Northern California, had already been visiting Jonah in New York on an unpredictable schedule set by the occasional fourteen-dollar specials on the Chinatown bus from Boston. He knew that was where the action was; he was intrigued by the challenge and charmed by the mysterious European who presented it.

Nick had moved to New York in the summer of 2002 himself. He took an apartment in a building full of young professionals that was, in the tradition of New York real estate, named SoHo Court because it was not actually quite in SoHo. It was just across Elizabeth Street from the grubby apartment Jonah had renovated when he moved to New York, though Jonah had lost the sublet months earlier and now lived a few blocks down Houston. Unlike Jonah, Nick knew exactly what he was doing there. In San Francisco, he'd been filling and refilling the columns of a spreadsheet in which he weighed the factors that would determine where he should live. Those columns included old friends, Hungarians, Jews, nature, the attractiveness of the men, business opportunities. While Jonah had drifted down to the city with only a vague idea of the industry he was in, Nick had come with the purpose of launching a new tech company that would change blogging, along with perhaps a couple of blogs to run on it. He had come to lead a media revolution. It seemed like what he was born to do. Certainly, by the time he walked across the room toward Cameron at SXSW, Nick already had the ideal qualities of a revolutionary: a deep understanding of the status quo, and an elemental desire to burn it down.

Nick was born in London in 1966. Though he was Jewish, he had a plausible claim to membership in the British Establishment: His father, Geoffrey Denton, was a formidable academic who, when Nick was a teenager, took a government job running Wilton Park, a grand old British country estate about fifty miles south of London. After World War II, the building had been turned into a kind of confidential conference center, a place for quiet, off-the-record meetings on difficult subjects in global politics. Western and Soviet diplomats, and black and white

South Africans, met there under Geoffrey Denton's watchful eye. Geoffrey kept their secrets. Meanwhile, he mounted a campaign to upgrade the quality of the staff, whom he once referred to as a "disorganized rabble," and of the threadbare furnishings. A later history of Wilton Park credits him with improving the ambience and with antagonizing his bosses in the Foreign Office, who viewed him as a "bulldozer."

Nick was close to his father, and if there was something Oedipal in the fact that he would spend his life chasing traffic by revealing the kinds of secrets his father kept, that was buried deep. But we all choose our stories; Nick, who had a particular fondness for narrative, identified himself far more strongly with his mother's inheritance. Marika Denton was a Hungarian who escaped the Holocaust with her own mother when she was eighteen. She met Geoffrey when she was his graduate student in economics, and she went on to become a psychoanalyst. The Jewish history she passed on to Nick was mostly dark—she would show him any Holocaust movie available. He identified most of all with his grandmother, Anna Bernholz, a survivor in every sense. She'd been raised in a Jewish orphanage in Vienna, and built a raincoat-selling business that was confiscated by the fascists, then the Communists. Nick's grandfather died in a labor camp on the eastern front, and Anna's lover was then hanged for sheltering her, according to the stories Nick was raised on. She followed her daughter to England at the age of forty-five, and worked as a cleaner, then a bookkeeper. Nick admired how she "started from nothing, again and again." He used a word for her that otherwise barely passed his lips: "hero."

Nick attended the University College School, a day school in the liberal section of North London where a Hungarian Jew wouldn't particularly stand out, a place not all that different from Jonah's College Preparatory School in Oakland. Nick was as a child much as he was as an adult: remote, a little Machiavellian, "distinctly calculating," according to a London friend, Jay Rayner. "He was famous for not committing to a Friday- or Saturday-night plan unless he could be certain that he had alighted upon the best option. As a result, if you ended up at the same bar or party as him, you were left with the sense you were in the right place, which was both reassuring and profoundly irritating."

Nick's friends knew he was gay, but he didn't actually tell anyone until Oxford; later his friends realized that may have been the source of his sense of distance, of being an outsider despite his comfortable place in the British elite. He edited the Oxford student magazine *The Isis*, but he didn't take the easy path that credential offered into Fleet Street. Instead, he chose to be an outsider, and went to Hungary to practice his trade as a journalist. As a cub reporter in 1989, Nick drove his blue Mazda across the border to cover the violent Romanian revolution for the conservative *Daily Telegraph*—the right-wing outlet, rather than the danger, horrified his father. Geoffrey was relieved when Nick started writing for the *Financial Times* in London. Nick's high-wattage social skills and manipulative tendencies were built for cultivating sources at investment banks, but he was pulled again toward the new, and he talked his way into a job in a city the paper barely cared about, San Francisco.

To his bosses, Nick was there to cover the tech boom, in full swing in the late 1990s. Instead he found himself wanting to join it. On April 18, 1998, he wrote a colorful portrait of the startup scene in all its flawed glory: The big money, the high risk, the lack of diversity, the punishing working hours, the desperate socializing. It could be, he quoted one denizen saying, "pretty depressing." But, Nick continued, "no one dwells on that." At a Silicon Valley party, "all anyone sees is someone, obscenely young, having fun, making it, someone they want to be, someone they can be, damnit."

Then the article took a turn: "Including me: I am leaving the *Financial Times* after eight years as a journalist to join a small internet venture with big ambitions. The Silicon Valley stories may be airbrushed. But like so many others, I want to believe them."

That was Nick: the improbable combination of irony and romanticism, the willful self-delusion, the will to create his own reality. He saw a commercial future in news aggregation and distribution, and had written a memo for his bosses at the *FT* pushing for what was then a revolutionary tactic: linking to competing publications when their stories were better. One startup guy he met, Joel Maske, had launched a company, iSyndicate, licensing articles from places like *The New York Times*, selling them to websites, and sharing the revenue with publishers. Nick was particularly excited about the possibility of allowing partners to put links to news articles directly on their own sites. Nick had made some money renovating and selling a flat in Clerkenwell, so he invested and joined the company as one of its first ten employees, and Maske helped him get the H-1B visa he needed to stay in the United States after quitting the *FT*. Almost as soon as he got that visa, however, their relationship soured. Nick told Maske he wanted to be bought out. "Fuck you, I'll buy you out—get out of my face," the American recalled replying, and sent Nick away with $250,000. Nick remembered it differently, saying he parted because the company "struggled with software," and he saw a better path through the same space with tech friends in London.

Nick's next venture began with a side hustle: he was great at throwing parties. It was the core of his personality, really, the exterior of a smooth insider with the calculation and thin skin of the outsider he sometimes felt like—gay and Jewish and half-Hungarian. He had the connections to get the right people to come, and the neurosis to care whether they did. As the tech boom reached London in 1998, he'd turned his hobby into a business called First Tuesday. The series of "matchmaking" events for startups that began with fifty people in a pub that October eventually grew to a global business. The business model was to take a 2 percent cut of the $147 million in financing First Tuesday claimed to have generated for the entrepreneurs who showed up at the parties.

Nick was a student of status, and he spiked the events with a dash of humiliation. *The Guardian* sniffed that Nick had adopted the crass American practice of "tagging" attendees, red for investors and green for entrepreneurs. Journalists wore yellow dots. But he managed, in those heady days, to get the events business valued as a tech company. A few months after the air had begun coming out of the bubble in San Francisco, he found some Israelis who hadn't yet gotten the news, and sold it to them for £50 million in July of 2000. Their company would collapse along with the rest of them the following year.

Nick gave the impression that he'd made millions on First Tuesday, but in fact much of the sale came in what would soon be worthless equity in the Israeli spin-off venture, which he'd split with three partners. But the deal got him, above all, the patina of an internet exit, and the credibility to present the version of himself he preferred: the entrepreneur at the intersection of media and tech. So he moved back to San Francisco to work on what he saw as his real project, a website to change the way people consume news, called Moreover. He imagined consumers going to a single, centralized feed of news, rather than skipping from website to website—an early version of Google News—and worked on a technology called NewsBlogger that would allow readers to become *writers*, as the blogger Jason Kottke, a keen observer of the era, noted.

Nick threw some great "Eurotrash" parties at the French consul's house— San Francisco was, he later said, "a very easy place to be the party giver or the party scene-maker. It wasn't very competitive at all." But he never quite took to the city. He had returned at a moment of retrenchment and caution in a tech scene still shell-shocked from the crash. The first bubble had seen preposterous content plays—from space.com to thick, glossy magazines like the unfortunately named *Red Herring*—collapse, and whenever Nick started talking about Moreover, it sounded a little too much like the dreaded business of hiring people to write things. There was also his personal life to think of: "The biggest problem with San Francisco was that there were no Black guys," he said later.

Nick had brought Moreover to San Francisco to home in on what was clearly the next big thing in tech and media: blogging. The site's name was borrowed from a section of *The Economist* magazine that aggregated other stories. Nick saw the revolutionary quality of a technology that lowered the barrier of entry to zero and let anyone publish directly to the web. Blogging could be the beating heart of Moreover; he could turn Moreover into blogging's hub. He approached his board with an idea: they'd use their remaining cash to acquire the obscure publishing company Pyra, which had built a piece of software called Blogger.

Pyra's founders, Evan Williams and Meg Hourihan, were slightly confused by the British accents and boundless enthusiasm of the Londoners, Nick and David Galbraith, a University College School classmate who had become his business partner. But Williams and Hourihan were flattered to be taken seriously. As they began running out of cash, the deal began to sound better. Nick's charm had made him a demon fundraiser—he was sitting on a pile of money and could have absorbed their company and kept their team together, while giving Moreover a powerful publishing tool. But when Nick shared his plan and the work he'd already done with Pyra with his investors, they vetoed it. A board member told him, "We want to know the strategy as long as it has nothing to do with blogging." That was his cue to leave San Francisco. As the depth of the tech bust became clear, Moreover—like many internet companies of its generation—pivoted from trying to become a mass consumer product to offering "web intelligence" at "internet speed" to corporate subscribers.

The new world of news he'd glimpsed at Moreover left Nick persuaded that blogging was the future, and also that he couldn't put himself in the hands of venture capitalists again. He had also started a blog himself, where he expressed conservative politics that lined up with the times. "Try focusing some attention on Islamic family planning policy, which is some variant of: woman, it's babies back-to-back or you're moving into the basement," he mused.

Nick made two different kinds of impressions when he got to New York. He was thirty-five when he arrived, and the people his age and older often saw something desperate, damaged even, in his cool reserve, his casual cruelty and obsession with the social scene. "Some part of me wanted to take care of him," recalled John Johnson, Jonah's boss at Eyebeam and a major investor in the downtown art-and-tech scene. (Nick's boyfriend during his early New York years, the artist Douglas Boatwright, also worked at Eyebeam.) Johnson projected a certain noblesse oblige; he would host a launch party for one of Nick's blogs at his apartment because he thought that Nick seemed to be "suffering on some level."

But Nick spent most of his time with the young bloggers, to whom his affect was worldly—a "mysterious Count Dracula European-style thing," in the eyes of Jake Dobkin, the co-founder of the New York City blog *Gothamist*. Nick loomed large in the New York blogger scene of the early aughts in the way that the older guy buying the drinks can in a small world of people who are at once profoundly insecure in their own youth and outsiderness and sure that they've just discovered something real, just struck oil. The clubhouse of that scene was, as much as anywhere else, the Magician, a noirish bar on Rivington Street that only took cash and whose heavy Venetian blinds half screened the world outside. The characters there ran blogs whose URLs were their own names—Nick would sometimes post a dozen things a day to nickdenton.org, which was pretty impressive. Lock Steele covered the doings of the neighborhood on lockhartsteele.com, and without really thinking about it invented what would become twenty-first-century real estate coverage, with its mix of nostalgia for the shop that closed, obsession with the new bar, and pure curiosity about what might be happening behind the plywood at the shuttered storefront. Jason Kottke mostly wrote about design and cool things he saw on the internet, though he'd seen his traffic double—from ten thousand to twenty thousand a day—when he "live-blogged" the terror attacks of 9/11. His girlfriend was Meg Hourihan, the co-creator of Blogger, which Nick had tried to buy in his Moreover days; she was also a blogger known as "Megnut." Elizabeth Spiers wrote acerbically about finance on her personal blog when she wasn't writing up reports for investment bankers.

Nights that started at the Magician sometimes ended at Camp Bowery, as AJ Daulerio and his roommate called their nearby apartment. AJ had co-founded an online journal with literary ambitions called *The Black Table* (named for the color of a piece of furniture, not the diversity of the staff). Strikingly handsome with a dark complexion and light eyes, he'd moved up from Philadelphia in 1999 to drink at the Magician and write for the internet. He had one of media's great boring day jobs at *The Bond Buyer* (sample headline: "Moody's Downgrades Schenectady, N.Y., to Ba3"), and poured his heart into *The Black Table*—a full-time job, he later said, 5:00 p.m. to 5:00 a.m. The site carried the proud tagline "Updated daily." Nobody got paid. AJ's own specialty was over-the-top, crude interviews with members of their own small scene. "Would you rather let George Wendt pee in your mouth or have Shelly [sic] Long wear a strap-on and ram you in the hiney for 22 minutes?" he asked Spiers in one interview, riffing grotesquely on the television show *Cheers*. He illustrated the interview with Spiers wearing a T-shirt with the words "I Fucked The Black Table" photoshopped onto the front.

Nick, for his part, was a pretty good blogger, and it was cool when he linked you, and he was grateful when you linked him back. That was certainly enough to get him through the door at the Magician. But he also felt to the young blog crowd like something larger—a businessman, a guy who'd made it in the tech boom, and someone whose horizons stretched beyond theirs. The *Gothamist* co-founder Jake Dobkin would always call Nick when he needed some exotic concept—say, stock options—explained by someone older and wiser. He would also be shocked from time to time by his new friend's cruelty: Nick would suddenly sneer at Dobkin for being "so interested in a small stupid thing like NYC," and he'd always look over your shoulder at parties for someone better. "Nick's a spiritual vampire," Dobkin, the child of Communists from Park Slope, Brooklyn, finally concluded. "He's trying to fill this black void in himself."

Nick told his new friends that blogging was the future, but that the big money was in his real business, technology. Moreover had finally folded, and he was onto something new, which he called the Lafayette Project after the location of his new loft. It was another shot at building the technology that would undergird the new generation of media. While Cameron Marlow toiled away creating a platform for them, Nick started making actual blogs. The first, Gizmodo, was a gadget-review website that launched on July 1, 2002; John Johnson hosted the party at his downtown penthouse, upstairs from David Bowie (with whom he generously shared his T1 internet connection).

. . .

Nick and Jonah approached the new internet from opposite directions. Jonah was obsessed with how to make a single idea—often, a single joke—travel, regardless of its content or the identity of the person who originated it. Nick had the inverse obsession: he wanted people coming back again and again to his blog. The reader he imagined was a gadget-head, bored at work, refreshing Gizmodo. That meant starting early and posting all day, ensuring that your audience would have something new every time they hit refresh.

One way to look at Blogdex was as a kind of a technical measurement system, a new system to game. That's how Jonah had always seen it. But it was also a kind of a social X-ray, a guide to who in the blogosphere really mattered, who belonged on the Excel spreadsheet that Nick carefully maintained, hundreds of names long, of acceptable guests at his parties. But it proved harder to build the new platform than Nick had hoped. Marlow left town at the end of the summer, the project half-finished. He handed it off to Hourihan, who had sold Blogger to Google and believed she could build a new front page for the internet in a way that was more methodical, less shoot-from-the-hip, than the earlier wave of startups. But Nick didn't give her control over the project's budget, and kept nickel-and-diming her on engineers.

He had gotten distracted from the tech again, drawn to the content. Nick was working on a sister site to Gizmodo, a New York media gossip hub that would be called Gawker. He hired Elizabeth Spiers, the finance blogger, to run it, and though she'd sometimes come down and work out of his loft on Lafayette Street, even she couldn't really tell how seriously he was taking the whole thing, because he seemed to think Gizmodo was primarily a good way to market the software that was his real focus.

Gawker was going to be ten hours a week for her, a little money on the side, and some fun with their social circle. "We didn't think it was going to be a real business or anything."

Though the tech company would never truly get off the ground, Gizmodo had thirty thousand views in its first full month, August of 2002—one thousand a day! By December, it was getting one hundred thousand views a month—more than some top tech websites of that time. And while the tech platform of Nick's dreams could grow inexpensively to serve millions of people and make him a billionaire—just look at the founders of contemporary titans like Yahoo!—Gizmodo's growing blog views translated much more directly into money. The unit of measurement in advertising was the CPM—cost per thousand views, with "thousand" confusingly represented by the French word "mille." In 2003, Gawker's sites began selling advertising, charging CPMs ranging from about seven dollars to about nine dollars. The technology was simple, noninvasive. Advertisers paid publishers for a raw number of impressions—counted each time someone's browser landed on the page. Neither side of the transaction knew much about exactly who was visiting the website, but they could deduce the characteristics of the audience the way the media industry always had: from a site's content. If you wanted to selling rods to fishermen, you bought ads in *Field & Stream*. This was a simple and lucrative business, just like magazines and newspapers had been in their glory days.

There were signs, though, that things could change. There was a new kind of middleman, the "ad network," which took the problem of selling ads off publishers' hands in return for a small commission. Technology companies, led by DoubleClick, which had been founded in 1996, did the cumbersome work of displaying and measuring digital ads for everyone from *The Wall Street Journal* to MySpace. In 2003, an analytically minded DoubleClick salesman quit to found a company called Right Media, and started down the path to offering something different to advertisers: slots across many websites that would be able to target an individual consumer looking for fishing rods or cameras, regardless of where he or she was browsing. But marketers were skeptical of that kind of wizardry, and its associated technical challenges remained complex. For now, the best that most advertisers could do was try to match their product to a website's brand. A tech blog like Gizmodo was a logical place to advertise the latest digital camera or iPod, which was why the tech blog commanded the highest rates among Nick's websites.

Gawker couldn't command the top CPMs Gizmodo could, but it had something else: the attention of the media it covered and tormented. Gawker captivated the New York media scene immediately, its buzz drowning out the steady revenue of Gizmodo and other, more lucrative sites Nick would launch. Nick had a sixth sense for social success; he knew Gawker had arrived when Kurt Andersen, the co-founder of *Spy* magazine and the previous generation's cheeky alternative media baron, turned up at a party he hosted for the new site. That felt like victory to Nick. Gawker turned Nick into a celebrity, and made his company the focus of the new scene, although, he'd later come to believe "New York exposure comes at a price."

3

....

Black People Love Us

Nick had learned in San Francisco that the nascent internet could be a business, and he'd come to New York to build his own. But to Jonah, the internet was still a playground—a place to troll and jam mainstream American culture, to try out jokes and conduct social experiments. Jonah's best pranks still got more traffic than Nick's blogs. His last great one had come just as Gizmodo was taking off, in the fall of 2002, when more than 600,000 appalled and amused people found their way to a website called Black People Love Us! There, a white couple named Sally and Johnny bragged about their cross-racial social skills, and included testimonials: "Johnny calls me 'da man!' That puts me at ease," writes one supposed Black friend. "It makes me feel comfortable, because I am Black and that's how Black folks talk to one another." The couple are fake, of course: Jonah had created the site with his little sister Chelsea, who had moved to New York to make it in stand-up comedy. Cringe! But clearly, Jonah was some kind of genius.

At least that was what Jonah's friend Duncan Watts, a sociologist he'd met through their shared obsession with the way information traveled on the new internet, was trying to convey to his companion at an expensive Manhattan lunch in early 2003. Duncan, who had the bearing, courteous deference, and weathered good looks of the Australian naval officer he'd been before turning to academia, was sitting across from a rich and powerful man who believed, rather improbably, that Duncan could have the power to defeat the National Rifle Association.

Duncan's lunch date was Kenneth Lerer, who would become Jonah's partner and mentor. Kenny, as everyone who knew him called him, had already played a central role at the peak of the last internet boom in linking the worlds of political power and new media money. Once a cagey New York PR man, he was the executive vice president at AOL in 2000 when the company that popularized email and mailed you CDs had used its inflated stock to purchase Time Warner, the cable and media giant. Kenny held the ear of three CEOs—Steve Case, Gerald Levin, and Richard Parsons—through the iconic, disastrous merger of the first internet boom. The bubble burst in 2001 and the deal became a symbol of the idiocy of the era, but Kenny walked away with a sack of cash, a part-time role advising Parsons, and a sweet office overlooking Central Park.

Kenny believed in a digital future, but he also knew that the internet was over—as a business in itself, at least, to the investors who had made and lost a fortune on it. After the market crash of 2001, nobody was going to be making any financial bets on that future anytime soon. Which was all right. He had a family foundation. As 2002 turned to 2003, Kenny decided to turn his energy toward a personal obsession: he'd take some of his payout from AOL and see if he couldn't make some trouble for the NRA, an organization he'd always loathed.

Kenny had read the book Duncan had just published, *Six Degrees: The Science of a Connected Age*. Duncan had reexamined the famous "small world" experiment from the 1960s, a landmark study in which strangers mailed letters to one another through friends of friends. Back then, the researchers concluded that Americans were on average separated from one another by six nodes. They claimed that certain key individuals, dubbed "influencers," played an outsize role in the networks. That idea of "influencers" would become central to the way political consultants, marketers, and influence peddlers of all kinds—and Lerer was a bit of all three—thought about how to change minds. When Kenny told Watts he knew that the key to destroying the NRA was somewhere in that 384-page tome, Watts told him he was pretty sure it wasn't. He was quite familiar with the contents of his own book, he said. He referred his intense new acquaintance to a section that disproved Kenny's idea. Watts had indeed confirmed—in a study of 24,163 email chains—that we are separated, on average, by six degrees. But he had debunked the notion that certain individuals had special influence. In fact, his book was as much about the randomness of those connections as it was about their power. To his mind there was no way to control the crowd, to turn it on a target the way Kenny wanted.

But, Watts added, not everyone was so skeptical. He had one friend who seemed to think he could harness the internet's strange new powers. Duncan tried to explain Black People Love Us! to Kenny, who wasn't particularly impressed. But the next time Kenny summoned Watts to his office to talk further about his obsession, Watts told Kenny that he'd broken a leg, and so travel was difficult, and that what's more the guy he was really looking for was his friend, Jonah Peretti, whose profession Duncan couldn't quite describe but who was "the most interesting guy you'll ever meet." Kenny didn't really care about Duncan's friend, but he said he'd send his driver to pick them up and let them keep the car for the day, which the two young men thought was pretty cool, and so they turned up at Carnegie Hall Tower for the brainstorm in late spring.

Jonah stole the show. He was twenty-nine by now, his brown hair swept back and his thick-framed glasses right on the line between hipster and nerd. He couldn't stop telling jokes. Kenny hadn't been taken with Black People Love Us!, but the story of Jonah's email prank now got his attention.

When people identified Jonah at all, they tended to use the word "prankster" or even "activist" (though the former word missed the depth of his thought, and the latter didn't capture that he was more interested in the process than the result). John Johnson called Jonah a "culture jammer," in the jargon of the time. Jonah was immersed in the blog scene that Kenny could feel was the future. He had begun dating a blogger, Andrea Harner, who was working as Johnson's assistant at Eyebeam, and whose work occasionally made it onto Gawker.

Kenny saw something novel in Jonah's pranks. They operated at the exposed edge where corporate sanctimony and liberal hypocrisy converged. Jonah seemed to be developing a new kind of tool, a weapon, that might be deployed in the interest of politics or commerce. He had discovered some new source of cultural power in the ability to gather and steer internet traffic, but he wasn't sure which direction he should turn it in next. Kenny had the answer. The National Rifle Association was fighting to end Bill Clinton's ban on assault weapons. With Kenny's money and Jonah's brains, they'd find a way to stop this campaign. They decided to circulate a petition, but one infused with Jonah's insights into what, in those days, he was calling "contagious media"—things like that Nike email that spread on their own, hand to hand and mouth to mouth, like a virus. Kenny had started paying Jonah and a few friends a small stipend and covering pizza for the weekly meetings of what they were calling the Contagious Media Working Group. They'd developed something called ForwardTrack, which allowed you to sign a petition and then forward it to friends. Then you could see who had signed based on your forwards. Essentially, the idea was to turn email forwards into a kind of competition, and into something measurable—essentially creating a social reward for online organizing.

Stopthenra.com got hundreds of thousands of signatures on a petition demanding the assault weapons ban be renewed in September of 2004, part of a campaign that failed only when Republicans took Congress. This was a big number back then, but the effort never gave rise to a movement. Its highest impact came through *The New York Times*. A powerful columnist, Bob Herbert, wrote about the effort, and Kenny had personally taken out a full-page ad that listed prominent figures—John McEnroe, Walter Cronkite, and Bruce Springsteen—who were featured on an NRA "blacklist," and invited readers to get involved. The website already offered a bottom-up iteration of this same argument; still, Jonah was amazed by his partner's ability to project his voice into the elite media.

The Contagious Media Working Group, which met at Eyebeam, came up with another curious technical mechanism, called the reBlog. It was a clever little open-source script that, installed on your blog, allowed you to pull in a post from another site and promote it yourself. It was a version of an idea that Nick had been playing with at Moreover. Tim Shey, Jonah's old roommate, liked reBlog enough to install it on his own blog and showed it to a young programmer, David Karp, who would implement it on a website he was developing, Tumblr. That technical trick drove Tumblr's success, and was copied by other social networks—Facebook's share, Twitter's retweet. It would become the basic mechanism for a generation of amplifying everything from clever jokes to lies about elections.

Neither tool was exactly going to stop the actual NRA, though. Ultimately, Jonah and Watts concluded that their message had failed to reach the wider universe of what Jonah called the "Bored At Work Network" of office workers forwarding emails. Their project never went viral. But the *Times* ad got so much attention that Watts and Jonah revised their theory about how content could travel on the internet, arguing in a *Harvard Business Review* article that a "big seed" could be a crucial part of a marketing campaign. The power of a splashy *Times* op-ed may seem obvious, but Jonah and Duncan argued that the combination of a big megaphone and social sharing had special power: even if a message, or an ad, didn't go totally viral, some sharing could drastically cut the average cost of spreading your message.

Nick was thinking about politics too. But for Gawker he wanted something other than the breathy, earnest bursts of personal opinion then known as political blogging. That was the world of Howard Dean, who drew his energy in part from the "netroots," a collection of bloggers who opposed the Iraq War, and who helped force the Democratic Party to open up to anti-war views. Though Dean nearly won the Democratic primary, there was something painfully juvenile about his campaign and its appeal. The small set of voters getting their information from the internet found some insightful analysis and a lot of flame wars among partisan bloggers. The liberal blog *Daily Kos* yelled at *The New York Times*, right-wing bloggers yelled at *The New York Times*, and nobody brought in much new information.

Nick knew what he wanted. The Gawker scoop of his dreams had always been to out a gay, Christian Republican senator, and thus reveal right-wing hypocrisy in its most naked form. In January 2004 he hired Ana Marie Cox, a young ironist from one of the bastions of the first wave of internet writing, suck.com, to skewer Washington in the same way Gawker did New York. Their new site would be called *Wonkette*. Nick told her he wanted the inside dope, but he couldn't help her find it. He had heard the gossip in New York and San Francisco (and London and Budapest), but Washington was a foreign country. Ana knew she wouldn't be able to deliver, because she didn't actually have any sources beyond her husband's friends at *The Washington Post* (in, unhelpfully, the book section). So she found something else that would get traffic: an outrageous sense of humor. In her writing, she developed the persona of a "weird drunken housewife" who had become enraptured with the doings of politicos and journalists—"obsessive and breathless, but cynical." She cracked jokes and turned bloggers and congressional staffers into minor celebrities. These were people ignored by the older forms of Washington gossip: the coy *Washington Post* Style section, and the dry morning newsletters arriving by fax announcing who was going to chair the Agriculture Committee. Ana was glad that Nick, whom she found mysterious and a bit frightening, ultimately didn't pay much attention to her work, with a single exception: he wanted her to pass on a long-standing Washington rumor that a politician was gay.

She refused.

In any case, Ana believed she had something better to print. Her great break-out story introduced the Washingtonienne, a young woman whose obscure online diary she discovered, elevated, and transformed, as she put it, into "a Hill-based Belle de Jour." The Washingtonienne, who turned out to be a legislative assistant to an Ohio senator, was juggling eight men, whom she helpfully indexed by initials:

> FD=The intern in my office whom I want to fuck; X=Married man who pays me for sex. Chief of Staff at one of the gov agencies, appointed by Bush; T=Lost my virginity to him and fell in love. Dude who has been driving me crazy since 1999. Lives in Springfield, IL. Flies halfway across the country to fuck me, then I don't hear from him for weeks; HK=Dude

from the Senate office I interned in Jan. thru Feb. Hired me as an intern; Broke up my relationship w/ QV (see below); QV= Serious, long-term boyfriend whom I lived with since 2001. Disastrous break up in March, but still seeing each other; P=AKA "Threesome Dude." Somebody I would rather forget about; YZ=My new office bf with whom I am embroiled in an office sex scandal. The current favorite; K=A sugar daddy who wants nothing but anal. Keep trying to end it with him, but the money is too good.

The diary distracted official Washington from the mayhem in Iraq and the Democratic primary, which John Kerry had mostly locked up, for a few weeks in the spring of 2004. Cox, learning to report in public, guessed at which official could be which man, and eventually brought the thing to a climax by naming the author of the blog, Jessica Cutler, whose adventures got her fired but landed her a $300,000 book deal. It was what Nick seemed to have been looking for, a gleeful and relentless unmasking of a more interesting version of Washington than the mainstream media depicted. That's how Cox saw it: she was revealing that "politics is kind of stupid, and everyone should know that."

But for Nick, *Wonkette* proved to be a dead end. Cox never got another story like that. Instead, she left to write a novel about her Washington world. The young bloggers of Howard Dean's campaign proved fleeting too. The new thing after the 2004 campaign seemed to be earnestness and hope—not Nick's forte—embodied by a young Illinois senator named Barack Obama. *Wonkette*'s traffic peaked at four million views in November of 2004 and then started falling. Further to his detriment, Nick found that all traffic wasn't equally valuable. Advertisers were allergic to politics, it turned out—an old problem for hard news that would only intensify online.

. . .

Jonah and Kenny Lerer, on the other hand, were delighted by their early experiments in the politics of the internet. But eventually Kenny's attention began to wander as well. In November, George W. Bush defeated John Kerry and Republicans took control of the Senate, dooming the assault weapons ban and other liberal priorities. Democrats were in a state of grief and panic. Kenny got an invitation from a friend who wanted to do something about it.

Arianna Huffington invited Kenny to a gathering on December 3, 2004, at her Brentwood home, a four-bedroom Italianate palace that served both as the home she shared with her sister and two daughters, and as the headquarters for an only-in-America public career. Huffington, born in Greece as Arianna Stassinopoulos, had been a star of London's conservative intellectual scene in the 1980s, and come to the United States on the arm of a wealthy California Republican, Michael Huffington. He ran for Senate in 1994 and lost, while his wife cultivated figures like Newt Gingrich and a circle of conservative intellectuals in Washington who fulminated bitterly against Bill Clinton. But in 1997 she split with her husband, who came out as bisexual in 1998, and reinvented herself as a liberal and then as a fiery critic of George W. Bush. She had run for governor of California in 2003 on a platform that blended attacks on Bush and Arnold Schwarzenegger with promises of plentiful hybrid cars and independence from political parties.

Arianna's real superpower was her personal capacity for starting and maintaining relationships, for building a social network in real life. Her contact list contained nineteen thousand names. When Kenny arrived at her brightly lit home, with its faux-marble dining table and private office hidden behind a set of bookshelves, even he was impressed. The room was full of Hollywood royalty: David Geffen, Larry and Laurie David, producer Brian Grazer, writer Aaron Sorkin, the statesmanlike Norman Lear, Meg Ryan. Kenny spent most of the party trying to talk to Meg Ryan and listening to a litany of ideas that were, at best, kind of obvious: The internet was going to be important. Blogs were starting to matter. And perhaps most of all, the left needed its own version of Matt Drudge and his website, *The Drudge Report*.

Amid all the power players in that room, Arianna and Kenny turned out to be the ones who mattered most to what would come next. They shared an obsession with Drudge, a reclusive, gay Washington gadfly who had built his one-page site into the biggest and most important thing on the political internet, sprinkling just enough fresh gossip and witty headline writing on top of a quirky and partisan selection of links. He was the single most important force in traffic to news articles in America, driving some forty thousand views for a link in small Courier font on his site, and as many as a million—an unthinkable number, enough to crush most servers—for a big headline on the top of the page. That traffic meant that *The Drudge Report* wielded cultural power: Television producers looked at *The Drudge Report* to decide what to put on the air. *New York Times* reporters obsessed over its links. Ever since Drudge had broken the news, on January 17, 1998, that *Newsweek* was hanging on to a story about the president and an intern, Drudge had been the center of the world. And Drudge was a right-winger! He'd taken his talking points directly from the Bush campaign and had managed to propel unfounded claims that John Kerry exaggerated his Vietnam War record into the mainstream media. A leading political commentator of that moment, Mark Halperin, opined that Drudge was the Walter Cronkite of the aughts. Drudge was the man who set the agenda.

Kenny and Arianna wanted that kind of power, for themselves and for Democrats. Over the next few days, they resolved that they would build it together. Kenny was the moneyman, though he still wasn't sure if this was a real business or just another political hobby. He found them office space down on what had become known as Silicon Alley, a couple of blocks of lower Broadway between Houston and Spring, where the lavish French bistro Balthazar was Nick Denton's favorite place to bring bloggers he was trying to impress. Kenny put in $1 million of his AOL money. Huffington brought the social connections and media attention. People like the actor John Cusack and the historian Arthur Schlesinger Jr. agreed to blog for the new venture, even if they only hazily knew what a blog was.

Kenny and Arianna each had a young man in mind who could help. For Kenny, it was, obviously, Jonah. John Johnson, Jonah's boss, was happy to loan him to the venture, and to consider investing a small slice of his own fortune as part of the $2 million with which they launched. Jonah got started in the beginning of 2005 building a platform with the software Movable Type, creating a front page that would both highlight the hottest blogs and provide space for editors to write Drudge-style headlines on other outlets' stories.

Huffington's young protégé was Andrew Breitbart, who had worked in her rotating cast of researchers and assistants back when she was a conservative. He was brilliant and frenetic, and brought both a deep knowledge of the internet and a different set of relationships in Los Angeles. Most intriguing, Andrew had a connection to Drudge himself: he was quietly running *The Drudge Report* eight hours a day! There would be four partners in the business: Kenny and Arianna, who split the bulk of the shares fifty-fifty, and Jonah and Andrew, who each got 5 percent. The senior partners had emerged as dominant media figures during the first decade of the internet. The two junior partners would shape the decade to follow.

4

Drudge

Arianna wanted Andrew Breitbart for the simple reason that he held the key to what *The Huffington Post* needed: traffic. Andrew was Matt Drudge's minion—or assistant, or silent partner, depending on whom you asked. For eight hours a day, Andrew wrote and rewrote the simple HTML code that could drive one million views to an article. *The Drudge Report*'s true power was that it told the story of American politics to millions, and set the agenda for news organizations whose editors and producers were forever refreshing the site.

Andrew had paid a strange, heavy price for that power—a decade of anonymity and even humiliation at the hands of his boss and idol. To most who knew him in Los Angeles, Breitbart was a frenetic, overweight fleabag of a man, an underachiever who'd grown up in Brentwood, barely made it through Tulane, and washed out in Hollywood. It was, in retrospect, classic Arianna Huffington to believe that, with only her connections and a dash of fairy dust, she could turn Andrew Breitbart into a leader at 2005's hot new left-wing website. But she did have something to offer him: the chance to be his own man. She'd shifted her own politics, so why couldn't he? And she and Kenny needed some of that traffic. First, though, she'd have to pry Breitbart loose from Drudge.

Andrew never forgot the moment he met Matt Drudge. It was a sunny day in the summer of 1995 when Drudge pulled his shitty little red Geo Metro onto Carroll Canal Court, a street in Venice, California, that neither man could possibly afford to live on. But Andrew's girlfriend's father was a famous comedian, Orson Bean, and so Andrew had invited his hero to their family's glamorous address. Andrew was working on the fringes of Hollywood then, a rich kid back from partying his way through college, now building websites for the embarrassingly trashy E! network. Andrew had always had trouble paying attention—he was later diagnosed with ADHD—and he spent much of his day on the nascent internet, in particular on a set of bulletin boards called the Usenet. Posters on one of his favorite boards, alt.current-events.clinton.whitewater, would often cut and paste in an email digest called *The Drudge Report*, a list of links that included the newest political scandals, the big news of the day, and various oddities its mysterious author had uncovered. The newsletter "was like a tour of one man's short-term memory," Andrew later wrote. He was obsessed with its author, and finally gathered up the courage to send him an email. "Are you 50 people? A hundred people? Is there a building?" he asked.

Matt Drudge was, in fact an obscure, sallow, twenty-nine-year-old gossipmonger working as a clerk for CBS—which meant, in reality, folding T-shirts in the gift shop, eking out a living. At night, though, he was a new kind of journalist, emailing out a news digest that ranged from political scandal to early Hollywood box office numbers.

The two men connected intensely and immediately, spending four hours talking about politics and media, peering into the future from their vantage point deep inside the early internet. Drudge's biographer Matthew Lysiak later reported that Drudge had offered Andrew a 25 percent stake in the website version of his email newsletter that he was launching. But Andrew wasn't willing to give up his industry job, much as he hated it, for such an uncertain venture, and so they parted instead with a handshake deal that *The Drudge Report* would be Andrew's side hustle. Between 9:00 a.m. and 3:00 p.m., Andrew would be the one posting its links, and Matt would pay him "what he could." Andrew was awed by the meeting. "That guy is going to change the world," he told his girlfriend as the Geo Metro drove away.

Working for Drudge was a dream of relevance and power. From that day in 1995 forward, Andrew Breitbart had a front-row seat to the birth of the internet, as Drudge channeled the anger and resentment of their favorite talk radio host, Rush Limbaugh, into a riveting and simple page of links. There was right-wing politics and celebrity gossip, and other subtler strains that tickled America's id: stories of loony liberals, terrifying Muslims, extreme weather, and weird science. Slowly but surely, the minor scandals that dripped out of newsrooms to the reclusive blogger became major ones. Andrew had been the silent force in the Clinton scandals, watching as the media raced to catch up with Matt's (and his) obscure, ugly website.

Drudge made Monica Lewinsky's name, and his own, famous with that story. He became the model of how traffic could mean money, power, and independence from any of the norms or controls that had traditionally come with a successful media venture. A generation of American conservatives, and a generation of political junkies, developed the habit of typing his URL into their browsers. And media companies began to see that thousands, then tens of thousands, then hundreds of thousands of readers would follow a Drudge link. Clever reporters would email Drudge directly with their stories; cleverer ones would guess what Drudge might like, then write a story that fit his interests.

Drudge was the force Kenny Lerer and Arianna Huffington sought to rival; he was a veritable pillar of the early internet. He was powerful and famous. Andrew had some of the power, but none of the fame. He eventually quit the job at E! but still couldn't quite explain to people what he did for a living. After Andrew married Susannah Bean and moved back to Brentwood, few of his friends and neighbors had any idea of his power. One neighbor watched the 2004 Super Bowl with him, and saw Andrew grab his laptop when Janet Jackson's famous "wardrobe malfunction" revealed one breast. Andrew termed what she was wearing beneath it a "solar nipple medallion," and the neighbor realized that "for the next couple of hours you could see that phrase popping up on all the broadcasts. I couldn't believe how quickly they could influence the Zeitgeist of the world."

Andrew also felt the excitement of the insurgent new internet, an allegiance that sometimes trumped his politics. Back then, right- and left-wingers online had a common bond: they were allied against the old establishment. So when Gawker took a shot at launching a Hollywood blog (called *Defamer*) in 2004, Nick saw Andrew as an ally. "At the time, we were all bloggers of different political complexions—in opposition to a stultifying mainstream media," Nick wrote.

While working for Drudge provided intoxicating access to power, it also meant a constant stream of humiliation. Drudge, born in the liberal Washington, DC, suburbs in 1966, had moved to LA in his twenties and existed as a spectral, digital presence. He didn't want to be Andrew's friend. He didn't even want to talk to him. They'd hand off the web page in the silence of the internet, and communicate by instant message when they communicated at all. Drudge would occasionally tell Andrew he was taking a few days off, without explanation. Months would pass without their speaking. Drudge mostly got in touch when Andrew missed a big breaking story, to chide him. Andrew's favorite stories would sometimes quietly disappear from the site: management by silent passive aggression. In 2004, Andrew and another conservative journalist published a book attacking liberal Hollywood. They'd promised the publisher that the book would be promoted on the powerful *Drudge Report*, and Andrew dutifully posted up a link. His co-author was thrilled—until it quietly vanished minutes later, with no explanation from Andrew's boss.

Drudge was bringing in millions of dollars a year in advertising against view counts that could break a hundred million a month. But Andrew subsisted on irregular personal checks from his boss, sometimes for a few thousand dollars. It was barely enough to cover his expenses. His friends wanted him to confront Drudge, but he never would. Even in 2005, when Andrew told his new colleagues at *The Huffington Post* that he was leaving Drudge for the new venture, he never quite quit: Andrew's Instant Messenger still would light up with links from nine to three, and he was still posting them to the site. In Andrew's later tellings of his own personal mythology, he was a hero of the early conservative internet, but in a flash of self-loathing, Andrew described himself to *Reason* magazine as "Matt Drudge's bitch."

At *The Huffington Post*, Andrew would be a partner, not just an anonymous minion. Arianna had been an early friend and ally of Drudge's, and the two stayed close even after her politics moved left. Andrew convinced himself that he could help Arianna with a celebrity-focused site without forgoing his decade-old ties to Drudge. And Huffington, with her infinite capacity for understanding, got what this hyperactive pig-pen of a right-wing lunatic, whose belly hung out from underneath his ratty T-shirt, was about. Kenny at first saw Andrew as an idiot savant, but quickly began to loathe him, both because he couldn't shut up and because when he spoke, it tended to be right-wing bullshit.

Jonah, who was in the office more than his *Huffington Post* colleagues, at first enjoyed his new partner's nonstop stream of ideas: To charge commenters $1 apiece, to create a phone line where celebrities could call in blogs, to have an eye out for stories breaking in the early hours of the morning in London. He also benefited from Andrew's self-confidence: After Jonah learned that the right-wing blogger had managed to extract a $250,000 annual salary from Huffington for . . . it wasn't clear what exactly, Jonah went to Kenny and demanded at least $150,000 for himself. It was still puzzling what Andrew was supposed to be doing in exchange for all that money. He didn't have the attention span to build anything, Jonah concluded.

Andrew, his new partners found, was hard to even have around the office—distracting, distractible, jumping from idea to idea. "He would spend hours playing fantasy baseball during the day. He was incredibly good at fantasy baseball," Jonah told me years later, recalling that Andrew spent much of his time talking to another *Huffington Post* employee about starting a fantasy baseball company amid the *Huffington Post* launch.

Andrew was also at war with himself, Jonah realized. Andrew was desperate to preserve his relationship with Drudge even as he was working for what everyone else knew was the left-wing alternative.

"He was terrified of the idea that *Huffington Post* was a competitor to Drudge. He thought that *Huffington Post* could be bipartisan and that Drudge would love the idea of these big boldface names blogging because he understands the value of that," Jonah said.

Eventually, Kenny, viscerally revolted by Andrew and his politics, was the one who pulled the plug. Before *The Huffington Post* even launched, he bought Andrew's 5 percent for $250,000 and dispatched him to Los Angeles. Andrew went crawling back to Drudge, and to the right-wing outrage and anger that Drudge bathed him in. He explained his departure to a gossip blogger that summer in ideological terms. "I think it boiled down to this: mustache notwithstanding, I think John Bolton is a pretty swell guy," he said. "And, for the life of me, I can't fit all three of my kids into a Prius. Lord knows I tried." That August, Andrew gave up on his dreams of true independence and launched a sad little website called breitbart.com to supply *The Drudge Report* with the articles Matt preferred to link to from his screaming headlines—stripped-down, easy-loading links to wire stories. Andrew was able to convert that stream of traffic into dollars from the growing business of digital display advertising, which had made Drudge rich. Matt indulged him. "I want to help him out," Drudge told CNET News in 2005. "Hopefully he can make a living from it."

Andrew told his own version years later, in a memoir called *Righteous Indignation: Excuse Me While I Save the World!* In his account, Andrew hadn't been the minion of the most powerful conservative blogger: he'd been his own man all along, a conservative who saw through the lies of liberal Hollywood, an agent behind enemy lines. Andrew's story was so far from reality that the other *Huffington Post* founders couldn't decide if he was joking or just lying. It was probably some of both—plus the fact that with his severe attention deficit disorder, Andrew had left most of the writing to a bright young assistant named Ben Shapiro. But the book offered a glimpse through the looking glass of the early internet, and a good sense of how the new Right, for a decade, would view the web that Facebook and Twitter, *The Huffington Post* and Gawker and BuzzFeed had created.

In that telling, Andrew had abruptly discovered how intolerant the Democratic Party was—how obsessed with irrational hatred of George W. Bush and irrational opposition to the invasion of Iraq. He had realized that conservatives in Hollywood would be ostracized from the entertainment industry if they expressed those views, and that his highest mission would be to build a kind of underground social network of Hollywood conservatives. And "at the exact time when I was undergoing the fundamental recognition that my neighbors in West Los Angeles were acting to undermine national cohesion in a time of war, which put me in a perennial state of psychic dissonance . . . at exactly that point, I got a phone call from Arianna Huffington."

"Do you have any ideas for a website?" he claimed she asked him.

Andrew jumped at the opportunity. Not because he was Arianna's old intern, an ambitious misfit looking to get out of Drudge's shadow. In this telling, he was a spy!

While he decided what to tell Arianna, he wrote, he conferred with his new, anonymous friends.

"What if we can get the collective left that we have dinner with, cocktail parties with, the left that talks crazy in private but only expresses itself at the Daily Kos under pseudonyms—what if we can get them all to put their names next to their crazy ideas? What if we can make it a one-stop shop for exposing liberals for who they are?" he asked. Then he presented the idea to Huffington, and told her "she should set up a salon for likeminded thinkers."

His true goal, Andrew wrote, was to expose left-wing lunacy. He compared his three months at *The Huffington Post* to working as a CIA agent. Then he quit—rather than being forced out by Kenny—when "I realized that I wasn't going to be a spy but their manservant."

"I couldn't live with myself or with my true friends," he declared.

Andrew isn't alive to defend himself, but even people who loved him and worked closely with him at the time noticed the strangest omission from his book: Matt Drudge himself. Drudge was the one who had brought him to his two loves of politics and the internet, the one who got him hooked on traffic. Traffic-hungry bloggers knew about Andrew—they knew that his tastes ran more toward a slashing style of right-wing politics, and that unlike Drudge, he hadn't been charmed by Barack Obama. They knew you saved those links for the afternoon, for Andrew, if you wanted a taste of that traffic. When Drudge himself got online, those links and the traffic that came with them would silently disappear.

In fact, Andrew had devoted a chapter in his memoir to Drudge—to how they'd met, what he'd learned, and how they worked together. But he couldn't afford to anger Drudge—his career had always depended on that relationship—so before he sent the draft to his publisher, he sent it to Drudge. Drudge vetoed it, said he didn't want to see any of that in print, and so Andrew cut the chapter. All that remained was the first line of the short book's last paragraph: "Three years ago, I was mostly a behind-the-scenes guy who linked to stuff on a very popular website."

Andrew would later emerge as a kind of John the Baptist to Donald Trump, seeding the ground for a new Right that would direct its anger at the media itself. But he was also just the most visible of many strange points of contact between what would be, ten years later, two totally distinct political movements separated by an online abyss. Obama and Trump, *The Huffington Post* and breitbart.com—it's hard to imagine that they'd have much in common. Yet both movements were rooted, in part, in the new way of thinking about people that came when you saw them as traffic—measuring interest and intent, and channeling it into action. So perhaps it's not so surprising that Jonah Peretti and Andrew Breitbart worked out of the same office for a couple of months in 2005.

5

....

Contagious

The *Huffington Post* launched on May 9, 2005. It got a lot of attention, most of it negative, and nearly two million page views in the first week.

The site landed, in fact, as a bit of a joke. It was the sort of thing Jonah would once have spoofed, not published. Arianna had persuaded her friends to "blog." Getting that request from her was, the writer Michael Wolff later noted, a bit like being asked to pray for someone. You couldn't refuse. The site was plastered with predictable screeds by Arianna and her Hollywood friends, including John Cusack and Ellen DeGeneres. The substance was pretty much whatever was on the mind of Hollywood's liberal elite, including a satirical article by Larry David on why he supported George W. Bush's nomination of the right-wing foreign policy figure John Bolton as ambassador to the United Nations. The Hollywood scoopster Nikki Finke pronounced the site dead on arrival, "such a bomb that it's the movie equivalent of *Gigli, Ishtar* and *Heaven's Gate* rolled into one" or perhaps "a sick hoax." AJ Daulerio had written Huffington off on *The Black Table* as a "five-star crackpot."

Despite all that negative attention, or perhaps because of it, *The Huff-*

ington Post's best day of traffic was its first one. The fantasy of million-view Drudge links had vanished along with Andrew. And technically, the site was essentially just the front page. After reaching 1.9 million views in the first week, the site fell to 1.1 million in the second, 960,000 in the third, 845,000 in the fourth. The only thing going viral was Arianna's name. But *The Huffington Post*'s revenue would depend on bringing in growing amounts of traffic at steady CPMs, taking advantage of what seemed like the inevitable realization among advertisers that shoppers had moved from newspapers and magazines to the internet. So Jonah went searching for ideas. Among the people he looked to for inspiration was Nick Denton. Because while Jonah had spent his time thinking about how to make an idea spread, Nick and Drudge were the masters of something else: how to make a website "sticky." They were masters of the refresh.

The crude traffic metrics of 2005 didn't even distinguish between a view to a specific article and a view to the whole website. By counting the times a single pixel, connected to an advertisement or a web page, had been downloaded from a server, a simple measuring tool could do what the business needed—crucially, telling advertisers how many times their little square or rectangular image had loaded. And like Drudge, Nick and his bloggers at an empire that was now anchored by Gawker were focused on a reader who woke up in the morning, went to the website, and kept visiting throughout the day. Nick was obsessed with commenters, too, and tried to make them into an exclusive club, sending out invitations by email to a select elite who were the only ones, at first, permitted to comment. He told the Gawker writers that they would know they'd succeeded when Kurt Andersen, the *Spy* co-founder, became a commenter.

Over coffee, Jonah asked Nick how he thought about traffic. Nick said he was beginning to think about it like compound interest—that if you could set a goal for a percentage of growth every month, pretty soon you'd see an exponential curve. That left an impression: Jonah thought of this often as he compared traffic totals from month to month with an eye toward a line that would go to the top right corner of the chart.

Jonah saw Nick back then as the man to beat, and eyed him with a mixture of admiration and competitiveness. He wasn't alone. Everyone in and around the media business was interested in Nick. He'd used Gawker to catch the attention of the media's power brokers—often with an edge that seemed to reflect his own personality. The former finance blogger Elizabeth Spiers infiltrated the Condé Nast cafeteria camouflaged as a *Devil Wears Prada*-era assistant in "a wrap dress and 'fuck ~~me~~ you' boots" and wrote at length for Gawker about a company culture that revolved around a grand cafeteria with high school politics. Another early initiative, Gawker Stalker, displayed Nick's cruel edge. It purported to use reader tips to track minor New York media celebrities, and panicked its subjects. The idea existed largely in the minds of angry publicists and celebrities, because even Nick's staff wouldn't quite go along. When Meg Hourihan mentioned walking past Gwyneth Paltrow's landmarked West Village town house on her way to work, Nick hounded her to add the actress's home to the stalker map. "Suddenly I was super protective of Gwyneth Paltrow," she recalled. Gawker Stalker ignited an early moral panic over what would come to be called, and loathed, as doxxing, but Nick was unconcerned. The media elite might despise him, but they knew who he was.

Jonah, meanwhile—well, *The Huffington Post* site was up and running, and he loved the feeling of building something new, and the drama and power his senior partners, Kenny and Arianna, carried with them. But while Nick was notorious, cool, and mysterious, Jonah was anonymous. The site was named after Arianna; nobody really knew who Jonah was. When he went to one of Nick's parties, the write-up would mention his sister, Chelsea, not him. Nerds like Duncan Watts knew he was special, but even they had a hard time explaining quite what Jonah did with his time. One of the few people who noticed Jonah, in fact, was Nick, who saw in him just the sort of person he liked to collect: a clever outsider trying to make his way in New York. He didn't like what he saw as Jonah's indifference to the substance of what he published, but he didn't see him as a threat either.

Nick had followed Jonah's viral stunts, like Black People Love Us! and the Rejection Line, a 212 number women could use to blow off unwanted suitors in the pre-Tinder days, with his own mix of admiration at the cleverness and revulsion at the goofy disconnect from any coherent argument. On May 19, 2005, ten days after *The Huffington Post* had launched in an enviable fury of media buzz, Nick found himself explaining Jonah to Gawker's skeptical sales guy, Chris Batty. Batty had come to Gawker licking his wounds from the layoffs at CNET, then a giant tech news site, that followed the bursting of the first internet bubble. Now he was working on a much smaller scale. At CNET, he'd been scoring seven-figure buys; now he found himself pumping his fist when he closed an $18,000 deal with Mini Cooper for Gawker. But the engagement of Gawker's readers, even then, made Batty's job feel powerful and real, and he knew the market would catch up. Now his boss was explaining internet jokes to him as they took a cab westward to the Contagious Media Showdown.

The Contagious Media Working Group, that small gathering of friends Jonah had started, still met weekly at Eyebeam on Kenny's dime. They gathered in a glassed-in office based on the MIT Media Lab's famous Cube, built with John Johnson's pharmaceutical fortune in a gallerylike space on far West Twenty-First Street. The group included Chelsea, along with Andrea Breanna, the star student in a class Jonah was teaching at NYU, the designer and researcher Ann Poochareon, and a gifted coder named Michael Frumin. They were joined by a rotating cast of early internet brains including the digital artist Cory Arcangel and a wild-eyed video-maker named Ze Frank, who had begun producing sharply edited monologues with a tight focus on his own face, a format that would later be known as vlogging. The group laughed a lot, often in wonder at the possibilities of the internet. They were creating a new science of hoaxes and pranks on the wide-open internet—a science because, for once, they had found a way to measure culture, measure the volume of outrage or the success of a joke. The group studied projects like Breanna's "Dog Island," in which she placed ads on Craigslist for a below-market apartment that you could rent on the condition that you give your dog to the idyllic Dog Island—which, as appalled internet sleuths followed Breanna's bread crumbs to discover, was owned by the former proprietor of a dog meat processing company. It was a hoax, funny if you were in on the joke. If you weren't, it was shocking and outrageous. Either way, you needed to tell someone about it, which is what made an idea "contagious."

Jonah had come up with the Contagious Media Showdown while building *The Huffington Post*'s bare-bones website. He needed a space where he could push ideas too weird, embarrassing, or likely to blow up in your face for *The Huffington Post*. The Showdown was an attempt to turn these apparently harmless online pranks into a kind of competitive sport. The metric, of course, would be traffic. Jonah sent word through emails to friends and through blogs like Jason Kottke's of the coming contest, and soon enough sixty teams were registered to take their shot at the $2,000 grand prize. The strongest entries used tactics that remain familiar. Forget-Me-Not Panties was an outrage: it purported to be a GPS-enabled product that jealous husbands and protective fathers could use to track a woman's location and body temperature. Delivr.net was a useful—and social—technology, allowing you to send postcards made from the service Flickr. And Crying while Eating was simply an inspired meme, a collection of short videos of people reliving difficult memories while scarfing food.

The crowd gathered in folding chairs in front of a low stage in Eyebeam's cavernous office that May 19. Jonah sat to one side of the stage, operating the screen behind him from his Mac laptop with mock seriousness, his hair thick and shaggy and his undershirt poking out from beneath a rumpled gray button-down. He had a panel of internet notables arrayed to his right. Chelsea was seated next to him in a sleeveless yellow dress, cracking jokes. Nick, natty in a gray sweater over a pink dress shirt, sat beside a bunch of nerds, including the co-founder of Hot or Not, James Hong. The big question Jonah was posing was the same one he and Cameron Marlow had been asking each other for two years: Could they predict who would win a cash prize, before the entries even went online? As an invitation asked: "Can they anticipate the tastes of the unwashed masses?" Entries played on a large screen, and the crowd shouted out approval for a few, including a clip of children at an amusement park over a soundtrack of Édith Piaf's "Non, je ne regrette rien" and loud fart sounds. Jonah thought Blogebrity would win the grand prize. That project played to bloggers' egos, treating them as celebrities and assuming they would inevitably link back, which would drive traffic. He took the others' predictions, and then announced with great fanfare that, simultaneously, all sixty sites had just launched on subdomains of Eyebeam's website. And then—well, nothing happened. It was a bit of an anticlimax. Nobody had smartphones. YouTube hadn't taken off yet. The crowd, awkwardly young and generally just awkward, milled around and picked at the wine and cheese. Some headed for the exits; others migrated into Eyebeam's office space and started sketching out on whiteboards their theories for how a prank could really go viral. To Hong, it was "nerd heaven."

There was no standardized way to measure traffic in 2005, which was why Jonah had insisted that the projects all be hosted on Eyebeam's site. Simple code recorded visits, and Frumin ran a crude script on those logs, counting the hits, page views, and unique visits to each page. When Frumin finished counting, the winner wasn't one of the ones anyone predicted: it was the sinister Forget-Me-Not Panties, the fake marketing materials of which boasted that, "unlike the cumbersome and uncomfortable chastity belts of the past, these panties are 100% cotton, and use cutting-edge technology to help you protect what matters most."

The project had managed to get global attention; its inventors had created a fake PR firm and manufacturing company to bolster the myth as journalists and would-be distributors reached out. The site got 122,000 unique visits from Japan alone, for a total of 615,562 visitors over the next month. But there was a problem. Most of the people who reacted to the project, with delight or outrage, didn't quite seem to get the feminist joke. This phenomenon was something that would later become painfully familiar: a bit of trolling would generate a wave of outrage from people who weren't in on the joke. The inventors' goal—to get consumers to question their own values and absorb a feminist message—remained out of reach. Even its co-creator, Leba Haber, couldn't figure out how to unravel the disturbing reaction.

The Showdown runner-up, Crying while Eating, had a different problem: people loved the site—and kept asking the creators how they planned to turn it into a business. "So what are your careers?" a puzzled Jay Leno asked them on *The Tonight Show.* (The stunt made it that big.) "Say you get a hundred million hits—you still don't get any money?!"

Batty, Nick's sales guy, had the same question. He couldn't figure out why he was at the Contagious Media party. Whatever it was—comedy? art?—it wasn't business. There were certainly no ad buyers at the event, which felt to Batty like some kind of college party, "super lame." But most of the attendees loved the noncommercial ethos. Andrea Breanna recalled, "We were total weirdos. It didn't tie to business. Nobody thought this would end up replacing or be the future of journalism or media or any of that. We didn't know what it would become."

Jonah, though, did have a glimpse of where it was going. He saw no tension between the noncommercial spirit of the Eyebeam event and his other career—which few at Eyebeam knew or cared about—as a partner in the promising new business of *The Huffington Post*. *The Huffington Post* was new then—but it was also, essentially, an old idea. It called itself, for God's sake, "The Internet Newspaper." With its echoes of *The Drudge Report*, *The Huffington Post* would be among the last of its breed, a great destination on the old web. Jonah would perfect the stickiness there that Nick pioneered, finding ways to make *The Huffington Post* the destination not just for a generation of baby boomer liberals who wanted their politics reaffirmed, but also, crucially, for a new slice of readers who would come to the site through Google. But even then, as Jonah saw it, his endgame was elsewhere: it was in contagious traffic to a single idea, which would travel through the world under its own power, cutting a wide swath.

6

....

Valleywag

S ay one thing about Nick Denton: he hosted better parties than Jonah. He was cheap when it came to booze, and his idea of hors
d'oeuvres was White Castle hamburgers, but he had a killer hand with a
guest list. He drew from his spreadsheet that contained the names of 679
"influencers"—minor media personalities—sorted by gender, but also
knew that it was all about whom you left off: one of his own staff, un-
predictably, for each party, along with most of the khaki pants squad his
ad salesman Chris Batty wanted to invite.

Back in 2005, Nick's SoHo loft held a special place in the downtown
imagination. In a world of Brooklyn walk-ups, Nick—who had finally
gotten a real Silicon Valley exit when Moreover was sold for $30 million
in 2005 to an unglamorous internet service provider called Verisign—
inhabited a sprawling 2,556-square-foot loft on the corner of Spring and
Crosby in a building where Harvey Weinstein also owned an apartment.
As he took New York's media world by storm, Nick threw huge Hal-
loween parties and launch parties, and smaller gatherings for writers

and entrepreneurs. His writers smoked weed on the balcony, and snorted cocaine and Adderall in the bathroom.

The guest of honor at Nick Denton's loft on September 21, 2005, a few months after the Contagious Media Showdown, was Arianna Huffington, but the center of attention was Jessica Coen. Jessica was the center of attention at most of the parties she came to and covered that magic year. That had a little to do with the rarity of a young woman with a big voice in the male-dominated early blogosphere, and something to do with the way she'd steered the voice of Gawker. The site was getting traffic, more traffic than Gawker had ever attracted before.

Traffic, to Nick and to Jessica, was something pure. It was an art, not a science. Traffic meant that what you were doing was working. It meant that someone was reading your blog, instead of all the other blogs, most of them personal diaries with no readers at all. Jessica's own path embodied her era of bloggers. She'd gone to school in state, at the University of Michigan, but then she moved to Los Angeles and got a glamorous-sounding job as an assistant on the 20th Century Fox Television lot in Culver City. In reality, she was working for the company's business affairs officer, and her most important duty was fetching an omelet from the commissary for her boss each morning. The highlight of her time there was the 2003 Christmas party, where she thanked Rupert Murdoch personally for airing *The O.C.* Coen realized quickly that she didn't want to be there, and started her personal blog to stave off the boredom and get into shape for Columbia Journalism School, where she'd just applied. But when she blogged about a minor tidbit relating to a speech at the Emmys and other blogs picked it up, she felt a sense of vertigo at how suddenly an unverified bit of gossip could spread.

Jessica made friends online—her New York blogger friends called her "Foxy Jess"—and when she came to New York to visit Columbia's campus, the local bloggers threw her a party, where she met the Gawker crew and other figures of that early blogosphere. Within a week of moving to the city, she had made her way to Camp Bowery, where she met AJ. He talked her into writing short items for *The Black Table*. But her sarcasm and outsider posture—her Michigan roots showed—caught Nick's eye, and he persuaded her to give up her slot at Columbia for the blog dream job, at $24,000 a year and no health insurance, at the age of twenty-four. Now, at his loft just a year later, her gimlet eye had made her central to that moment in New York, in the way a young journalist can briefly be central.

It's hard to capture just how riveting her work was. Blogs are conversational, not meant to be preserved. Their style, and their subjects, date fast. Take as a sample her spoof of *New York* magazine's annual "Reasons to Love New York." Jessica's entries included "5. Because we get to push tourists if we're late for work" and "57. Because everyone's got a blog." Jessica was the voice of an aggrieved creative underclass, raging against the pompous, decaying big New York media. She had sources, too, and that was part of the drama. *The New York Times* wrote about it when Condé Nast fired a researcher for forwarding Gawker a memo Jessica then published. A student at the University of Utah, Foster Kamer, found Gawker's window into a seductive downtown world so addicting that he dropped out of school and moved to New York, found a job as a busboy, and angled for years for a job at Gawker.

Nick liked his writers feral, and Jessica was the model. She lived by the hourly updates provided by Site Meter, a one-man company created in 1998 whose invisible code, embedded on Gawker, reported how many people had been reading her blog the previous hour. Even this was a new level of immediacy. Jess's main revelation was that if you started early, readers would check the site before work and then again when they sat down at the office, and keep hitting refresh through the day. She'd get back to her sixth-floor Lower East Side walk-up after midnight most nights, but she woke up at 6:00 a.m. and shot straight from her bed to her desk to cruise through the morning papers for tidbits. She'd hit refresh to see how many people were reading what she'd posted. When the morning was going well, and she felt like she had a shot at one hundred thousand views on the day, she'd allow herself a brief nap at 11:00 a.m. That was the spirit that had pushed Nick's growing blog empire beyond a million views a day by the beginning of 2005, his half dozen blogs amassing a total of 31.5 million views that January.

In the spring of 2005, AJ Daulerio, the *Black Table* co-founder and now Jess's boyfriend, managed to persuade Nick that he was an expert in gambling, and got hired to start a gambling blog called Oddjack. In fact, AJ knew nothing about gambling. ("Do you understand you've hired somebody who has no knowledge of gambling whatsoever?" one gambler who glanced at a beta version of the site asked Lockhart Steele, then Nick's deputy. But in those days, this didn't seem like a fatal flaw.) AJ didn't know much about blogging, either, so Coen became his tutor. Gawker didn't yet have headquarters—just Nick's loft and the office on the top floor of a Franklin Street walk-up with no air conditioning, sweltering on hot summer days as engineers labored to build a tech platform Nick had begun calling Kinja. Steele arrived at Franklin Street in the morning of June 1, the day Oddjack was to launch, to find that AJ had been there all night, frantically trying to populate the website. He was dripping with sweat. Coen helped as best she could. (Nick would ask the editor of another of his growing fleet of blogs, Nick Douglas, to break the news that two of his writers were dating, but Douglas let Jessica talk him out of it, an early sign he wasn't ruthless enough for Nick Denton's employ.)

Jessica welcomed AJ to the Gawker fold that afternoon with a post announcing the new site. "Much like any family-friendly company, Gawker

Media prides itself on vice. We've covered porn and gossip, but our lawyers are getting tired with the boring old libel and obscenity suits," she wrote. "Edited by AJ Daulerio, Oddjack covers everything you need to know to fuck up your life."

Traffic was intoxicating, but it wasn't the only substance available. Coen was at that party for Arianna Huffington in the company of the two other "fucked-up musketeers," Steele and Coen's Gawker co-editor, Jesse Oxfeld, so christened by Nick because they were rarely sober at the parties they covered nearly every night. Sometimes Nick tried to help out: Coen recalled him once inviting her to "go skiing" with him—even then a ludicrously old-fashioned invite to use coke.

That night she and the other musketeers hadn't required any help. They watched as Nick stood on his coffee table, dressed in black jeans and a tight black shirt, to welcome a competitor to the party. He read out the abuse that had been heaped on Arianna Huffington by one rival, who called the site "horrific" and predicted that its failure would be "unsurvivable" for her.

"I think contrition is in order from the doubters," he said to applause.

Then Huffington kicked off her shoes to join him on the coffee table. Nick Denton, she pronounced, measuring his value in the language of power, was "the Rupert Murdoch of the blogosphere."

Huffington didn't entirely mean it. She never said no to an invitation, but she also didn't think Nick's gossip sites added up to much. Anonymous kids writing for one another, with no impact on politics and no entrée to the world of celebrities. She was the one who would validate blogging by bringing the big names—even George Clooney!—to the internet.

There were, though, some false notes, suggestions Arianna didn't quite speak the language of the world she was entering. In particular, the bloggers noted, she kept using the word "blog" to mean what they called "blog posts"; it was like calling a newspaper article a "newspaper."

But even if the musketeers rolled their eyes, Nick's welcome wasn't feigned: Huffington's arrival validated their small world. She was a real celebrity, not the sort of threadbare one Gawker had created out of minor downtown scenesters. She was a real millionaire. She'd lived two lives: her version of that downtown scene had been London pubs in the 1980s, where she and Tina Brown had reigned as brilliant young writers and editors.

Gawker, Nick thought, was ready to take its own place in the cycle of media booms, as the inheritor both of that London scene and of the 1980s New York of Kurt Andersen's *Spy* magazine. Nick had the numbers to prove it. That same week, he'd taken *The New York Observer*'s influential media writer, Tom Scocca, to Balthazar. Nick sat on the red banquette, opened his laptop, and gave Scocca the view. Nick's empire cruised past thirty million views a month in 2005, though he'd begun focusing on a different metric: the "unique visitors," individuals who kept coming back and clicking, addicted to a blogger's voice. That summer, the tech site Gizmodo had reached 537,000 unique visitors a month; Gawker had 456,000, and Nick's charts showed Scocca that they were growing steadily. *Wonkette* had fallen off since the election to about 250,000 unique visitors a month, and the porn blog *Fleshbot* had hit 519,000. (It was sort of cheating to do a porn blog, but Nick liked introducing himself at parties as a pornographer.) *Lifehacker*, a blog of tips that would turn out to be Nick's most valuable property, had just launched and was growing nicely.

"No one can really argue with the data," Nick told Scocca. "I can't argue with the data. The writers can't really argue with the data."

Nick took Scocca on a tour of Gawker's biggest successes. Paris Hilton in March. Jude Law. Kate Moss. Hurricane Katrina.

"You can't pretend to yourself that people actually have highfalutin taste," he said. "Nobody ever searches for 'Inequality in America.'"

And so Nick, looking at traffic that reflected a combination of Coen's cutting wit and people's prurient interest in celebrities, was privately skeptical that Huffington's project could work. Safe and vapid celebrity blogs would get old, he told friends. But the money and the glamour Arianna had brought to the party lent Gawker cachet. Her low-profile partner, Jonah, meanwhile stood by a window while his sister, Chelsea, told jokes to Chris Batty.

To welcome Arianna was also to affirm Gawker's centrality. Nick was the host, and if he was basking in Huffington's reflected glory, he was also asserting his own. *The Huffington Post* was merely joining a party that he had started; he saw no path for this clunky new thing of hers to overtake him.

What felt to everyone at the time like Gawker's ascendancy was, in retrospect, something like its peak. Gawker's staff would quickly go back to ignoring *The Huffington Post*, except for the increasingly cruel jokes they made about Arianna. But *The Huffington Post* was playing a different game, in more ways than one. They had none of Gawker's pride in playing by instinct, and no illusion that traffic was the same as quality, or had any real connection to the things that young New York media people cared about. Jonah and *The Huffington Post* would increasingly turn traffic into a science. And they'd be the first in a new wave of media, funded by the venture capital Nick had forsworn and taking an analytical approach to traffic that offended his tastes and undermined his belief that the underlying mechanics of the internet would point toward a raw new truth.

One person who did glimpse that future was Rachel Sklar, a young Canadian lawyer who had moved to New York and fallen for the nascent glamour of blog reports on parties just like this one. She showed up at Nick's September party as a reporter for the media gossip blog *FishbowlNY*, but she saw that Arianna and her website were ascendant and she wanted to be part of it.

So Sklar bought a fancy red tube top, with sequins. (This was, after all, 2005.) She accessorized further by convincing her ex-boyfriend, an eye-catching model, to accompany her, and got a Greek friend to teach her how to say, "Welcome to New York." She swooped in, said the magic words, and felt for a moment the warmth of Huffington's charisma. She later learned that the way she pronounced it, she had called Huffington a "fucking masturbator," but the spirit was enough—the interaction won her an invitation to a party Huffington was giving for Nick in Los Angeles a few months later, and Sklar said, why, of course she'd be in town, before scrounging the money for a ticket.

Their conversation was interrupted abruptly by Nick, who wanted to introduce Huffington to Coen, who had also scored an invite to a Huffington party a couple of weeks later.

Nick liked to be efficient, so the parties weren't just about influence: they were content too. Two days later, Coen posted twenty-eight pictures by Gawker's photographer, writing that "Gawker publisher Nick Denton decided to be a little less selfish than usual and threw a soiree in honor of Arianna Huffington" who "was in town to distribute air-kisses and feta cheese."

The pictures have the poignancy of something in its happy youth. They also capture the homogeneity of New York's rising media class in 2005, not all that different from the classes before it: all fifty-nine people photographed appear to be white.

The photographs also indicate how obscure Jonah still was, not among the fifty-nine most important people at Nick's loft that night. Though Coen did mention his sister. "Before night's end, Chelsea Peretti will be carrying Jakob Lodwick's seed," she wrote of a picture of the comedian with Vimeo's co-founder. Batty had been hanging around Chelsea Peretti, too, but he'd only gotten her first name, and when the party cleared out, he asked Nick who she was. He was shocked to learn that she was the sister of the dork from the Contagious Media Showdown.

A couple of weeks later, Coen answered Huffington's invitation to meet her at a penthouse off Astor Place. The guest list there was made up of bona fide television celebrities, not the hacks and flacks from Nick's spreadsheet. Huffington introduced Coen to the kind of people that Jessica had been taking potshots at and Arianna knew on a first-name basis. When she brought her to meet Star Jones, a host of *The View*, Coen felt the other woman recoil when she was introduced as a writer for Gawker. Jessica tried to remember through the fog of celebrity and alcohol what she'd written to insult her. So much of her stuff was mean—mean-funny kept her safe, and besides, Nick liked it.

Coen felt utterly out of place. It was part of why her writing was so good, her eye so clear. She was a force in her small world, a celebrity in her own right who graced the cover of the downtown magazine *Animal New York*, leaning against a wall in a green T-shirt, hands thrust into her pockets. But she felt like a total outsider there with Huffington. She was wearing hand-me-downs from the *New York Post* gossip writer Paula Froelich, who was—like so many those days—cozying up to Gawker.

She felt even more out of place when Arianna hustled her downstairs into a taxi up Lafayette Street, across town and to an apartment building on Central Park West and West Eighty-Eighth Street. Huffington swept Coen past the doorman. The elevator doors opened directly into Kenny Lerer's apartment, a duplex. "I should not be here," Coen thought. The feeling got worse when she spilled red wine on the carpet.

When her head cleared, she was talking to John Cusack, the iconic Gen X actor. He wanted to pick *her* brain. In particular, he had a blog post he wanted to write about politics, and his advice for the Democratic Party.

"I want to call it 'Waiting for Dems,'" he said. "What do you think?"

She thought it had to be one of the worst ideas for a blog headline she'd ever heard. Nobody would click on that. She couldn't decide if that meant that *The Huffington Post* was a joke, that this would never work. Or alternately, if it didn't matter if anyone clicked, if *The Huffington Post* could run on some fuel other than traffic. The little club of bloggers wasn't exclusive or countercultural anymore. John Cusack had arrived, with a very dumb headline. However *The Huffington Post* was getting traffic, this wasn't it.

History doesn't proceed evenly; it moves through scenes and moments. The history of the twenty-first century's technological revolution has been written almost entirely from the West Coast of the United States, where the great companies that dominate our lives—Facebook and Google and Netflix in San Francisco, Amazon and Microsoft in Seattle— were founded and based. But those middle years after the crash were uncertain ones for Silicon Valley, and heady ones in SoHo's aspiring Silicon Alley, where a wave of companies seemed poised to blend culture and technology with a lighter touch than the crude monsters of the early web, dial-up specialists like AOL and CompuServe. The New York companies were Gawker and *The Huffington Post, Business Insider* and Etsy and Foursquare; while none would ultimately challenge the giants, the new connections between technology and society that these companies created—in the forms of things like share buttons, reblogs, and meetups—remain central to the economy of platforms and creators that emerged years later.

For Jonah and Nick, 2005 was the year it all accelerated. In the space of eighteen months, Jonah went from being seen as a kind of mad genius tinkerer to the visionary behind first one, then two, of the most exciting new media companies in town. Nick, for his part, went from being the envy of a few downtown bloggers to the embodiment of media's relentless future.

One place Nick and Jonah diverged was on the question of financing. Jonah had watched Kenny and Arianna raise that first round for *The Huffington Post*, and he was confident that when the time came to strike out on his own, he could tell the kind of story that attracted venture capitalists in New York and San Francisco alike. But Nick didn't want to raise money from Silicon Valley. He'd been there before, had his board shoot him down when he was right on the verge of a real tech deal. He'd been talking to friends about doing a startup already when he was covering Silicon Valley for the *Financial Times* in the late 1990s. He spent more than a decade fantasizing that Kinja, the tech platform, would be his real business—not just a bunch of blogs.

Maybe that explains why Nick decided to launch Valleywag. It's hard to explain it otherwise. The site never got much traffic, peaking around two million visitors a month. It didn't sell many ads. It didn't even generate the kinds of anonymous comments you'd see on Jezebel or Gawker—too many tech workers understood how IP addresses worked, how traceable they could be. It was, Nick always knew, "never commercial." The advertisers in lucrative Silicon Valley publications were venture capital and law firms—not the consumer brands Batty sold to.

But Valleywag was, in some ways, the most personally significant of the Gawker sites to Nick Denton. He had never quite been able to make it in San Francisco himself. His friends always speculated as to why not. Maybe he was too much of a perfectionist, too obsessed with loading Kinja up with cool little features to actually launch much of it. On Valleywag, Nick targeted the people he might have been, had he stayed out west, had Moreover turned into the giant news platform Nick had dreamed it could become. But if it was the least successful of his ventures, the blog about Silicon Valley was what would destroy his company.

Valleywag channeled Nick's frustrated ambition. It embodied New York's scorn and resentment for Silicon Valley. It was obsessed with exposure in a tech world that valued its privacy, even as it would end global privacy as we'd known it. Nick had always produced traffic flow by giving people the things they wouldn't admit they wanted, and by publishing the things that nobody else would. The purest form of this was the sex tape—the embodiment of prurience, of the thing you'd never admit to watching but couldn't help yourself from clicking. The sex tape brought out the worst in people; that is to say, it revealed people as Nick had always assumed they were.

Sex tapes were a regular feature of the aughts internet. Those were the late days of analog privacy, of normal people's assumptions that they could have secrets. Sex tapes were exotic, something that happened to someone with fancy equipment who went to the trouble of making a movie; not something on everyone's phone, not something that could happen to you. Paris Hilton's tape helped cement her celebrity. Most mainstream media ignored the ones that appeared in dark corners of the internet, but to Nick these tapes represented a breakthrough in honesty, transgression, whatever. In February of 2005, Jessica Coen had seen one going around featuring—that is to say, violating the privacy of—the front man of the band Limp Bizkit, Fred Durst. She posted the Durst sex tape, and it was the first in a series on Nick's websites that would grow to include the quarterback Brett Favre's penis and the wrestler Hulk Hogan having sex with his best friend's wife.

The rules about sex tapes were pretty clear back then, if you were a celebrity: you had to pretend not to mind, maybe suggest you'd pro-moted it yourself. Durst didn't understand that at first, and he threat-ened an $80 million lawsuit against Gawker and the other sites that had posted the tape.

"There's an old saying around the Gawker offices, coined by our wise Hungarian goat-herding ancestors: you're nobody until somebody hates you," Coen posted in response. "But we had it wrong. It turns out that you're actually nobody until some other nobody sues you. Thank you, Fred Durst and your fabulous band of lawyers, for setting us straight. . . . We'll see you in court. Or not, if you want to kiss and make up in the meantime. If your flowers are freshly cut, we can be rather forgiving," she concluded.

Gawker did take the video down, after ensuring that anyone who was interested had seen it. And Durst decided he didn't want to fight with these dangerous new internet kids. Incredibly, he did send flowers, with a handwritten note. "I never meant the suit to include you guys," he wrote.

Silicon Valley didn't have sex tapes. But it had sex, something that the staid business coverage of the Valley to date had avoided saying out loud. Valleywag launched with a bit of a bang: by disclosing the open secret that Google co-founder Larry Page had dated the company's head of search, Marissa Mayer.

"Marissa Mayer used to date Larry Page. There, we said it," the site began on February 2, 2006, justifying the report immediately by saying that while "the relationship shouldn't be a big deal . . . the real embarrassment is that of the Silicon Valley's toothless press corps," who had never reported on the couple's existence.

It was classic Nick, and he wanted more. His unlikely champion was Nick Douglas, an aspiring writer from a Christian college in Pennsylvania, whom Nick Denton saw as the kind of pure outsider he wanted to enlist for his assault on Silicon Valley.

"It was like some dipshit college in Pennsylvania and he's a fucking retard anyway," Batty recalled. "So I'm like, 'He should definitely leave college.' And he does!" They left him in San Francisco to round up the news during the day, and to show up at parties and try to gather gossip at night. It was an incredible ride, Douglas remembered later. Once he walked up to Mayer at a party at Oracle founder Larry Ellison's lavish mansion, and she literally ran away from him.

For the young blogger, it was "a sick, undeserved rush of power."

One particular target was the young founder of Facebook, Mark Zuckerberg. "We Want to Know If You're Single Mark Zuckerberg so We Can Contact You Maybe," read one headline soon after the blog's launch. "Mark, get some shoes—bitch," Douglas advised after Zuck turned up at a conference in November 2006 wearing sandals.

But Douglas couldn't quite get the hang of it. He wasn't getting the quality of gossip that Nick Denton wanted, and he didn't seem to have much grasp of the business story, the only reason anyone cared about the Valley anyway. Eight months later, Denton flew to San Francisco and fired Douglas, which he wrote about in one of the ice-cold personnel memos that truly scared his young staff.

"Nick Douglas, the kid we plucked from college to launch Valleywag, will be a great journalist," Nick Denton began. But the young writer lacked the journalistic chops that Denton still thought would beat either bloggy commentary or the technical tricks that *The Huffington Post* was beginning to pioneer in the race for traffic. Denton was "looking for someone with, ideally, some background in reporting. An old-media career, useful in the sparkling new world of blogs. Who would have thought?"

Nick Denton seemed a little chastened after his protégé's failure. "We're going to tone down the personal coverage of civilians, because they haven't done anything to seek out attention, and their personal lives aren't that interesting. Unless they are. Anyway, more money, a little less sex: that is Valleywag's new gossip mantra," he wrote, adding that he himself would be taking over writing the site. "Okay, so I was bored running a business."

While he was in town, Nick Denton ran into one of those Silicon Valley tech journalists he so scorned, Sarah Lacy, who had just had a big *BusinessWeek* cover on the founder of Digg. Nick and Lacy were in the hallway of San Francisco's Palace Hotel for the Web 2.0 Summit (the theme: "Disruption & Opportunity"), listening in on speakers who included Jeff Bezos, Eric Schmidt, and Arthur Sulzberger Jr. Neither of them could afford tickets to the exclusive hallways where deals got done. So she was wearing a badge that the venture capitalist Marc Andreessen had lent her; the Englishman who introduced himself to her, she noticed, was wearing someone else's badge too.

A week later, right after he announced that he'd fired Douglas, Nick blogged about Lacy, tagging the post "VALLEY FOXES."

There is, he wrote below a picture of the smiling reporter, "one salient fact about Sarah Lacy that most commentators are way too politically correct to mention: she is the hottest reporter in the Valley.

"Not saying that's the reason for her success," Denton leered. "The fact that she and Jeremy Stoppelman of Yelp are both attractive, and know each other, does *not* mean that they're having an affair, or that she sleeps with other tech execs."

Then Lacy got an email from Nick Denton, the gist of which was "Don't you love that I wrote that?" She was incredulous. He had no idea how hard it had been to get any credibility on the beat. "He always had this sense of somehow I'm making you, somehow I'm doing you a favor," she recalled. The post got seventy-five thousand views. And the message from Nick was pretty clear: fuck these people, their faux utopianism, and the journalism that bought into it. Their money might have put a veneer on their greed and their standard-issue quest for sex and power, but with X-ray cynicism they'd learned from their boss, the bloggers back in SoHo thought they could see right through it all.

Plateau

W hen *The Huffington Post* launched in the spring of 2005, Jonah
drew a line on a whiteboard for Kenny to illustrate what he expected the site's early traffic to be like. It showed a single spike in the first
week, then a plunge almost all the way back down to zero, then a plateau,
and then a long slow climb back up. Jonah had secretly worried that the
site—like so many viral stunts—would flatline after the first week of
media buzz, which included Arianna's appearance on the *Today* show
and promotion by her celebrity friends. The traffic did follow the pattern
Jonah predicted, impressing Kenny, but it didn't fall quite as far as he
feared. With the Iraq War raging and Republicans firmly in control, liberals *did*, as Kenny and Arianna had predicted, want their own *Drudge
Report*, and some of the people who'd visited *The Huffington Post* on
that first day came back, and shared, until the site was reaching a million
people a month.

The Huffington Post founders were still a little short of the $2 million
they'd planned to raise for launch, despite Kenny's putting up half and
friends of Arianna's closing most of the rest of the gap. John Johnson,

Jonah's patron at Eyebeam, had been interested, but Jonah quietly told him to hold off. After a few days of traffic, he called John to tell him it would be a surer bet, and John's investment closed the first round.

Still, the plateau presented a problem, and the problem was the whole idea of *The Huffington Post* as a platform for famous voices and liberal politics. This was Arianna's side of the operation, the side that would hire Rachel Sklar the next year to both cover the media and recruit new bloggers—celebrities large and small, who would write for free and talk up their connection to *The Huffington Post*, creating buzz and social currency and thus, Huffington claimed, traffic.

But, as Coen had intuited in that moment with John Cusack, that couldn't really be how *The Huffington Post* worked. Arianna brought elite attention and talent to the site. But even as Huffington went around talking to anyone who could listen about how millions of people wanted to read an alternative view on the Iraq War, Jonah and his team knew the truth: nobody was reading that stuff. In fact, not that many people were reading *The Huffington Post* at all. At this rate, its liberal founders would run out of money before they could get a Democratic president elected.

So Jonah began scrambling for that missing element, traffic. While he played the role of chief technology officer and general internet expert all through 2005, his domain had been limited. *The Huffington Post*, back then, was really just a single web page. It still took *The Drudge Report* as its model, and most of the links went out to other sites, with just a column for the celebrity bloggers Arianna had posting directly to the site. Kenny, who knew how to catch the attention of the political and media class, was personally writing the giant "splash" headlines, and everyone knew the site had attitude. But there was a limit to how many times you could hit refresh. That slogan, "The Internet Newspaper," pleased investors but made younger staffers cringe. At best, it looked back to the previous decade, the previous boom; it was just a portal. This was how Yahoo! and AOL had built their massive traffic: by funneling users of their dial-up or email services to a single, organized page through which you could find the whole internet, a page to which you'd turn many times a day. Yahoo! and AOL were deadly boring, though—everything to everybody. *The Drudge Report*, at least, was interesting: an oddball juggernaut driving a right-wing narrative through the internet back to mainstream media, drawing people back and back with the newest news and provocative angles. But Matt Drudge was just one guy in Miami. He had influence—the thing Lerer craved—but he wasn't trying to build a giant media business capable of doing more than providing himself a luxurious lifestyle.

This, in 2005, was what the *Huffington Post* team was worrying about in the huge open room that looked out on Crosby Street. They were a couple of blocks north of Nick's loft, in space Kenny had rented to house the new online news site along with his own venture fund, and assorted other investments including his son's men's style newsletter, *Thrillist*. Writers could tell that Jonah had some kind of special power because of how often he walked from his corner over to Kenny's office on the relatively rare occasions both were in at the same time. What they were talking about was usually how to defy the expectations that Nick and many others held that the site would ultimately merely be Huffington's latest vanity project.

Nick had launched his own portal the same year, called *Sploid*. It was intended as a kind of dense, juicy internet tabloid—a new front page for the internet that people really wanted to see. Lockhart Steele, Nick's deputy and Coen's boss, sneered at the competition from *The Huffington Post*: "This is the worst idea we have ever heard, and it has the stupidest name ever. It's trying to do the same thing we're doing, but in the dumbest way possible, and we are going to fucking obliterate *The Huffington Post*," he thought.

But Jonah had some tricks up his sleeve. There was another way to get traffic, he realized. It was to stay out of sight—away from the clever and political front page, and Huffington's eternal cocktail party circuit, where she described a project that bore only a passing resemblance to an actual website. While Huffington talked a big game, Jonah tinkered. He began filling in the bottom of the page with the sorts of stories people clicked on, even if those didn't exactly fit the site's carefully manicured image. He traded links with other big websites of the era, forgotten traffic springs like fark.com. He noticed the big patterns, like the fact that Digg's young users were obsessed with Barack Obama and would upvote the stories that made him look good.

Huffington liked to hire big-name Washington journalists who would promote her site on television and at Georgetown dinner parties, figures like *Newsweek*'s Howard Fineman. They showed a benign interest in Jonah's increasingly frantic scramble for traffic, but wrote the same stories they'd always been writing. They cared *who* was reading, not *how many*. They measured themselves by the old standards of journalism: power, relevance, impact.

By the beginning of 2006, *The Huffington Post* was turning into what Arianna wanted it to be: a buzzy platform for her famous friends; and what Kenny wanted it to be: a political force. But the home page, with screaming political headlines about Iraq and celebrity bloggers opining, interested Jonah less and less. He found himself being introduced to people in meetings as "the tech guy," even asked to help with people's machines.

Jonah still thought the real future was purely online—without reference to the old ways of doing media. He wanted to mine for traffic in ways that were too weird, too close to the edge for "The Internet Newspaper" that *The Huffington Post* aspired to be. He began plotting an escape. On January 6, 2006, almost exactly five years after the Nike email,

Jonah incorporated a new company, Contagious Media LLC. He told Kenny and John Johnson that he was restless, that perhaps he should move on from *The Huffington Post*. They, in turn, saw an opportunity in Jonah's discomfort. Kenny invested—$100,000—in Jonah's new company and became chairman of his board. Johnson paid the bills month to month, eventually putting in about $1 million. To Johnson, the money constituted a pure investment in Jonah, a bet that whatever he touched would turn to gold. For Kenny, it was a way to keep Jonah on his team. He justified the unusual arrangement as a kind of skunkworks—like in the Stop the NRA days—with Jonah channeling his project's findings back to the real business, *The Huffington Post*. Jonah wouldn't leave his job, or his $150,000-a-year salary, but he'd forgo raises and equity while he spent more time at the new company.

That February, Jonah made a run at merging his ambitions and *The Huffington Post*'s by bringing Mark Wilkie on board. Wilkie, a sturdy, amiable jack-of-all-trades (or "full stack developer," to put it technically), had worked for everyone in that small world, including being part of Meg Hourihan's team in the early days of Kinja. Now Jonah hired him at *The Huffington Post* as a consultant to help the overwhelmed lone developer Andy Yaco-Mink on the rollout of the Contagious Media Festival, which Jonah was trying to revive as a *Huffington Post* feature. There would be monthly competitions, which served the dual goals of keeping Jonah entertained and generating traffic for *The Huffington Post*—2.5 million views in February alone. The contest, hosted on a hacked-together subdomain, had gotten off to a slow start at the beginning of the month, with a rapping ostrich competing with what Jonah described, in a post pleading for more entries, as "a hilarious animated spoof on wiretapping." Shortly after Wilkie started, however, the news cycle provided perfect viral fodder when Vice President Dick Cheney shot a man in the face. A Philadelphia man named Vance Lehmkuhl threw together a flash game called *Quail Hunting with Dick Cheney* (try as you might, you always wind up shooting your friend in the face) and used Wilkie's interface to upload it to *The Huffington Post*. Jonah loved it. He found in Wilkie the kind of collaborator he liked: a big laugh, a tinkerer's heart, and a game willingness to implement ideas so crazy or trolly they just might work.

Jonah kept promoting the festivals, but his content was experiencing a key feature of viral media: decay. He first noticed it in one of the great early viral videos, "Numa Numa Dance," in which a young man from New Jersey dances ecstatically to an Eastern European pop song. The first video got hundreds of millions of views and so the young man made a second, which got tens of millions. Numa 3 just cleared a million. It had become cringe.

The Contagious Festival—indeed the whole idea of "contagious media"—seemed to be decaying too. The victorious Vance Lehmkuhl enjoyed his prize—a dinner with Arianna and John Cusack—but the quality of entries kept declining, and their sheer weirdness didn't comport with *The Huffington Post*'s increasingly serious sense of itself.

Jonah brought Wilkie to his new company, where Wilkie and Frumin began building tools to track media objects as they traveled the internet, smarter new RSS feeds that would tell you what was hot. This was a version of what Nick had tried to do at Moreover and Kinja. Wilkie's scripts crawled blogs and news sites and aggregators like Digg and Reddit, identified popular links, and grouped them together as trends. The tool did not discriminate between news, a silly joke, a video, or a photo of a surprised-looking animal with a quote over the top—it was all content, all measured by a single, clear standard.

About six months in, Jonah decided they needed a website where they could show off their findings—a feed of all the buzz they were tracking, called BuzzFeed. They hired another jack-of-all-trades, a quiet graphic designer named Chris Johanesen to build it. Johanesen wanted something that looked modern, in tune with the rounded and bubbly design of Twitter and Facebook—but also bold and urban. So he combined their sans serif fonts with the brand's striking red color.

As the software kicked out lists of links, it became clear that while it could detect what was going viral, it would also detect a lot of junk. Jonah could pick out new trends from the spam and the obvious big news, but he needed someone to do that full time—a human editor. He scrambled to find one, emailing friends for ideas before he thought of Peggy Wang. She'd been a student at the elite private school in New Orleans where he taught before MIT, and she'd appreciated his California hipster taste and his dorky jokes—plus she had been really, really good at his subject, computer science. Her father was a programmer at Tulane, but she was most of all a music nerd. Her tastes were broad: she went to local punk shows, and she was also obsessed with MTV and had come to New York to make music.

While she'd made it to MTV, it was as a programmer—she was now twenty-six, building websites for its parent company, Viacom, and deejaying at night. She was an unusual character: quiet but not shy, confident but not boastful. To the extent she was dreaming, it was about her musical career. Jonah hired her to help with some JavaScript at *The Huffington Post*. Then he asked her to try out for the editorial role at BuzzFeed. Jonah had applicants fill out responses on an online form, which he submitted to a panel of judges; Peggy hadn't taken the process particularly seriously, and just put a few random trends her friends had been talking about into the list format Jonah was asking for. However, Jonah saw in Peggy's casual application exactly what he'd been looking for: a clear grasp on internet culture and no journalistic snobbery—in fact, no sense of herself as a journalist at all. He persuaded her to take a small pay cut—writing being a lower-value skill than coding—to be his third employee.

Jonah set Wilkie, Johanesen, and Peggy up in a small office in China-town, on the corner of Canal and Elizabeth Streets. It seemed a long way from the heady gamble he'd made with Marlow at MIT. The only bets being placed were by the old ladies in the mah-jongg parlors that shared the building, where—even in Mike Bloomberg's New York—laws against smoking and gambling went blissfully unenforced. The website they launched that November was a simple, reverse chronological feed—the basic look has never changed—under Johanesen's red logo and the motto "Find your new favorite thing." Lest a visitor to the site mistake it for just another list of links—something users voted on, like Digg, or editors populated, like Yahoo!—BuzzFeed strained to show off the technology under the hood. Each day's content was defined, at first, by a robotic-sounding header: "NEW BUZZ detected." And the top right of the home page offered a wordy explanation of what you were looking at. "BuzzFeed distinguishes what is actually interesting from what is merely hyped," it declared. "We only feature movies, music, fashion, ideas, technology, and culture that are on the rise and worth your time."

The text went on to emphasize that special "Buzz Detection" soft-ware "crunches the raw data from these sites to identify new buzz that's just starting to spread."

Then, in the next stage, "the editorial process transforms a messy jumble of buzz data and submissions into a quick, fun summary of the hottest new buzz."

Mostly, there was just a long, nearly endless list of lists of links. The "new buzz" was composed of each day's new posts—Peggy tried to do five a day every weekday—each with a deadpan headline. A sample from late November and early December of 2006 is a weird echo of the zeitgeist: "Global Warming Vacation Hotspots," "Funny Republican T-Shirts," "Radioactive Poisoning," "Cuddle Parties," "Photoshopped Images of Non-Existent Apple Products," "Rich and Skinny," "Quirky Hats," and

"Spray On Condoms." Under each heading was a brief, one-sentence summary of the trend. Click and you'd get a list of a few links—blogs, news articles—talking about it.

Peggy's great strength, to Jonah, was how hard she was to place. She had great taste and real technical skills, but she didn't see herself as a journalist or as a coder or a startup kid. She fit Jonah's management philosophy. He didn't like to give orders, just to let ideas percolate, to see what people would do with the toys he dropped off for them. Peggy didn't require much direction. She also wasn't sure this job would work out. But she had the sort of open mind required to show up at a Canal Street office that felt nothing like a caffeinated startup or a bustling media hub. It was barely a nine-to-five job. With the exception of the one time Jonah insisted that they show up before 10:00 a.m. because he was bringing by investors from the big uptown media company Hearst, the small staff kept bankers' hours. When Jonah appeared at 4:30 p.m., Johanesen would be torn between regret that he wasn't going to be able to leave at five to go home to his baby daughter and the charge of actually collaborating with his brilliant boss.

While Peggy kept the site updated regularly, Jonah posted all the time, too, dashing off pranks that he hoped would catch fire—posts that would be hard to explain later, when he was the CEO of a major media company. "Stop YouTube Porn!!!" one post declared, asking contributors to post porn videos in the comments. "This public service mission for internet decency is NSFW."

If you read Jonah's posts, you'd think he was a crazy person, or an idiot. But he wasn't either; he was simply immune to embarrassment, throwing internet spaghetti at the wall, waiting to see what would stick. He wasn't concerned with taste or quality or brand or consistency. He just wanted to know what would get traffic. When something did, he wanted to do more of it. Wilkie built tools for promoting BuzzFeed's posts, figuring out which got the most clicks and jamming that one into promotional units on the site.

Wilkie also kept close tabs on the most valuable slot of all, a small BuzzFeed widget Jonah had inserted into the right-hand sidebar of *The Huffington Post*'s front page. People might be coming to *The Huffington Post* for the left-wing politics, but every day, about 6,000 found their way to the small red box to click on something silly, or buzzy, or sexy. Peggy always knew not to respond too automatically to the sheer numbers, however, because a total focus on clicks turned the widget into the "salacious-meter" and simply encouraged linking to nudity.

When you asked Peggy what she did for a living, she said she worked for a blog, which was as true as anything else. She certainly didn't feel like she was part of the media scene that was busily documenting itself a few blocks north. She read Gawker religiously, and she thought its new editor, Emily Gould, who wrote about her personal and emotional life on the site, was the coolest girl ever. She didn't know who the minor media figures Gould was writing about were most of the time, and didn't really think of BuzzFeed as part of the media scene, but Peggy found Gould's writing sharp and funny. Peggy was starstruck to meet another Gawker editor when she deejayed a party at Eyebeam, and nervous when Jonah invited her and Scott Lamb, a former *Salon* writer with deep internet roots who was BuzzFeed's second editorial employee, to Nick's loft. The occasion was the October 2007 launch party for the book, *The Gawker Guide to Conquering All Media*. Jonah even introduced the staffers to Nick, who made clear that he had no interest at all in Jonah's minions.

The book was meant to take Gawker legitimate: the company reportedly brought in a $250,000 advance from a reputable publisher for it. But instead it exposed how narrow Gawker's appeal was. "WE'RE GAWKER; AND WE'RE LAME: BOOK ON 'CONQUERING MEDIA' SELLS 242 COPIES," Drudge gloated. The book's failure showed Nick he needed to find a broader audience for Gawker, even while the blog would never quite leave behind its primary fuel source, the rage of New York's creative underclass.

Jonah felt the edge of competition too. He often had lunch with Kenny at Lure, a wood-paneled tech-media cafeteria just down Spring Street from the *Huffington Post* and Gawker offices, and watched executives from other companies swirl around. You couldn't avoid the Gawker crew. When Jonah stopped into a trendy sandwich place on Mott to sit at the bar one afternoon in 2007, he overheard Lockhart Steele explaining plans to launch the geek blog *io9*. Jonah typed what he heard into his proto-smartphone, a Sidekick. *The Huffington Post*'s media reporter broke the news, and Jonah got to watch through *The Huffington Post* office window with glee as angry Gawker executives gathered in their glassed-in Crosby Street headquarters.

8

Sideboob

At first, the uneasy deal that Jonah made with Kenny seemed to be working: *The Huffington Post* was Jonah's job, and BuzzFeed was the mad scientist's laboratory. What he learned there, he brought back to *The Huffington Post*. Jonah was the child of a California divorce, and in BuzzFeed's early days he cast himself as the divorced dad, dropping in on his second family once or twice a week, often unannounced. He came bearing gifts—new ideas, theories, gossip that he'd picked up a few blocks north, along with sacks of bánh mì sandwiches. He wasn't there for the hard stuff. Wilkie and the team felt like the secret family of a traveling salesman. The real family, *The Huffington Post*, barely knew they existed. But he liked the rhythm of Jonah coming by to deposit ideas and then leaving him and a growing team to tinker and show their boss the results when he returned. Jonah's wife, Andrea Harner, looked through résumés and helped scout talent.

There was much that was frustrating about *The Huffington Post*, including Arianna's habit of bragging in public about all the traffic their Iraq coverage was driving, which wasn't actually true, and the way in which the interests of her friends and Kenny's political allies spilled into their shared project. But *The Huffington Post* had its hooks into Jonah, by way of that steady stream of visitors to the BuzzFeed icon with, always, the weirdest thing on the site—a little image (sometimes a butt) and a word or phrase—"Crack Is Whack!" or "Crawdaddy!" It was the pure weird internet, bubbling up around the edges of The Internet Newspaper. Jonah spent less time at BuzzFeed, but he loved it more.

And Kenny and Arianna had no cause to complain. Some of Jonah's biggest innovations at *The Huffington Post* grew up on BuzzFeed first. There was, for one, the "mullet strategy"—named because, like the haircut, it was business up front, with a party in the back. Jonah explained it bluntly in his own BuzzFeed post: "The mullet strategy is here to stay because the best way for web companies to grow traffic is to let the users have control, but the best way to sell advertising is a slick, pretty front page where corporate sponsors can wistfully admire their brands."

Jonah and Peggy noticed something else: if they quickly posted a few links about breaking news, and particularly about a new name in the news—a prize winner, or the victim of a lurid crime—Google might sweep it up out of nowhere and send one hundred thousand views to the page. BuzzFeed's tiny team wasn't fast enough to take advantage of this most of the time, particularly if the news broke after 4:00 p.m., but it was a perfect trick for *The Huffington Post*.

By this time, Jonah had stopped trying to explain himself to Arianna's Washington hires and found a journalist who understood what he was up to. Katherine Thomson was a Princeton graduate who got her job like many others at *The Huffington Post*—through a random connection to Arianna Huffington, who had picked up her name from an acquaintance at the Los Angeles hotel Chateau Marmont. KT, as she was called, arrived at *The Huffington Post* in March of 2007, too late to attend Nick's party. She probably wouldn't have gone anyway. KT wasn't a New York media star like Coen. She wore her blond hair long and straight. She was an introvert who geeked out over celebrity news. Most of all, she was obsessed with Google, the traffic it could drive, and the glimpse it provided into people's fleeting interests, from "Rihanna nipple" to "Tina Fey Sarah Palin."

Jonah and his partners had realized by then if *The Huffington Post* was going to keep growing after the 2008 elections, it needed to be more than a single front page with links to news and a set of blogs about politics—it needed sections covering things like entertainment and style, which launched in May of 2007.

KT was, nominally, *The Huffington Post*'s entertainment editor. But her real job was generating traffic—all the traffic John Cusack's political musings and the dispatches from Washington were definitely not getting. (She was, though, under orders to find positive angles about Cusack's new movie, *War, Inc.*)

KT knew, as well as Nick did, that bored office workers weren't clicking around looking for articles about inequality. They wanted to find celebrities, preferably naked or, at least, topless. In the mullet that was *The Huffington Post*, KT was the Arianna equivalent of the back half. And while a lot of websites were gossiping about celebrities, nobody was doing it with the discipline and speed of KT.

What she and Jonah figured out was that when big news broke, millions of Americans opened their Internet Explorer browsers and typed in "google.com." And when you typed, say, "Angelina Jolie" into Google, the search engine spit out a list of results based on a number of factors. These were the building blocks of what was, in the news business, the brand new practice of search engine optimization, or SEO as it would become known. Some were obvious: "angelina-jolie" in the URL of the web page. Most media sites back then still had URLs full of complicated numbers, so that was an easy one to adapt to. The same went for photographs: images across the web were often labeled with random codes, but *The Huffington Post* started putting names and other search terms into the image titles, and putting several of them on a page. Google crawled all that too.

Other elements weren't so straightforward. Like pac-manning.

Back then, hyperlinks were something bloggers used. You'd throw in a link to your sources, a link to a cool video on YouTube, a link to an article in *The New York Times*. But *The New York Times* would never deign to sully its Times New Roman web page with one of those messy blue links. Its reporters and editors wouldn't even have known how to. But Google had been built by people who read blogs, not by people who edited newspapers. So very early on, Google's designers decided to give a boost to pages that contained links to other reputable sources, which their algorithm took as a sign that the page had been constructed in a timely and authoritative way.

Pac-manning: Jonah made the discovery; Thomson coined the phrase. It meant linking to as many other high-performing, freshly updated news sites as you could, particularly the links that were already rated on top of Google. And when you ate the links, you'd swallow their Google juice. Then you'd keep adding links, and Google would see the new one each time it crawled the page. Essentially, the process faked freshness, and the machine fell for it. They thought of themselves as clawing their way to the top of search on the back of other outlets' articles.

KT, though, was aware of the eternal tension this kind of tactic produced: When you're writing for machines, you're not writing for people. All those big hyperlinks made it more difficult for users to actually read an article's content. But that's where *The Huffington Post*'s system was able to contribute. When she had a problem, she picked up her laptop and walked to Jonah's corner. They'd talk, he'd huddle with his team of three or four engineers, and they'd come up with a solution—in this case, a special feature of the content management system that allowed you to paste in links that would show up, with the keywords, at the bottom of the article pages, achieving the same technical trick but without getting in the way of reading.

It all moved fast. Two days after she'd asked for the new link feature, the code was written and the tool was live. By May of 2008, *The Huffington Post* had more than ten million unique visitors a month, and more than one hundred million page views.

Pac-manning gave *The Huffington Post* huge surges in traffic. Occasionally, a single post would receive more than a million views. When Tina Fey debuted as Sarah Palin on *Saturday Night Live* in September of 2008, *The Huffington Post*'s link to the video picked up more than 2.4 million page views, the site's biggest hit of the year. And the strategy of drawing traffic from search engines rather than from the home page had an additional advantage. KT was always afraid she'd receive a call from Arianna or Kenny telling her to dial it back. Her discovery that *Huffington Post* readers would click on the term "sideboob" and hang out on a page full of stories with the word, for instance, was not the sort of thing they wanted associated with their names. But with the new link tool, if she and Jonah did it right, they'd get a million views to a post that never showed up on *Huffington Post*'s home page, and so never risking embarrassing Arianna or Kenny.

....

9

$5 a View

Nick had a similarly straightforward view of traffic to KT, though without the inclination for technical trickery. He had a purer view of traffic. It told him what his audience really wanted. And it paid the bills, with straightforward advertisements displayed on the page and billed per view.

Nick had always been a pioneer in the field of digital labor. At first, he paid his writers by volume: $12 per post, meaning that if you really cranked them out, you could make $500 a week, maybe $25,000 or $30,000 a year. No health care or anything—everyone was a contractor. In 2007, he began experimenting with something purer: a base salary, and bonuses based on page views. Traffic, after all, was basically money, denominated in CPMs. Why not measure labor in the same terms? This could get Nick around the tedious matters of office politics or editors' tastes. Now, "a writer's contributions can be measured," he later wrote. He assigned each of his sites a page view rate, starting around $5. That meant that a writer making $2,000 a month would need to get more than four hundred thousand page views to start earning a bonus. A total of five hundred thousand views would get them a $500 bonus—but a huge hit could bring in thousands of extra dollars a month.

Valleywag, unfortunately, remained a bitter distraction from that quest for traffic. Only one writer had really figured out how to drive attention to it, and that was a goofily optimistic New Yorker named Nicholas Carlson. The answer lay not in the sex lives of unattractive technologists and financiers but in slideshows, and in particular slideshows of the awesome new offices that tech workers occupied—big open-plan spaces, with Ping-Pong tables and colorful couches. Valleywag readers couldn't get enough of *that*.

Nick Denton viewed that kind of coverage as "supine," an opinion that has now become conventional. His own coverage of some of the country's most powerful men was, if anything, ahead of its time. A decade later, the notion that Silicon Valley's power was dangerous and out of control would be widespread, and the tech press would swing deep into a correction in which all coverage of Facebook and Google became as deeply adversarial as Valleywag ever was. It took much of the press years to understand what Nick saw, enviously, at the time—that a new world of power and wealth was under construction, and that journalism would antagonize that new power.

But back in 2007, a wounded Silicon Valley was healing from the crash; it was a moment when it was plausible to think New York had a chance—that Google was fleeting and Facebook was going nowhere and the pendulum had swung back to the old, corrupt, careful media power in Manhattan. Nick, who at one point had wanted to *be* one of these Silicon Valley tycoons, had come from New York to bully them.

This was an obsession for Nick, and one of the reasons he began editing Valleywag personally. He never actually moved back to Silicon Valley—his boyfriend and his real life were in SoHo—but he tried to make his presence felt. When he was in San Francisco, he'd host dinners and blog about the tech tycoons, trying to give the impression that he was among them all the time. In fact, his eyes on the ground now belonged to a former bartender in Palo Alto named Megan McCarthy. Megan went to the Jell-O-wrestling parties put on by twenty-five-year-old millionaires in trucker hats—it was that era in the Valley—and fed the gossip she picked up to Nick, who put it in context.

Carlson, the office-space blogger, privately hated the nasty edge Valleywag cultivated and tried to avoid it. But the arrival of Owen Thomas, a tech reporter Nick hired away from *Time*, indicated that that edge wasn't going anywhere. Thomas reminded one of Nick's friends of a puppy that couldn't be trained not to bite. He was gay, too, and he and Nick had a similar preoccupation with the Valley's quasi-closeted elite, gay men who didn't think of themselves as famous enough that they had any public responsibility to be out, even as they led comfortable, openly gay private lives.

The most important of these powerful, private Silicon Valley gay men was Peter Thiel, a standoffish Stanford graduate who in 1998 had co-founded the company that would become PayPal. The wave of money that company threw off created the "PayPal mafia"—a group of investors who seeded another wave of companies. They had real money to invest, even after the crash. Thiel had bet early on Facebook—he was Mark Zuckerberg's first outside investor—and been rewarded massively. Thiel's combination of power and intense privacy made him a perfect target for Nick Denton.

On December 19, 2007, Thomas published a short item on Gawker under the headline "Peter Thiel Is Totally Gay, People." Thomas speculated that Thiel's sense of being an outsider had accounted for his business edge: "His disdain for convention, his quest to overturn established rules. Like the immigrant Jews who created Hollywood a century ago, a gay investor has no way to fit into the old establishment. That frees him or her to build a different, hopefully better system for identifying and rewarding talented individuals, and unleashing their work on the world," he wrote.

Thomas could, of course, have been writing about his own boss—Nick was a gay man who felt himself to be an outsider, too, and that, too, was his edge. "That's why I think it's important to say this: Peter Thiel, the smartest VC in the world, is gay. More power to him," Thomas wrote. No big deal. Just another open secret. Nick, Thomas would later write, was jealous of Thiel. And Nick himself had left a biting comment below the story.

"The only thing that's strange about Thiel's sexuality: why on earth was he so paranoid about its discovery for so long," Nick wrote.

Thiel was enraged. What gave this blog the right to say such things about him? Why should these kids be allowed to make him and his friends miserable? Many of Thiel's friends believed the same. It was universally accepted in the Valley that Valleywag was cruel, and cruel to private people, for no particular reason. The cheerleading tech blog *Tech-Crunch* wondered who would be the inevitable first "Valleywag suicide."

Thiel was not an ordinary enemy to have. He was a conservative who had waged confrontational political battles when he was at Stanford, a schemer who believed in revenge served cold, and one of the richest men in town. Thiel began a long and secret campaign against Nick that would ultimately destroy his company and remove him from the stage.

But Nick and Owen didn't know those wheels had been set in motion. The summer after they outed Thiel, Nick saw a *New York Post* headline about Thiel's continuing success and messaged Thomas that the investor "makes me sick." There was something about his boss's obsession that caught Thomas's attention, and so—this was the sort of thing Nick encouraged his staff to do in those days—he wrote another post about his own boss, wondering whether his boss actually wished he *were* Thiel.

Girly Gawker

Nick's respect for traffic was what saved Jezebel, at first. The blog wasn't quite to his taste, and it certainly wasn't what he'd had in mind when he talked about "girly Gawker," an idea he'd been mulling over for as long as there had been a Gawker. It was a rational place to take his business: women's magazines have always been the biggest, richest slice of lifestyle media. Nick liked to talk to Chris Batty about *Glamour*, holding fingers to the width of a small phone book to show its thick stack of advertisements. The problem was that Nick's staff hated the idea. The last thing the women writing for Gawker wanted was to be dragooned into some second-tier blog about makeup. When Nick tried to persuade Jessica Coen to do it instead of leaving Gawker for a job at *Vanity Fair*, she was skeptical that he was the man to revolutionize women's media.

Over in actual women's magazines, however, it was far from the stupidest idea Anna Holmes had ever heard. There were, really, so many contenders for that distinction. But the actual stupidest idea, when she really thought about it, was the one she'd had to write for *Glamour*'s June 2000 issue: "What's Your Secret Sexual Personality? And His?" Holmes

cringed at her own advice, which featured gems like "once you've discovered the dominatrix within, don't be afraid to assert your foxy fierce-
ness." But that was the era of *Devil Wears Prada* at Condé Nast, of
glamorous, imperial editors embodied by *Vogue*'s Anna Wintour, and
fashion writers using their parents' money to buy the right $500 shoes.
You weren't there to philosophize, you were there to sell magazines. At
least *Glamour* wasn't *Vogue*—you could wear jeans to work, as long as
they were the right ones.

Holmes wanted to write, but she'd never felt really at home in that
high-magazine scene. She was the daughter of a real estate agent and a
park ranger who had raised her in the college town of Davis, California,
in the hopes that a biracial kid could feel at home there, even if their income left them on the lower edge of the local middle class. She needed to
work for a living, and so she took a job at *Glamour*, whose politics seemed
to be going backward and whose idea of the internet was a pdf.

Holmes was among the legions of young women who went to work
every day at 4 Times Square, where Condé Nast operated its fleet of magazines. At *Glamour*, the boss was Bonnie Fuller, who had taken over the
magazine in 1998, shaved off its proto-feminist edge, and liked to tell
staffers that the things that moved sales were "sex and angels." "Get
Moregasmic!" one cover screamed. Holmes wrote those pieces like
everyone else, but she didn't let the culture absorb her. She dressed like a
tomboy and spoke her mind in meetings. She didn't actually have relationships with celebrities but was happy to act like she did, dragging her
lesbian friend Erin Bried, a fellow Condé Nast misfit, across the room at
a party to introduce her to Ellen DeGeneres, whom Holmes didn't actually know. "Ellen! I want you to meet my good friend Erin!" she announced. "You'll hit it off!"

The offices at 4 Times Square occupied vast floors, and at *Glamour*
the powerful editors sat at the center. Junior staffers walking to the

ladies' room or the elevators would walk the long way, around the big open office, to avoid those center cubicles occupied by Fuller and her creative director. Holmes walked straight through. But she never felt fully part of the place. She seemed to know the handful of other Black people working on the magazines by name—a woman in the next cubicle and *Vogue*'s creative director André Leon Talley, and that was pretty much it. She couldn't help noticing that most of the other Black people in the building were mopping floors, or serving her a sandwich in the cafeteria while her colleagues grazed at the salad bar.

Holmes had been in magazines for a decade by the fall of 2006 and was considering a job running the anemic *InStyle* website when Lockhart Steele, by then Nick's managing editor, approached her. She told him she wouldn't consider working for internet peanuts. She'd need at least $90,000 a year to consider it. They both assumed that was a deal breaker. After all, Steele himself, Nick's most senior employee, was making just $60,000. But to his surprise, Nick told him to pay Holmes what she wanted. She was an editor with a magazine pedigree and a Gawker edge. While she and Nick brainstormed themes and names (among the rejects were *Dishslap*, pottymouth.com, and *Bitchery*). Once they settled that, Holmes would take the 7 train in from Long Island City, and pace outside with Steele as she drafted a memo to Nick on what exactly the site would be.

Steele had just one clear piece of advice to give Nick's newest employee. When Holmes laid out her vision of the site, he blanched at her use of "the f-word." Feminism wasn't Nick's sort of thing, and Steele urged her not to mention it to the boss. But the rest of her vision—to talk the way young women really talked to one another, and to get under the skin of the pompous and unreflective magazine industry—those were right up his alley. Holmes filed Steele's warning away. "I'll show him—I'm going to do it anyway," she thought.

√ It can be hard to fully remember what the internet was like back when feminism was a dirty word. Women's messy lives were public sport on television and across the internet. Britney Spears's pain was America's joke, as was the gay kid yelling, "Leave Britney aloooone!" The top gossip blogger was Perez Hilton, who sometimes illustrated his posts with crude drawings of semen on female celebrities' faces.

So there was no real framework for what Holmes was doing. Sure, there had been pioneering magazines like *Ms.* and *Bust* and *Sassy,* and there were some earnest feminist blogs. The old slogan that the personal was political had been popularized in the 1960s, but Jezebel made that *real.* The site would take identity and make it politics. It would build a community that rejected the old structures of gender and power, and tried to shape new ones. Jezebel would channel all that anger—Anna Holmes's anger accumulated over fifteen years in women's magazines, just for starters—into fuel for social media and for a new generation of politics.

Anna had a premonition of what that power might be. She knew she would be burning her bridges—if this thing failed, her career in women's magazines would certainly be over. Her ambitions were at least as big as Nick's: at particularly adrenalized moments, she punched up wildly, seeing the landscape as a battle of the Annas, her versus Wintour. But how do you recruit a guerilla army? Nick had high hopes for what he had told Holmes would be a "site about sex and celebrity and fashion," so he gave her two full-time hires, meaning the site would immediately be bigger than Gawker, though not as big as the lucrative Gizmodo. Batty met with Anna early on to learn the lay of the land, and asked her which cosmetics brands she expected to cover favorably. That prompted Anna to offer him not a list of potential clients but a musing on sexism. She asked him why she needed to "put paint on her face to get fucked," he recalled her saying. "Ruh roh," Batty thought.

Anna found a team that thought her way. When Gawker announced that Jezebel was hiring, a standout résumé came in over the transom. Dodai Stewart had, like Anna, been a magazine journey-woman—they'd crossed paths at *Entertainment Weekly* years earlier—and, like Anna, she was one of the relatively few Black women in such a role. Stewart didn't even know that her old acquaintance would be running the site, though, when she sent a cold email seeking a job on February 8, 2007, under the subject line "Writer and magazine junkie seeks full-time job, love from Anna Wintour." In the email, she compared Wintour's *Vogue* to an "evil, undermining, elderly and wealthy great aunt." She zeroed in on the homogeneity of its pages: "As a black woman who adores fashion, I feel personally slighted by nearly every issue. . . . January '07 has one black person in its editorial pages, and she is Zahara Marley Jolie. . . . But do I stop reading *Vogue*? No. My old Aunt Anna has me hooked on her elitist rag, and I find myself looking forward to her cold, loveless issues, clinging to her words of wisdom, searching for a scrap of approval or affirmation, even though I know better." Stewart was delighted to find that Anna *Holmes* was the one reading it, and was promptly hired. Anna then added to the roster Jennifer Gerson, who had been the assistant to *Elle*'s top editor, which made her a bit of a score for Jezebel. Moe Tkacik came through another door, one that you have to put yourself back in 2007 to even imagine. Somebody in marketing at the company that makes K-Y Jelly had been reading about how brands go viral, and had paid one of the Gawker bloggers, Doree Shafrir, to host a party for influential young New York women that January, to drink and eat and talk . . . about K-Y. "Basically, they will ply us with free wine and food (and, er, goodie bags)," the invitation promised. Shafrir invited Tkacik, then working part time at a local business publication, and knew immediately she was what Nick and Anna were looking for. Shafrir connected her to Holmes, and she was soon on the job, with a plan to give voice to "secret thoughts that girls have."

There were columnists too. Tracie Egan was a sex blogger with an anonymous site, *One D at a Time*, where she posted musings like "I kinda like getting my asshole licked." She came to Jezebel pseudonymously, at first, as "Slut Machine," walking the line between feminism and voyeurism, and became a sensation even before she began writing under her own name.

Their project was a hit from the moment it launched, on May 12, 2007, with a $10,000 bounty for the unretouched images of a fashion magazine shoot. It was a big bet on the idea that there was an audience that wanted to pierce the magic of the magazine covers—"female forgeries, what with all the computer-artistry involving airbrushing, contouring, and, sometimes, outright body-part swapping," Holmes called them when she placed the bounty.

"But calling out magazine editors for their deception is one thing; showing it is another," she wrote.

Two months later, an attractive courier showed up with an envelope holding an ordinary-looking photograph of the country singer Faith Hill, who appeared on the cover of that month's *Redbook*. Tkacik produced "the annotated guide to making Faith Hill hot," an imaginary internal memo with instructions including "You know what we need here? Some more frickin hair" and "More lines! Ugh: What's this bitch do, *move her mouth into unflattering positions for a living*?" and "ASS: Chop."

Holmes wrote a long editorial explaining "why we're pissed." She marveled that in the era of the internet, where you could browse endless galleries of celebrities looking normal, women's magazines insisted on reshaping them.

"In a world where lying, deception, and the fudging of facts has become endemic in everything, all the way up to the highest levels of government, this is yet another example of a fraud being perpetrated on the public . . . and the public, for the most part, is not yet in on the joke," she wrote. "Magazine-retouching may not be a lie on par with, you know, 'Iraq has weapons of mass destruction,' but in a world where girls as young as eight are going on the South Beach Diet, teenagers are getting breast implants as graduation gifts, professional women are almost required to fetishize handbags, and everyone is spending way too much goddamn time figuring out how to pose in a way that will look as good as that friend with the really popular MySpace profile, it's fucking wrong." When fashion week arrived in the fall, Jezebel's staff handed out branded vomit bags, making their stance—of disgust with the industry—clear.

What do you call this? Journalism? Activism? In retrospect, it was a new kind of cultural politics that would reshape America when social media really came of age. (If you squint at 2007 Jezebel, you can see 2020s Twitter more clearly than anywhere else on the internet of that era.)

The glossies were incredibly vulnerable to attacks of being overpolished and hypocritical, having been produced by women who knew that there was something fake about what they were selling.

Jezebel's attacks on photoshopping stung, and creative directors began dialing back their most extreme editing practices. Stewart's work, in particular, had another particularly direct effect on the fashion industry, when she and Holmes began calling out fashion companies and magazines for their utter lack of Black models. They wrote nineteen articles under the heading "black models" in Jezebel's first year, but the most powerful thing they did was simply to comprehensively, pedantically tally up the number of Black women in the pages of each major women's magazine, each month. They also publicized that Black models were far more likely to appear in the advertisements of midmarket fashion retailers than of high-end brands or in the magazines' own shoots.

In October of 2007, when Stewart showed up to cover a panel on the topic, nobody mentioned Jezebel—a bit of a taboo subject among fashion editors. But they were all citing the site's statistics on the ethnic breakdown of the models.

This was the frontal assault on the glossies. The rest of Jezebel was simply a showcase for brutal, funny honesty that served as a refreshing contrast to the magazines' manic forced cheer. There was electoral politics first of all, more than you'd see in a straightforward way on any of the other Gawker sites or at Condé's women's titles. Anna ran a far tighter, more organized ship than any of the others—a hangover from her magazine life—and so at 10:00 a.m. every weekday, there was an update on the Democratic primary in the form of an off-the-rails exchange of messages between Tkacik and a colleague. This, too, presaged something a little new. The women's-magazine internet was all for Hillary, for pantsuits and girl power. Moe was skeptical of the Clinton 1990s that hadn't seemed to leave her generation any better off than their parents, and skeptical of the whole Clinton vibe. The biggest voice on the internet's most important feminist venue, she supported Barack Obama. And there was the war: every Friday afternoon, Gerson, who'd been hired from *Elle* to write about fashion, tallied up that week's casualties from Iraq.

This was, needless to say, not exactly what Nick had in mind for girly Gawker.

He asked Anna from time to time whether "you really need to do so many posts about periods or abortion or rape. Why don't you do some about makeup?" She mostly ignored him.

"I was aware of the fact that he wasn't thrilled, but here's the thing—we had great traffic," she said. By August 2007, they had five hundred thousand page views a month; by the next March, they were at over a million. Holmes couldn't help gloating when their numbers surpassed Gawker's.

And Nick didn't really mind. He'd learned that his editors needed to rebel against the man, and that he was the man. "A lot of it was theater—wasn't it?" he asked, years later.

Anyway, he reflected, "It's pretty natural and obvious that you set up an online women's magazine for a new generation and it's going to go—it was predestined to go—in a more political, more feminist direction." And Nick loved success and relevance even more than he loved money; Batty knew he'd never win a fight with Anna as long as the site was a hit.

The Jezebel women were following Nick's logic of honesty and exposure to a logical conclusion. It was just that, as Stewart realized, when women—and Black women—were being honest with each other, they weren't exactly having the same conversations. Sometimes the Jezebel writers would slip down from their small apartments after work to drink at a bar downstairs from Public on Elizabeth Street. Stewart and Coen were standing outside one evening talking to Nick when he brought up a favorite hobbyhorse, how he despised the constant pressure to be politically correct. "Think of it this way," Stewart told him. "It's politically correct not to call me a nigger. Think about the things that people say that are not politically correct about gay people." She felt that, if only for a moment, a lightbulb had gone off.

Anyway, they had the traffic, the answer to any question he could ask. And Jezebel had something else, too, something Nick had from the start valued to a degree that perplexed his writers, that looked prescient only in retrospect. Jezebel had a community, a real one. The comments the site attracted appeared on Gawker's own platform. In those comments, women called themselves "Jezzies"—which made Anna uncomfortable—and they had a sometimes disturbingly intense relationship with the writers, logging on to lecture their favorite authors on sex or politics. It was one of the earliest flares of what would, a decade later, become social media. When the writers veered off the rails, their commenters would vent wild, disproportionate anger at them. Tkacik, in particular, was a serial veerer, with posts including one musing on how she understood why men fetishized an idealized Asian woman. The comments were brutal. But the commenters' anger came from their connection to Tkacik's writing, and their commitment to her causes—from the honesty of the site, and the fact that these were the things you would never, ever read in *Glamour*. The commenters drove the writers as much as Anna did, making clear that this wasn't normal journalism, or blogging. It was something closer to emotional guerilla warfare, typically conducted in a ratty T-shirt from the tiny Lower East Side apartment that you never managed to leave while Anna shouted about deadlines over Gchat. Tkacik's most widely remembered post of that era is, still, probably the one that she warned her readers was "beyond gross."

"Its sole redeeming trait is that it involves a scenario we've all feared before—the one where you get a tampon stuck up inside you for a treacherously, perilously long period of time," she wrote, beginning an odyssey that begins with her taking drugs at her best friend's wedding and ends with her squatting on the floor of her apartment, receiving deadpan advice over AOL Instant Messenger from Holmes, who offers cheering commentary including "it's a good thing you don't have a dog!"

The ruthless exposure and self-exposure sometimes teetered between liberation and exploitation. Nick chased traffic in the same direction over on Gawker, where Emily Gould had become a new kind of mini-celebrity, headed for a new kind of public flameout as she blogged about dating a colleague. At times, the whole thing seemed out of control—certainly when a Gawker video producer, and former romantic partner of Tkacik's, posted a video to YouTube insulting Tkacik's looks. The women of Jezebel, most of whom stayed out of Gawker's offices and worked from home, often felt a kind of leering misogyny from inside the house.

They were also the subject of endless fascination from elsewhere, including from the hot, macho media company Vice, whose explicit sex writing—usually by men—had been part of the environment Jezebel was both responding to and assimilating into. Tracie Egan, who wasn't posting as "Slut Machine" anymore but under her own name, wrote a piece for Vice about hiring a male prostitute to simulate "raping" her. Gavin McInnes, the charismatic, attention-seeking co-founder of Vice and author of *The Vice Guide to Sex, Drugs, and Rock and Roll*, liked the stunt so much that he booked himself on Tracie's podcast, and the two became friends.

As 2007 became 2008, Egan hosted a New Year's Eve party at her apartment in Williamsburg. Nick even turned up, with a bottle of wine—though she spotted him taking the bottle with him when he left, before she passed out from drinking. She woke up to a trashed apartment and sent out a furious email. A Gawker blogger posted the whole thing on the site, illustrated with an image of Egan's cleavage.

The women of Jezebel all went back to work after that, dialing everything up. Tkacik embraced Obama and ignored the angry comments. Egan pushed the limits of self-exposure, without the sense of irony that protected other writers. It was a feature of that era of online feminism, something that would reach a fuller and more toxic flowering a few years later, on websites like *xoJane*. It's also something many of the writers regret in retrospect. During this era, women spoke more frankly than they ever had in American journalism. But they also pretended to be tougher than they were, and editors and readers alike pushed them beyond their limits. Egan said she reached hers in Las Vegas, where she'd been dispatched to cover the Adult Video News convention, America's leading annual porn gathering. "Maybe I should try to fuck a porn star," she'd remarked to Holmes before she'd left New York—but she then began to feel that her editor might not realize the comment hadn't been entirely serious. Holmes says she didn't intend to pressure Egan, but when she asked if Egan had found the right porn star yet, Egan, who was then twenty-seven, got uncomfortable.

"I felt pressured to fuck someone and write about it so I did," she said. Not an actor, though—the guy was a nominee for Best Soundtrack. She'd gotten her hips bruised on the marble counter of her hotel room bathroom, and the post "got a ton of traffic and did what it was supposed to do, but I think Anna was disappointed that I didn't fuck a porn star."

Nick loved that self-exposure, and the traffic it brought. Holmes sometimes had to protect her writers from his excesses. Once, Nick caught wind of a date of Gerson's that had gone horribly wrong. "Oh my God I heard about your date, you've got to write about that," he told her, and she realized that "if you were working for Nick, traffic was your life."

One thing Anna and Nick shared was a manic work ethic. Nick at one point turned down a request that writers be given BlackBerries on the grounds that they should never step away from their computers long enough to need the devices. That intensity, layered on top of their breakout success, almost guaranteed that the moment couldn't last. It ended while Anna was away on her honeymoon in Australia. The long, golden year of Jezebel's electrifying launch came to an end with a loud crash on June 30, 2008, in a 130-seat basement theater on the Bowery. There, Lizz Winstead, a comedian who had co-created *The Daily Show*, hosted a weekly faux-news program called *Thinking and Drinking*, which had a cult following. She was a feminist of the previous generation and she liked Jezebel, though she didn't read it much; younger TV producers, she knew, were obsessed with it. Her show, which began with satire, always ended with an interview with a serious journalist. Bill Moyers and Rachel Maddow had been on. So she thought she was doing Egan and Tkacik a favor when she invited them to come by and sit on the couch to her right under a big double image of Jezebel's triumph, the Faith Hill Photoshop get.

The women of Jezebel got there early, took the show's name seriously, and started drinking. They came onstage with two red Solo cups and a can of Budweiser. And they started, disastrously, drunkenly, making jokes about rape. Recalling a man who had date-raped her, Tkacik said she "got very mad at him, but I wasn't gonna fucking like turn him in to the police and fucking go through shit."

"Why not?" an agitated Winstead interrupted. "You see that's the problem, why not? I am just curious."

"Because it was a load of trouble and I had better things to do, like drinking more," Tkacik replied.

The conversation went on like that, and by the time it ended, Winstead was appalled. Recriminations and disappointment over the incident quickly spread in the feminist blogosphere. Anna, for her part, returned to find a gathering storm. She rushed to Winstead's apartment to apologize, to say that the two women's words didn't represent her vision for Jezebel, and to plead with Winstead not to post the video of the evening online. But Winstead couldn't stop thinking about the evening, and she posted the video and a transcript on *The Huffington Post*, under the title "Jezebelism."

Her gist was that these bloggers had become too big to be so irresponsible. "They do not understand the influence they have over the women who read them, nor do they accept any responsibility as role models for young women who are coming of age searching for lifestyles to emulate," Winstead wrote.

The writers themselves were unapologetic; they believed they'd been set up, gotten drunk and trapped by an older and worldlier journalist into a kind of ritual generational embarrassment. Even if the truth was simpler—that the alcohol and drugs that had fueled so much of Gawker's culture also made it obviously vulnerable—they were mostly just angry. Egan took it out on Winstead directly, taking to her Wikipedia page to call her a "cunt."

Nick was delighted by the controversy, the exposure. But Anna hated it. She and Stewart were furious and embarrassed. Anna, in particular, understood the way in which a media brand is a public performance. She had kept the whole thing on the high wire for more than a year; now, suddenly, Jezebel had fallen off. She couldn't make Egan or Tkacik apologize—and later wished she'd fired Egan—but instead wrote her own sort-of-apology to readers.

"Some blame the format, or the participants, or generational differences, or alcohol, or the provocative subject matter, or unrealistic expectations, inarticulateness and lack of preparedness. I believe that *everyone*, however, can agree that the whole thing was a fucking shame," she wrote.

Still, the commenters lost their minds. Their disappointment, expressed in more than a thousand entries into the commenting system that was Nick's pride and joy, spilled over into the rest of the internet, tainting Jezebel's image. After that, Holmes forced her bloggers to grow up. Less performance art, less self-exposure, more caution. But what Nick and Anna and Moe and the rest of the early Jezebel crew had unleashed would eventually reshape American media and social media. A generation of women who worked at Jezebel, and who read it, would reshape journalism, too, bringing a feminist vantage point to news organizations and television writers' rooms, and they'd build the groundwork for what would become the #MeToo movement a decade later. On Jezebel, too, were the earliest stirrings of new online identity politics that would, a decade later, dominate social media. The bloggers' fury at the media's two-dimensional, virtually all-white portraits of American women would migrate from the blog and its comments section onto

Twitter, which was founded in 2006, the same year Lockhart approached Anna about the job at Jezebel. So much of it started on Jezebel. But Twitter and Facebook, the latter of which was making its way from college dorms to America's public spaces, would host the big social movements that changed how Americans saw race and gender. The darker elements, the rage and poison of the comments section, would become more visible later, too, as righteous social media rage at the system often targeted a single individual—something Jezebel's writers had gotten an early taste of.

They'd all been shaken by these new cultural forces. To Tkacik, "It felt like we had unleashed something that was more volatile than we realized."

....

Politics

Nick backed into politics through Jezebel. *The Huffington Post's* roots were political, and the site embodied the mainstream politics of the internet in the mid-aughts, when online politics was basically synonymous first with opposition to President George W. Bush and then with the name of a young senator from Illinois, Barack Obama.

The Huffington Post's three founders came to Obama by different routes. Arianna had soured on Hillary Clinton back in the 1990s. She wrote that during the Monica Lewinsky affair, the First Lady became "enabler-in-chief." Later, Arianna added Iraq to that critique. Obama sought Kenny out, paying him the respect due to a new power broker of the internet age: the Illinois politician invited Kenny to a drink at an East Side bar before he was even sworn into the Senate, the sort of gesture Kenny appreciated.

But Jonah found Obama through Digg. That site was, in that era, a simple list of blue links on a white page, chosen by users who could vote to elevate—"digg"—a story, or to "bury" it. And as the primary campaign between Senators Clinton and Obama got rolling in late 2007, Jonah noticed dramatic spikes in traffic on Digg for a particular kind of story: one that made Obama look good. This was, in its way, the side-boob of politics. Obama was, simply, a lot more viral than Hillary Clinton. Sure, you could get people to click on a story about Hillary if you put it on the front page. But a good story about Obama would really travel—around people's emails, around the blogs and email groups that had yet to be swallowed by social media, and, if you nailed it, over to Digg.

Jonah knew about the Obama phenomenon by then, because Andrea Breanna's new dashboards had told him. Breanna had been Jonah's student back at NYU, where her "Dog Island" prank had bought her a seat in the Contagious Media Working Group. Now she was the chief technology officer at *The Huffington Post*. She had a different name and gender then, and square-jawed nerd good looks paired with a mop of brown hair and a vibrating, insistent alto. Breanna surprised people when she talked about her identity—"I'm Mexican but I'm white"—and was wrestling privately with deeper questions. On business trips, Breanna would buy women's clothes at H&M to match her true identity, pose in them, then throw them in a dumpster. A decade later, she'd change her name, and live as a transgender Chicana. Her internal struggles back then translated into a kind of hyperkinetic work ethic, an energy that seemed to mirror the *Huffington Post* traffic flows Jonah had tasked his protégé to master.

Back when Jonah had done his Contagious Media Showdown, Michael Frumin ran over the site logs himself to measure traffic. Now Jonah was codifying that science. When Breanna arrived at *The Huffington Post* in March of 2007, the lone developer, Andy Yaco-Mink, was doing what he could to provide relatively crude measures of traffic—unique visitors, page views, the ups and the downs of a "bored at work network" of people who arrived at the site in predictable patterns: when they sat down to work at 9:00 a.m., and when they broke for lunch.

For the first two years of *The Huffington Post*, they'd ascertained this data in the usual, cumbersome ways: a meter on the site that updated every hour with a crude summary of traffic or, worse, the cumbersome monthly pull of server logs by Yaco-Mink.

Jonah wanted something better—something that could change writers' and editors' behavior, that would drive them to get more traffic. And on December 12, 2007, he finally figured it out. That's when the long late-night conversations between Breanna and Jonah took concrete form in a dashboard that updated live and divided traffic into three new categories: One was "Seed," the basic traffic that came to *The Huffington Post*'s front page, which Jonah and Duncan Watts had defined years earlier as the starting point for any viral project. The second was "Extra"—traffic from email or Digg or "anything but Huffington Post," Breanna explained in a follow-up email. The third was "SS," which, Breanna had to explain to the staff, stood for Jonah's "special sauce." SS was the most important measure of all. It was a formula reflecting what share of any item's overall traffic was extra, was beyond *The Huffington Post*'s technical control—basically, how viral you were. "Basically, it's all fine to distribute traffic around the site, but [what] we really want is new traffic," Breanna wrote.

After the initial confusion about the categories, Breanna renamed them: "Seed" became "recirculation," and "special sauce" became "viral." "Recirc," as they called it, simply meant that an editor had slapped a link to your story on the *Huffington Post* home page. Viral—well, that was the traffic you earned yourself—the kind KT won from men's private searches for nude photographs, or from noticing that some people looking to read about late actor Heath Ledger had his first name wrong, and were searching "Keith Ledger." KT's team quickly included that misspelling in the set of "tags" that helped Google know what was on a page.

But the goal of the new traffic system wasn't just to explain what was going on. It was to create an incentive. It was "the first time a room of editors had an instant view of the stats on each article," Breanna recalled. "It made the whole room stop competing just for front page placement and start focusing on bringing in traffic from the web, and really growing our audience." The shift wasn't instant, but it was "a gradual unstoppable force of stats informing" the journalism.

"That was the moment we went from mushroom hunting to farming—and when we opened Pandora's box," Breanna said.

Jonah and Paul added other incentives to the *Huffington Post* system. They created a "click meter," which allowed editors to check every ten minutes to see which stories, and which headlines, were engaging to readers. The system included a default setting that would remove poorly performing stories from the page. The problem was that many of those were good-news stories about Arianna's friends, or reflections of one of Kenny's political angles. Editors kept a running list of them to keep on the front page and passed it from hand to hand at shift change, the only way to bypass the new algorithmic pressure.

Versions of Breanna's charts are now everywhere. Virtually every media company, from TikTok to *The New York Times*, uses a similar system. But these were dark arts back then. Serious journalists sneered nervously at the idea that you'd allow your news judgment to be replaced by crude clicks—that is, by the fast-shifting attention of your audience. When visitors came through the office, Kenny or Jonah would tell Breanna to turn her screen to the wall. They were disturbed when they learned that an investor, John Borthwick, who ran a company called Betaworks, was building a similar product to license to other companies. Jonah's team didn't want to give up their edge.

The traffic they measured meant political influence, and it meant advertising dollars. But elsewhere in the industry, other, more sophisticated dashboards were sprouting. The "ad tech" arms race that had begun between DoubleClick and Right Media in 2003 had become the focus of some of the brightest minds of a generation of graduates of Stanford's computer science program. On April 14, 2007, Google bought DoubleClick for $3.1 billion. Later that month, Yahoo! spent $680 million to buy Right Media. Publishers began to realize that the faceless tech middlemen, which they'd seen as mere tools to simplify the business of selling digital ads, threatened to reshape their industry. In March of 2008, the chairwoman of the online publishers' association, Wenda Harris Millard, rose at a trade conference in Phoenix to deliver a dire warning. "We must not trade our advertising inventory like pork bellies!" she declared. Chris Batty applauded from the audience. His business was booming as traffic increased, even if the price of an ad impression stayed worryingly constant. But while Millard's defiant speech captured the industry's anxiety, the threat still seemed abstract to many in the publishing business. The American economy was strong, buoyed by a bubbly real estate market. Dollars kept flowing to digital media, and a presidential election was about to truly play out on the internet for the first time.

Back in 2008, one big story Jonah's and Andrea Breanna's charts tracked was the Democratic primary, an epic contest between the establishmentarian Clinton and the young insurgent, Obama. Everyone could agree, if for different reasons, that *The Huffington Post* needed to get on board with the young Illinois senator. Jonah loved the traffic, Kenny the politics, and Arianna needed an alternative to her old enemies, the Clintons. This produced a rare and much-needed consensus among the site's occasionally feuding factions, the staffers variously loyal to Kenny, Arianna, and Jonah.

The Huffington Post's office on Broadway was a humming, peculiar place whose politics reflected the company's three founders. The place was full of the founders' protégés, hired not through some human resources process but through acquaintances and connections. Kenny recruited Katharine Zaleski, who would translate his political instincts into headlines, in the lobby of his apartment building, where she'd grown up. Huffington installed her former research assistant to recruit bloggers. The young staffers fought proxy battles over the limits of taste and the company's identity. Arianna's team schmoozed with celebrity bloggers, Kenny's wrote barbed political headlines, and starting in 2007, Breanna and a team of four developers hunched over their keyboards. Lerer was in almost every day, obsessing over headlines, while Arianna phoned in from Brentwood and Jonah shuttled between *The Huffington Post*, BuzzFeed, and his apartment at SoHo Court. (Though Nick left the building before Jonah moved in, Jonah had lent Nick his place in 2004, to put Geoffrey Denton up on a visit to New York.)

It wasn't always clear who was in charge. Zaleski, who spent her days fielding Kenny's headline changes, saw Jonah at his computer in the early days of the site, and asked, "What's your deal?" "I'm just here building things," he said, laughing. But when she started complaining about how much work she had, she found an edge below the half-joking surface. "If you don't like it, you can walk down the street to Gawker," he told her. Soon, Kenny was forwarding her Jonah's late-night memos. Eventually, the thing they said above all was more Barack Obama.

Journalists had already been catering to the invisible power of big bloggers for a few years at this point, especially the biggest of all, Matt Drudge. They knew his interests—right-wing politics, but also weather and health and aliens—and he served as a kind of secret assignment editor, rewarding writers with between twenty thousand and a million views, depending on where on the page he put their links. The *Huffington Post* front page was beginning to gather a little of that gravitational force: many political reporters knew the email address of the front-page editor.

But Digg was also the beginning of something new in political media.

For decades, journalists' incentives had been set pretty much by their editors: you wrote what you were assigned to write, or went where the natural evolution of a story took you. The blog years, and the early flickerings of traffic, had produced a new kind of media powerhouse, in which obscure and partisan figures like Drudge could reward you with traffic if you wrote stories he liked. But Digg represented an evolution of that idea, an assignment editor who wasn't a person at all. Digg's power came from an opaque blend of community and algorithm, and it was beginning to shape not just what got read but how the news was written. The tail had begun to wag the dog; the story had begun to chase the traffic. You'd publish a story with a pro-Obama headline and *boom*, forty thousand views, so Jonah and Kenny crafted headlines to feed the mechanism, often responding to the controversy of the day: "Experts: Obama-Ayers Ad May Be Illegal," read one headline upvoted in Digg. Another suggested that Clinton had darkened Obama's skin in her advertising. Katherine Thomson once slipped in something with a bit wider appeal: "Obama Bodysurfs in Hawaii (PHOTOS)."

Online Democratic politics had begun with Howard Dean's angry bloggers. But the Obama age was—to use one of the candidate's favorite words—more hopeful. Jonah found ways to translate that hope into traffic from sources like Digg. And nobody could really control it. The energy that would fuel Obama didn't come from media power players, old or new. It was more distributed, more social. And as large a change as it represented from the stodgy old media, it also represented a puzzle for Nick Denton's dark vision. Obama's supporters didn't seem to want the inside story, or to rip off his mask. They were there for cheerleading and affirmation, and *The Huffington Post* could give them that.

Digging Obama

Barack Obama realized he'd need to tap into that digital energy source. As he started moving toward running for president in 2006, he and his aides knew they'd need huge support from young people and that they'd have to find those young people where they were, on this newfangled technology called Facebook. When an Obama aide messaged Facebook for help setting up the senator's official Facebook page, Chris Hughes wrote back.

Hughes had been Mark Zuckerberg's roommate at Harvard. He'd been a French history and literature major, not a coder, and his main product contribution had been coming up with a much-mocked early form of Facebook communication, the wordless "poke." But he'd handled the crucial human side of the business, managing relationships with other colleges as the company spread to them, and dealing with press as the company began to explode.

Now Hughes, a fine-featured Southerner with sandy blond hair who looked even younger than his twenty-three years, wasn't just talking to Ivy League student newspapers. Facebook had captured the attention of some of America's most voracious and opportunistic communicators: politicians, who were always on the lookout for a competitive edge. It was a fair exchange. Politicians were always trying to reach the audience of a hot new medium, and new media always craved the legitimacy and the newspaper headlines that a political figure bestowed. That was the deal Bill Clinton made in 1994 when he gamely appeared on MTV to cheerfully answer questions about whether he wore "boxers or briefs" in exchange for access to a young audience that wasn't watching the evening news. And Hughes, who had the best social skills of Facebook's intense young co-founders (a low bar), was tasked with handling relationships with politicians early on. Which is why he was the one walking Obama's staff through Facebook's simple interface.

Obama chose a good time. His staff was talking to Hughes right around the moment that Facebook made a monumental shift, opening its platform to anyone over thirteen years of age with a valid email address. The platform went from just twelve million monthly active users in 2006 to fifty million in 2007. Hughes helped Obama's staff add information about his favorite musicians, including Stevie Wonder, and his top movies (*Casablanca*, *The Godfather I* and *II*), to his official profile. A breathless *Wall Street Journal* article on Hughes's effort, headlined "BO, U R So Gr8," noted that the page immediately caught the attention of college students, one of whom posted the first message to the page: "Run for president! Save us!"

When Obama's presidential campaign launched the following February, Hughes called the senator's aides back to ask for a job. He met another Obama aide over coffee at Union Station, and was hired on the spot. In 2007, he left Palo Alto for freezing Chicago.

Hughes was a multimillionaire on paper when he arrived in his bare office overlooking Michigan Avenue, but he couldn't buy or sell his shares in Facebook, then merely a promising little startup, so he shared an apartment with a colleague and took the El to work. Obama liked him—liked the idea of him too—and would single him out whenever he walked across the big office to say hi to the new media staff. The press team teed up favorable profiles of their pet whiz kid to show how in tune with young people and technology their candidate was.

The age of social media politics had been stirring in the comments section at Jezebel, and in Jonah's charts at *The Huffington Post*. Facebook was promising then, but not special—it was one of a dozen platforms to be aware of, from the Black social network BlackPlanet to the immersive Second Life. The microblogging service Twitter launched in the summer of 2006 and started growing exponentially, but to the campaign staff in Chicago, Twitter's users seemed mostly to be journalists, and its main utility was keeping an eye on what members of the press were saying to one another. Facebook was bigger than most of its competitors, though smaller than MySpace, and it skewed helpfully young. The campaign's digital director, Joe Rospars, thought it was worth the effort to build an embassy and interact with the denizens in their native language. But he and Hughes were also bumping up against the limitations of Facebook. There wasn't much more you could do than put up a page and send messages to your fans. You couldn't buy ads, you couldn't cross-reference data or collect email addresses or even raise money, which was the main thing political campaigns were using the internet for in 2008.

Because Facebook wasn't quite ready, Hughes went to work, building a social network specifically for the campaign. Mybarackobama.com allowed Obama supporters to create accounts and pages, organize events, and raise money. Its users were active—they organized more than two hundred thousand events for the Illinois senator. Its power to move people from the internet to the ballot box stunned even Obama's aides, who would arrive in obscure states to find that volunteers had already created a campaign apparatus—places like Idaho, where Kassie Cerami, a local woman who'd been working in marketing, quit her job, found one other Obama supporter online, and threw her life into the campaign.

Facebook's executives were watching their platform expand in all directions, and it was certainly cool to see America's political leaders coming to visit their young audience. They saw flickers of an uncontrollable new future, just as Anna and her team at Jezebel had. But what inspired the execs, what really gave them the sense not just that their platform would make them billions and change life for American college kids, but that Facebook could change the world, was happening two thousand miles south of Washington, DC. Social media politics as we know them in the early 2020s didn't begin in SoHo or Chicago or Washington, but in Barranquilla, Colombia, where, on January 3, 2008, a young civil engineer read news of the latest developments in a high-profile kidnapping.

Oscar Morales Guevara, like many Colombians, was captivated by the saga of a presidential candidate, Íngrid Betancourt, and her campaign manager. They were being held captive in the jungle by the leftist rebel group known as the FARC. The group had begun in 1964 promising to fight on behalf of the country's impoverished peasants, but now the FARC were dangerous guerillas, fighting for their own survival at the cost of civilian lives. That winter, they were trying to earn public approval by announcing that they'd freed the little boy the campaign manager had given birth to in their custody, named Emmanuel. Guevara read that instead of actually returning the boy to his family, however, the guerillas had simply abandoned him with a peasant. Many people were happy the child was safe, but Guevara and others like him were just angry.

And Guevara had a place to take that righteous anger. When Facebook opened itself to users beyond American college students a year earlier, it had exploded out among educated internet users all over the world, among people like Guevara. He'd been spending time catching up with friends on the new platform, and he searched for the word "FARC," assuming there would be some way for him to get involved in the cause. There wasn't. And so without much forethought, just after midnight on January 4, 2008, he started a group called A Million Voices Against FARC.

He went to bed at 3:00 a.m. and woke up to find the group already had 1,500 members. By January 6 there were 8,000 members, and a sense among them that they had to do something. The group announced plans for a national rally, a show of solidarity to send the message that the armed revolutionaries had lost popular support. Hundreds of thousands took to the streets. It took your breath away.

On his first trip to the United States, Guevara visited Facebook's headquarters on Hamilton Avenue in Palo Alto. The first outside speaker the company had ever invited in, he showed the employees photographs of the crowds, near tears himself as he told the story. Facebook had been building a cool little app that college kids could use to hook up. Now, as 2008 began, its employees knew they were changing the world. Guevara's story shifted Facebook's view of itself. And it changed how the world saw social media. Facebook executives loved to talk about Oscar and his visit as the moment when they realized it could be something more. The visit would lead to the first, and most optimistic, book ever written about the company, *The Facebook Effect*. And it ushered in a moment of fantasy—that the youth of Facebook would change the world. (Eight years later, their parents and grandparents would adopt Facebook and make stories praising their own candidate, Donald Trump, as viral as *The Huffington Post*'s praise for Obama had been.)

On February 2, 2008, less than a month after Guevara brought thousands to the streets in Colombia, Barack Obama arrived in Boise, Idaho. There, his new way of organizing on social media had taken the place of the usual expensive campaign apparatus. Cerami and another volunteer had scrambled to secure the largest venue in town. Local observers were stunned to find that more than 14,000 Democrats in the conservative state had turned up to hear him speak. Cerami had met Obama once before, begged him to come to Idaho to take advantage of what mybarackobama.com was building for him, and referred to the famous line in the movie *Field of Dreams*: "If you build it, he will come." Backstage the candidate told her: "You built it, and I came." In the Democratic caucuses three days later, Obama won nearly 80 percent of the vote, picking up fifteen of the state's eighteen delegates. It was his widest margin of victory anywhere over Clinton, and it was where it became clear that he had channeled the same kind of energy that Guevara had found in Colombia. Even without staff there, the complicated math of American primary politics had turned tiny caucuses like Idaho's into places where he could get an edge against the lumbering Clinton machine.

The power of the new social media politics was intoxicating to Obama's supporters, and to Facebook's executives in Palo Alto. It seemed also to coalesce around people like them—educated young folks with progressive social values. Few considered at the time that the tools were malleable, and that young progressives just happened to be the ones on the internet in 2008. As the year went on, Facebook executives grew thirstier for this stream of political energy. The company's leaders could also see that tiny Twitter had begun to channel it, tapping into the immediacy of breaking news and of social movements to grip the attention of users and the media alike. Twitter was growing so fast, Zuckerberg observed, that if it kept going at the same rate, it would soon surpass Facebook as the largest of the social networks.

In October 2008, Mark Zuckerberg met with Twitter's executives and offered them $500 million for the company. In an email to Twitter's chairman, Jack Dorsey, Zuckerberg also made a tacit threat: if they wouldn't sell, he'd continue to "build products that moved further in their direction." Twitter said no. Twitter's board believed their company could be worth more than half a billion, and they had qualms about Facebook's ruthless business practices.

It was a monumental decision, setting off a frantic wave of competition between the two platforms for this apparently positive and inspirational new source of traffic mined from politics and social movements. That frenzy would later draw in companies from BuzzFeed and *The Huffington Post* to *The New York Times*, all hungering after the traffic Facebook could send them. Facebook chronicler Steven Levy later wrote that after failing to acquire Twitter, "Facebook tried to copy a number of Twitter's features, including a real-time urgency and an increased viral pulse." He speculated that if Facebook had done the deal, it might not have felt so driven to compete with Twitter to mine the traffic and attention of politics, and that "maybe the News Feed would not have courted so much of the toxicity it became known for later on." But Facebook instead chased Twitter in a race to dominate the business of real-time news and overheated opinion, and journalists would find themselves pulled over the waterfall the two companies created.

13

$100 Million

The *Huffington Post* was drawing on the same energy as Facebook, riding in Obama's wake. Its traffic multiplied nearly fivefold between September 2007 and September 2008. But while the company had begun to turn views into advertising dollars, *The Huffington Post* was still burning money so fast that by the end of the year, absent an intervention, it would be done. Still, in the summer of 2008, the founders weren't worried. *The Huffington Post* was hot; someone would invest. Kenny had been talking to Bob Iger, the CEO of Disney, about a $25 million investment—the first really major round the company would take. The money would allow them to keep growing, and the involvement of the bluest of blue-chip media companies would also validate their project, validate the whole idea of news on the internet.

Jonah, too, had gotten interested in this new game of raising money. He liked figuring out new rules and new systems, playing new roles. And he liked winning, even if he sometimes gave off a disconcerting sense that he viewed the whole thing as a game, not really recognizing the stakes. Kenny and Arianna saw Iger as the ultimate blue-chip investor, and they handed off to Jonah the back-up project of the *Daily Mail*, whose salacious celebrity content—it was famous for the "sidebar of shame"—had been a source of traffic inspiration to KT. Jonah didn't understand that the company's reputation in media circles was, well, trashy, and that Kenny and Arianna were just humoring him in letting him carry on exploratory conversations with a rotating series of British executives whose names he never learned. (Jonah was awful with names.) His pitch: *The Huffington Post* and the *Mail* could "take over the English-speaking world." He was proud when the *Daily Mail* seemed ready to invest.

But Jonah was learning to tell a story. One person who was listening was Steve Bannon, a friend of his old partner Andrew Breitbart. Bannon, a banker turned right-wing activist with an interest in the internet, would be inspired by the angry stirrings and unhinged memes of Chris Poole's 4chan. He had met Andrew back in 2004 and grown close to him, and now Bannon surveyed the left-wing media landscape for things to copy. "I had looked over the shoulders of some of the private-equity guys who had put money into *The Huffington Post*," Bannon later told Joshua Green. "The one thing they told me to explain the huge valuation was that it was not a content play but a technology play. They had Jonah Peretti—guy's a genius—[who] at the time was walking me through the tech side of the business."

As Disney proceeded with its due diligence, the controlling narrowness of the Disney brand began to reveal itself. Iger told Kenny that Disney's powerful head of public relations, a veteran Republican operative named Zenia Mucha, thought *The Huffington Post* was too partisan. And Arianna's own relationship building also backfired. She had befriended Iger's wife, the broadcast journalist Willow Bay, and Bay had done work for *The Huffington Post* and had equity in the company—a red flag for Disney's compliance division. Meanwhile, a worrying decline in housing prices had started dragging down other elements of the economy. By the summer of 2008, Treasury Secretary Hank Paulson was begging Congress to bail out key government-backed mortgage lenders. In July, Iger called Kenny to apologize profusely: he couldn't do the deal. As the markets began to crater, the *Daily Mail* told Jonah that the British newspaper was out too. The *Huffington Post* founders were close to panic. "We were done. We didn't have any money left," Kenny recalled.

The founders scrambled. Arianna dialed up her network—first, the movie mogul David Geffen, who advised her that it was time to cash out. He sent her to his banker at Goldman Sachs, Scott Stanford, who listened to her pitch and disagreed with Geffen: He thought she should raise another round of money, as planned. He suggested they pitch a venture capitalist named Fred Harman, who had been an early investor in Demand Media, a company that went public based on producing unmemorable blurbs that ranked well in search engines, before Google caught on to the game and nearly destroyed them. Stanford knew Harman would be interested in the economics of *The Huffington Post*'s unpaid bloggers.

It turned out, though, that Harman had also taken a liking to the site's political coverage: although he was a Republican, he'd met Obama at a Silicon Valley fundraiser the previous June and been wowed by his intellect and charisma. And, the banker told Huffington, Harman was in Los Angeles. Arianna pounced. She called Harman and, when he demurred, saying he was on vacation with his family, she insisted they all come visit her in Brentwood. After all, she'd heard his wife Stephanie was Greek too! The Harman family received a warm welcome, complete with spanakopita, dolmades, and tzatziki—Harman's wife loved it—and he got a quick introduction to the pitch for "The Internet Newspaper" that Kenny and Arianna had thought Disney was going to invest in. The core of it was that *The Huffington Post* already had the traffic—4.5

million unique visitors that September, the most of any political website (though of course more of that still went to salacious celebrity content than to politics). They'd focused, like many new tech companies, on building an audience, not making money. But now that they'd amassed that digital commodity, traffic, they were confident they could sell it.

Harman returned home to the Bay Area excited about the deal and began working with Kenny on the formal diligence process, kicking the tires on The Huffington Post's traffic and revenue projections. He liked what he saw. And he liked that The Huffington Post, and its founders, had made an early political bet on Obama over Clinton, one that had already paid off in the Democratic primaries, distinguishing them from much of the rest of the media who had been trying to play it straight. The venture market was, like the stock market, competitive and fast-moving that summer, the rumbles of concern about subprime mortgages overwhelmed by excitement about an online economy that was finally coming into its own and attracting consumers. Harman knew he wasn't the only possible investor, so he pushed his team to work fast, and he agreed to value The Huffington Post at just under $100 million—fifty times the value back when it launched. The share that Andrew Breitbart had sold to Kenny for $250,000 was now worth something like $10 million. Harman and the Huffington Post founders reached a handshake deal in early September but decided not to hold a celebration; everyone was distracted by the ominous movements on Wall Street.

Then the sky fell. On September 10, Lehman Brothers announced it had lost $3.9 billion. On September 15, it declared bankruptcy. And another domino looked like it might fall: Morgan Stanley, where Harman had started his career and where his fund had its accounts. He wasn't even sure if the money he had promised to The Huffington Post was safe. Venture deals, meanwhile, were falling apart left and right—and the investors who didn't pull out entirely were insisting on renegotiating their investments. *The Huffington Post*'s competitors were cutting back. Nick, who prided himself on both his foresight and his pessimism, unceremoniously started shrinking, shutting down *Wonkette* and Valleywag, which was getting just two million visits a month at that point. Their combined traffic represented less than 3 percent of Nick's empire. Nicholas Carlson, bard of the cool tech office spaces, was the first to go.

Harman considered walking away from the *Huffington Post* deal too. There would have been no shame in it. But when Morgan Stanley and the other big banks got their federal bailout in October, Harman decided that *The Huffington Post* still looked like a good bet. He was surprised to learn, though, that his new partners wouldn't renegotiate. They wanted the $100 million headline valuation, and they needed the $25 million.

If Harman couldn't reduce his risk by knocking down the company's valuation, he decided, he'd find other ways to lower his exposure in the deal. He insisted on "preferences"—terms that meant that *The Huffington Post*'s early investors would get paid after he did, and gave them an incentive to ensure that the company would sell for more than $300 million.

And he told Kenny that he'd agree to the terms with one new condition: he'd invest only if Obama won the election. It made sense to Jonah, but Kenny was stunned. He'd never heard a condition like that. Harman wasn't trying to make a political statement: his considered view was that Arianna and Kenny would have special access in an Obama presidency, that the news site would be aligned with the zeitgeist. It might have been unheard of to do, he knew, "but it was a particular moment in time."

On November 4, 2008, Obama won the election handily. All of *The Huffington Post*'s bets had come through at the same time. And the next December, Harman tagged along to the White House holiday party as

Huffington's plus-one. When they wound through the holiday decorations to the front of the photo line, where Barack and Michelle Obama towered over most of their guests, the president greeted the publisher warmly. "Arianna, I want you to know that I don't agree with everything you say, but I read *The Huffington Post* every day," he said.

"That's pretty cool," Harman thought. "There's really a special connection here." Traffic might be the new currency, but, as Arianna had always known, proximity to power could also help pay the bills.

....

Unique Visitors

Jonah watched the financing come through for *The Huffington Post* with growing confidence that BuzzFeed's turn would come next. He'd threatened to leave *The Huffington Post* earlier in 2008, having gotten close to a deal with the venture capital fund at the center of the New York boom, Union Square Ventures, which had proposed to invest in BuzzFeed on the condition that Jonah move over full time. Kenny had reeled him back in by raising another $2.4 million of funding to his and John's investments, bringing in new money from SoftBank and Hearst. The investment round valued BuzzFeed at $6.4 million—not bad for a weird little website with no revenue—and included the condition that Jonah still split his time. Still, the status quo made less and less sense. Jonah was feeding the best insights of BuzzFeed to *The Huffington Post*, a few blocks uptown, because the latter had the staff to automate them. Jonah didn't really manage people in a conventional sense. Working for him was more like being managed by the oracle at Delphi: he'd make an observation, sometimes a cryptic one, about the future of the internet, and his staff would try to figure out what he meant and what to do. Jonah believed, above all, in a kind of freedom that meant both that he didn't like to be encumbered by managerial details and that he had an almost ideological opposition to telling people what to do. BuzzFeed, its offices still in the building with the mah-jongg parlors, was the sort of relaxed, chaotic environment in which Jonah thrived; *The Huffington Post*, with its bright, open office and hidden politics, increasingly felt like the kind of big, dysfunctional, political organization Jonah had spent his life trying to avoid.

Arianna was getting tired of Jonah's double life too. As she was finalizing Fred Harman's investment, she came to her junior partner with the bad news: it was time to kill the BuzzFeed widget on the *Huffington Post* home page, which was siphoning off traffic from *The Huffington Post* and was, when you looked closely at it, too weird and embarrassing for The Internet Newspaper. Jonah was taken aback. It was the first time anyone had told him to do anything in a while. But, at *The Huffington Post*, you couldn't ultimately say no to Arianna.

And so in the summer of 2008, Jonah started turning BuzzFeed into a real company, one that would ultimately rival, surpass, and purchase his main employer, where his colleagues still saw it as a tiny curiosity. At 1:30 a.m. on June 15, 2008, Jonah—who did his best work on late-night email—sent Johanesen, the designer, a memo titled "BuzzFeed Meme Machine: How to Open Platform so It Works for Power Users and Casual Fans." In it, he laid out a vision of BuzzFeed as a place where users—not, primarily, paid editors—could not just track trends but "launch buzz" in nine different formats, including "Trend Page (aka Classic Buzz)" as well as image, video, animated GIF, quiz, chart, or even a list of any of those things. "Let's go through the history of memes and web editorial to cover all the best formats!" BuzzFeed would increasingly aim to go viral, not just track virality. It would need to: in early October of 2008, that little red widget and its steady stream of traffic disappeared from *The Huffington Post*.

In April of 2009, BuzzFeed added code that allowed editors to jam a series of photographs or videos together to make lists and include short captions. BuzzFeed didn't exactly invent the list, but they did invent the thing that got dubbed the listicle.

For all the talk of automation, one of the team's problems was that the best mechanism for going viral was neither algorithms nor Peggy Wang's taste. It was still Jonah, constantly tinkering around based on his instincts about the psychological factors that made people share. People shared content that reflected well on them, he noted—they were more likely to share a post about earthquake relief than one about celebrity gossip. They shared content connected to their identity. They shared things that made them look clever and funny. And even the best content was subject to decay, as yesterday's novelty that showed how plugged in you were became today's cliché.

Jonah's approach was a radically new and abstract way of thinking about media—to focus on its psychological effect rather than on what it was actually about. This was the stuff he'd been thinking about since his time at Santa Cruz, the applied version of all that abstract talk of identity formation in late capitalism. Jonah's experiments didn't always work. Sometimes, they looked insane. Like when he tweeted in quick succession, "RT if you love Jesus!" and "RT if you think Jesus had some good ideas but is totally overrated," getting a total of three retweets and much head-scratching. A prank that worked better came in May of 2009, when he latched on to the mechanics of ego and celebrity that had motivated Blogebrity years earlier. After the actor Ashton Kutcher, who made his own reputation as a prankster in creating the reality show *Punk'd*, shared a BuzzFeed link on Twitter, Jonah wrote a post headlined "Yo Ashton! Thanks for Tweeting!"

When Kutcher didn't respond to that post, Jonah posted another one acting like a deranged fan. "You think you can just tweet a few BuzzFeed links and then just IGNORE me when I respond? When I offer to give you your own freakin' BuzzFeed badge??!!!! I was YOUR BIGGEST FAN!!!! How can you just IGNORE THE FANS who made you who you are?? That means you just turned your biggest fan into YOUR BIGGEST ONLINE NIGHTMARE. I am pleased to announce BuzzFeed.com's newest weekly feature. It is called———> F**K ASHTON!!!!!. BuzzFeed readers can email jonah@buzzfeed.com to suggest what I should post next week. And I will keep doing it until you apologize for ignoring me," he wrote, threatening a post called "TOP 3 THINGS THAT ARE LAME ABOUT ASHTON KUTCHER!!!!!!!!!"

Kutcher did not get that he was, this time, the subject of a prank. He called Jonah and left him a two-minute voicemail. "I want to ask for your forgiveness because I don't like having ill will," he said earnestly. The prank had worked. Jonah posted the voicemail to BuzzFeed, made Page Six, and got more than twenty thousand views on the website, triggering Johanesen's bright red "viral" arrow. The small team on Canal Street basked in the recognition.

Johanesen, the designer, felt kind of bad for the site's tiny editorial team. They were doing good work, training a system to create and spread viral content. But users were getting good at making their own viral content too. The big tech companies Jonah admired, like Facebook and Twitter, didn't employ editors. The best case for Johanesen, Jonah, and their investors was to become a tech platform like Facebook, not a media company. That's where you got the billion-dollar valuations and the effortless scale. For now BuzzFeed was somewhere between being a content company and a platform, but at some point, Johanesen speculated, Jonah would have to break the news to his editorial staff that their services were no longer required.

Meanwhile, the traffic climbed—four million views in August 2009, five million in November. As it did, Nick began to see his quirky friend as something more like a threat, something he expressed in the way he expressed everything: with blunt aggression. Jonah "is a bit of a dick," he tweeted on March 26. "But he's one of the web's few original thinkers." "I'm a dick to u bc of social mirroring," Jonah fired back.

It was a rare clash in the small, collegial early blog scene, much of which passed through that gritty Chinatown office. Jonah had learned at MIT and at Eyebeam the value of simply having smart, creative people in the same room, so he offered space in BuzzFeed's tight quarters to creative figures from the early internet. Jason Kottke came to work there and in BuzzFeed's subsequent offices for years, with a straight-backed chair that you borrowed at your peril. On June 18, 2010, Peggy returned from touring with her rock band to find a slight, soft-spoken young blond man installed at one of the desks. It was Chris Poole, known online as "moot," who had founded 4chan in 2003. "Oh man, it's my first day back at work and MOOT is here!!!" she messaged a friend.

This was particularly mortifying because Peggy had once suggested online that Poole was her "internet crush." But she was also surprised to discover that the founder of 4chan was so sweet and handsome. 4chan was disgusting—teenage-boy disgusting, to be fair—the source of much of the internet's early meme culture of lolcats and rickrolling, which was 4chan's own language, but the site was also full of racism and misogyny and sick jokes, which, back then, didn't put Poole beyond the pale. His peers in a mostly white, mostly male scene wrote the racism and sexism off as irony. The kids on 4chan were your little brother who you figured would eventually grow up, the way Poole had, and become a quiet, productive—hot—member of society; they weren't yet actual Nazis. Jonah knew Chris was running 4chan on the side but was more interested in helping him with his new, grown-up project, which eventually launched as a short-lived platform for remixing images and memes, called Canvas Networks. For the time being, Chris was glad to help out around BuzzFeed. He stuck around for a couple of years before going to work for Google.

The venture capitalists who had begun to shake off the crushing market collapse of 2008 were paying attention too. On March 1, 2010, Chris Dixon, a friend of Jonah's whose company Hunch promised to help people figure out what to buy on the internet, had emailed a venture capitalist he knew, Will Porteous, with a tip, subject line "BuzzFeed." "Great company, probably going to raise money soon. founder (Jonah Peretti) is brilliant and co-founder of HuffPo," he wrote, passing on Jonah's email address. The venture capital era in which investors courted founders, rather than vice versa, was just beginning, and so Porteous— an old-fashioned, square-jawed six-foot-three man who had rowed at Stanford, kept in shape, and prided himself on his sense of honor— moved fast. He was a newly minted general partner at the venture capital firm RRE, looking for his first big deal. BuzzFeed hadn't exactly been in his media diet, but when he called up the site and immediately fell down a rabbit hole of silly, warmly nostalgic posts about the International House of Pancakes, he felt that he'd found an addicting new kind of media. Porteous met Jonah for dim sum and was captivated by the founder's ambition, his drive to build a defining company of a new era, uniting the best of the tech and media industries.

Jonah had by then begun to articulate a clear vision for the business, one that drew on, among other things, Ken's experience working on the creation of MTV in the 1980s. The idea was that just as cable networks had provided the channels on which new media giants like CNN and

MTV's parent Viacom could sell content and reach audiences, so the new digital networks—from YouTube to Facebook—would one day be sources of revenue for a new generation of media companies. Back then, it seemed insane to imagine you'd make a living on those platforms—much less build a company on them. But Jonah had seen around a corner. There were, Porteous quickly realized, "a lot of ideas and not a lot of company," but the business of venture capital is betting on founders, and the scale of Jonah's vision drew him in. He offered Jonah a kind of a pact—that Porteous would stick with him for the long haul and not pressure him for a quick sale. He led an $8 million investment round that valued the company at $20 million, and the two celebrated the closing in May of 2010 over pancakes at the IHOP in downtown Brooklyn.

The money would pay for a new office on Spring Street, just a few blocks from Nick's favorite haunt, Balthazar. Over lunch there soon thereafter, Jonah made clear to Nick that he'd been making a study of Gawker's business. The Gawker Media sites, he told Nick, had gotten stuck in a "local maximum," as writers responded to page view bonuses by trying to drive up clicks and "overserve the regulars," as Nick later put it—at the expense of spreading their content across the wider internet and acquiring new readers. That bigger metric, the one that had supercharged *The Huffington Post* through the anonymous masses who surged in through Google links and viral stories, was "unique visitors." Those people, too, could learn to click repeatedly, if Nick could only draw them in. Nick took Jonah's advice and changed Gawker's core metric to unique visitors—a metric that encouraged you to make content for everyone. Indeed, unique visitors would become the core metric of the whole viral internet. It was, Nick later realized, "a technical change, but fateful."

Advertising agencies, too, had begun to look at their unique visitor numbers, concerned that their view counts meant that they were simply reaching the same users over and over. So back in the office, Peggy and Scott Lamb soon found themselves assembling white Ikea tables with the sort of person BuzzFeed had never employed before: a hard-driving moneyman. Jon Steinberg's strength, and his weakness, was that he simply had no veneer at all. Small and wiry and constantly in motion, he'd been a midlevel deal guy in Google's giant sales organization, but he'd wanted to run something himself. And he wanted what hustling young men like him all wanted at the time: an exit. He wanted to own a piece of a company, to build it fast and to sell it to a big, prestigious buyer—the dream, of course, would be the greatest media company of all, Disney, where he'd been an Imagineering intern when he was in high school in Manhattan. The BuzzFeed writers didn't really know what to make of his hunger and his hustle, but they could feel that his presence meant that things were suddenly more serious.

Privately, though, Steinberg knew he'd taken on a questionable proposition when he accepted Jonah's offer of equity in BuzzFeed in exchange for its top business job. While he dreamed of a big exit, his job was to bring in advertising revenue—but Jonah barely had a business. What he had was a big idea, and a great story. Jonah thought that the social web would bring with it a new kind of advertising—not the grim little boxes that lined websites the way they lined newspapers, but lavish, funny, and creative content that would recall the *Mad Men* era. This kind of advertising would be "native content"—native to the web, native to BuzzFeed. As he had learned from the NRA experiment, ads wouldn't need to go wildly viral in order to spread widely with low distribution costs, because at least some consumers shared ads with one another instead of seeing them only when someone paid to display them. This was an exciting new pitch to marketers, and a bespoke product that couldn't be mistaken for a commodity—it couldn't be turned into pork bellies quite as easily as the squares and rectangles of display advertising. But Buzz-

Feed had sold only a handful of campaigns so far; Jon would have to prove that the new model of advertising could scale.

Steinberg knew he was betting his young career on two things. The first was that this native advertising—such a fun story, such a good idea—would become a real business, and that the advertisements themselves could spread just as virally as BuzzFeed's best posts. The second was that BuzzFeed could benefit from Facebook's unprecedented growth. The social network had skyrocketed from 350 million monthly users at the end of 2009 to 608 million by the end of 2010. Only Facebook could send Jon the floods of traffic required to support his new advertising business. Jon was among the first in the media industry to understand the implications of the social networks' rise, and to realize that, while he was selling BuzzFeed as the future, he was also selling a future dominated by Facebook.

Breitbart Dot Com

ndrew Breitbart had left *The Huffington Post* in 2005 feeling pretty good about the $250,000 he'd extracted from Kenny for his 10 percent of the company. It had bought him, he'd tell friends, a new kitchen. But five years later, he was still in Los Angeles, watching all the new money flow to his old partners, Kenny and Arianna and Jonah. And Drudge was still treating him as a kind of minor feudal liege: he patronizingly let Andrew drive some traffic to wire stories on breitbart.com and collect a tiny fraction of the revenue Drudge earned from his huge front page. Andrew was still what he'd been all along: "Matt Drudge's bitch."

Watching the traffic flow through Drudge's site, though, Andrew knew something that the journalists and pundits telling the story of the Obama-era internet didn't. The story they saw was of the inexorable rise of progressive youth movements, powered by new technology, behind a new generation of leaders like the young American president. The giant platforms—Facebook first of all—were run by people who thrilled at the hopeful popular movements, from the One Million Voices Against

FARC in Colombia to Barack Obama's campaign, that their technology helped spawn. Mark Zuckerberg, Jack Dorsey, and the rest never quite grasped that there were people disgusted with the founders' new power. They'd never really considered that these same tools could be used against them.

And what did they all think of Andrew Breitbart? The pudgy fire starter didn't seem important to Jonah, or to much of what was then seen as the rising world of tech and media. His sad, performative attempt to swim against the tide wasn't getting him anywhere. He was a guy who had never gotten out of Drudge's shadow, and it seemed he would be remembered, if at all, as a footnote to Drudge's single-page, Courier-font website on a changing internet.

But Andrew had been busy since he'd flamed out at *The Huffington Post*, intent on securing his own place in the history of politics and the internet. He felt he deserved it. He had, after all, been Drudge's invisible right hand, there when Drudge broke the Monica Lewinsky scandal. Then he'd been there at the creation of the next internet juggernaut, *The Huffington Post*, only to get forced out by Kenny. Andrew was tired of being a local weirdo who worked on the internet, who couldn't even explain why he was important. Breitbart.com was going to fix that. The site had started as a way for Andrew to capitalize on his work for Drudge, who would occasionally use it as the landing place for a random Associated Press or Reuters article. Drudge never charged his protégé for the modest traffic flow he sent Andrew's way, a former colleague said. It was payment in kind.

Andrew's continued deference to the elusive Drudge, who lived in Miami and communicated with the world almost entirely through his web page, was a matter of necessity. Drudge was, for all intents and purposes, Breitbart's assignment editor in those early days. Drudge's power came from the traffic he could drive—forty thousand views for a modest link, two hundred thousand for a big banner. So Andrew knew he couldn't merely mimic *The Huffington Post*: the traffic machine was Drudge's front page, not his own. And in any case, he had his eye on a different model: Nick Denton's network of cheeky blogs. Andrew talked to friends about following Nick in giving a high-profile editor control of each one, and offering them bonuses based on the traffic their work produced.

In 2009, he borrowed $25,000 from his father, who owned a Santa Monica steakhouse, to launch the first of his network of blogs, called Big Government. Andrew still relied heavily on his mentor. "Hunting for Drudge links was essentially the way the site was edited," Ben Shapiro realized. So if Drudge was on an immigration kick, the Breitbart team would throw up all the links they could find to stories about immigration, and soon Andrew—mirroring *The Huffington Post*—began finding ways to add his own original content.

Andrew was in a hurry to launch the blogs because he had a hot story. A young conservative activist, James O'Keefe, had secretly recorded videos with employees of a group called ACORN, which mobilized poor Black people for political campaigns. O'Keefe had approached the group with a college student in tow, and had appeared to ask them for advice about how to handle their prostitution business; the ACORN financial advisers tried to answer. O'Keefe—who recorded an iconic introduction video of himself dressed as a prototypical pimp, though he never actually wore the costume into his stings—believed he could use the videos to destroy a pillar of the Democratic Party's institutional coalition, a group that just *must* be engaging in dirty politics, stealing votes, rigging elections—even if nothing in O'Keefe's videos actually showed any of that.

Andrew loved it. When O'Keefe told him, "We're going to take down ACORN," he responded: "No, we're going to take down the media."

This was what made Andrew different and important. Breitbart

.com's journalistic output didn't amount to much—a couple of take-downs and a lot of heavily hyped misses. Its traffic, though, was already the second largest in the conservative media, a by-product of Andrew's relationship with the largest, Drudge. And he saw with early clarity what would become the heart of a new online conservative movement: an ob-session with the media itself.

Andrew would later write as though that realization were with him from the start. But Andrew's fixation on what he saw as a hostile liberal media hardened after breitbart.com published its disastrous second partnership with O'Keefe in June of 2010, a video that appeared to ex-pose an obscure official in Obama's Department of Agriculture, Shirley Sherrod, claiming she'd discriminated against white farmers.

Andrew should have known better. The ACORN sting had faced widespread criticism over O'Keefe's deceptive editing, and the way in which a political attack had been packaged as journalism. But those were details—the attack had worked, and ACORN had collapsed under its pressure. So when O'Keefe showed up with another shot at exposing the corruption of Black politics, Andrew grabbed for it.

The video seemed so clear. In it, Sherrod, a Black Southerner, told of a time she was assigned to help a struggling white farmer. She wrestled with the idea, knowing how many Black farmers were struggling, and she "didn't give him the full force of what I could do." She instead sent him to a white lawyer so "one of his own kind would take care of him." This, Andrew declared, was as "racist" as you get. Andrew didn't actu-ally care much about Sherrod—her prompt firing was merely collateral damage. In his accompanying commentary, Andrew focused instead on media coverage of the Tea Party movement, and particularly on sugges-tions that the movement was (gasp) a racist backlash against Barack Obama. By publishing this video in which a Black Democrat was shown to be racist, Andrew was demonstrating that "the new media will not be silenced. It will not allow for the mainstream media to propagate hateful and hurtful lies."

Then it blew up in Andrew's face. The NAACP released a full video of the exchange, which showed that O'Keefe's video had taken Sherrod's comment wildly out of context. Sherrod actually had been talking about her path toward her current, anti-racist views; she was recounting how once, twenty-three years earlier, she'd felt animus toward a white farmer, and how she'd recognized it, worked through it, and ultimately helped him. The Obama administration offered Sherrod her job back, and the conservative media who had celebrated Breitbart's latest scoop turned on him, hard. In the cruelest cut, Fox News's most powerful host, Bill O'Reilly, apologized for carrying the story, and promised to be more careful. Then Sherrod sued for defamation.

Andrew was distraught, not about getting it wrong, though he was "pissed at O'Keefe"; he was infuriated, above all, that the conservatives who had hyped his story were now turning on him. Fox even blacklisted him. Andrew kept saying that he hadn't known the full context (even though the article began with "context is everything").

But the storm didn't die down. The media was calling Andrew "racist," and the label stuck. That was "the thing that drove him nuts more than any other single thing—that they called him a racist and continued to call him a racist," a friend recalled. Fox wouldn't let Andrew back on their programs. He was even banned from the front page of *The Huffington Post*, which he'd helped start. He never got over what he saw as the unfairness of the Sherrod episode. Andrew thought he, not Sherrod, was the real victim. The experience added a layer of anger and stress to the personality of someone who had been a happy warrior, a hyperkinetic embodiment of attention deficit disorder. At one point, when Andrew was hospitalized for the heart condition that would later kill him, he told a friend, Lee Stranahan, that he was keeping it private. "I don't want Sherrod to know I'm in the hospital because I don't want her to think she's getting to me," he said.

Andrew Breitbart, so easy for Manhattan's new media elite to write off for his slovenly style and his reactionary politics, now seemed really, finally, to be done. His desperate, racist stunt had backfired; an optimistic new media era would have little space for his darkness. But Andrew would keep watching his enemies on the internet, looking in equal parts for outrages he could mine and for tactics he could copy. And it was in observing Nick's empire that he found a lewd path to redemption.

Dicks

The years of the dick pic were 2010 and 2011. That's when the grow-ing new media, hungrier and more sophisticated than ever in its approach to traffic, and still totally unconstrained by any of the old norms, triumphed by publishing the penis pictures that twenty-first-century men can't seem to help themselves from sending to the objects of their desire. Andrew Breitbart would use one to save his career. But AJ Daulerio was the king: "The worldwide leader in sextapes," according to *GQ*, he had built an empire that was, in the words of *Esquire*, "all about dongs."

AJ had been one of the purest products of that 2000s New York blogging scene that Nick had extracted, one of the most vulnerable to its addic-tions, and one of the most committed to Gawker's uncompromising ideology of revealing the naked truth—down, in AJ's case, to the nude photos that had become commonplace with the rise of phone cameras. His first site, *The Black Table*, had been crude and ambitious, and like his apartment, Camp Bowery, it was at the heart of that early scene. AJ had his first turn with Nick back when he was dating the Gawker star Jessica Coen, and trying and failing to run the gambling site Oddjack. But that site got a pathetic two thousand views a day, and Nick had quickly shut it down back in 2005.

That same year, Nick, who had just sold Moreover, had money to put into an idea AJ's *Black Table* co-founder Will Leitch had for a sports blog, so they launched Deadspin, and AJ freelanced for the site occasionally. But needing a job and a place he could afford, AJ started writing for *Philadelphia* magazine, and left Camp Bowery for Queens with another co-founder of *The Black Table*, Aileen Gallagher. There, AJ's addictions started to become more alarming, his behavior more erratic. In January of 2006, Gallagher found herself helplessly weeping in the shower after waking up to find that her roommate had stumbled in drunk, fallen asleep on the couch, and then woken up and pissed all over her laptop. (AJ, unlike almost everyone else in this book, declined to talk to me, but he has spoken and written widely and movingly about his life, and I've drawn from those sources.)

Deadspin was thriving, however. By 2008, the site, with its outsider's voice and Leitch's sense of humor—gentler than Nick's but still scathing—was the world's biggest sports blog, with seven hundred thousand visitors a month. But Leitch quit in June of that year, already sick of Nick's constant pressure for more traffic. AJ, all swagger and insecurity blended visibly together, jumped at the opportunity, telling Nick that "he would give his left nut" to run the blog. "That kind of confidence or that kind of desire or ambition" was hard to fake, Nick thought.

AJ had been trying to get Nick's attention for years. He was in some ways the truest believer of all in Nick's vision—an uncompromising view, shared with Mark Zuckerberg, that Nick described as "the internet's most radical ideology, that information wants to be free, and that ✓ the truth shall set us free."

But AJ also looked back for antecedents in old magazine writers like Hunter S. Thompson. He believed in writing, in literature even. *The Black Table*'s sarcastic musings didn't get much attention, and that was okay. While Nick and Jonah were, in their way, idealists about traffic, AJ was a cynic.

The old Gawker editors had worshipped traffic as a kind of mystical god. AJ belonged to a new generation of Gawker Media editors who saw traffic as "something you inherit." He was openly dismissive of "doing the page-view chasing game," and talked about trying to publish great writing while grinding out whatever it took to get traffic on the side. By 2011, straining to compete with well-tuned machines like *The Huffington Post* and BuzzFeed, AJ thought about views with a kind of blunt cynicism that seemed to meet the new moment. "Traffic is a business problem that I need to solve," he said. But even as a first generation of Gawker employees soured on the idea of Nick as their surrogate father, AJ seemed willing to do whatever it took to impress him.

AJ's quest for traffic and for Nick's affection often led him to the internet's lowest common denominator, nudes. The writer Maximillian Potter, who profiled AJ for *Esquire*, noted that during his first few months at Deadspin his posts included one about a tight end for the Washington Redskins who had mistakenly posted an image to his blog showing his dick, a television broadcast that accidentally showed "some Viking locker room dong," and a photograph of a young cheerleader for the New England Patriots scrawling the image of a dick on the shoulder of her passed-out drunk friend.

Nick didn't really get it. Didn't get the Deadspin audience and its "puerile fascination with dick pics," in his words, and, to be fair, didn't even know what sport March Madness involved. But he saw the numbers going up, and so he didn't mess with AJ's formula. The internet of that day was pretty raunchy anyway, and questions around gender and exploitation hadn't begun to rise to the forefront, or split along polarized, political lines. Tracie Egan had been pushing its limits from a feminist perspective over on Jezebel for years, and when she got married in 2009, the Vice co-founder Gavin McInnes, by then a Republican (because, he told her, small government was a step toward anarchism), officiated at her wedding. "Tracking traffic makes everyone cynical," Nick later said.

AJ was doing what Nick had always said he wanted his blogs to do, what Gawker Stalker had promised, but rarely actually done—exposing everything, tearing the masks, even the clothes, off the powerful. AJ really was publishing the things nobody else would. The rise of digital technology meant that, suddenly, millions of people had intimate scenes on their phones and cameras that their enemies could easily send to a blogger. Society didn't really have words or norms for this yet, though it would come to be called "revenge porn"—and AJ had no compunctions about it at all.

It was also an old Gawker tradition. Coen had posted Fred Durst's sex tape way back in 2005. It made sense; the tape was the thing everyone was talking about and sharing, but nobody would admit to looking at. Publishing it was honesty. And it was only one part of a strategy that put Daulerio at the heart of sports journalism. He also broke news about the financial troubles of Major League Baseball and a pro basketball team, of feuds and dramas inside the linked worlds of sports and sports media.

When it was male athletes' nudity, posting them seemed harmless somehow—in some strange way like speaking truth to power. The Erin Andrews leak was something different. In 2009, the creepier corners of the internet lit up with a four-and-a-half-minute-long video of the ESPN sportscaster changing, which a stalker had filmed through the peephole of the door of her hotel room in the Nashville Marriott. AJ's Deadspin linked to the site that hosted the video. The episode was a grotesque invasion of privacy that left Andrews having to explain in court "why I'm insecure, why I'm humiliated, why I'm embarrassed, why I am obsessive about checking the Internet." The stalker would go to jail for two and a half years.

The next year, AJ published a video of a college student having sex in a bathroom in Bloomington, Indiana. It looked to many observers like rape. A woman—he thought it was the student—wrote to him begging him to take it down, and AJ refused, dismissing the video as "not a very serious matter." The student's father called next. "You gotta understand, I've just been dealing with watching my daughter get fucked in a pile of piss for the past two days," he told AJ. Deadspin did take the video down, though by then it had spread across the internet.

The video was extreme, and at the far edge of what even Nick Denton could stomach. It had nothing to do with sports, or with sticking it to someone powerful. It was mere cruelty, and voyeurism. It exposed the underbelly of what at other times seemed like a coherent ideology, a belief that the costs of this sometimes repellent transparency were worth paying. Dick-era Gawker was not solely about literal dicks. This was a broad assault on the idea of privacy—and, in particular, on people who Nick thought were hypocrites when it came to their personal privacy. The Bloomington video had been indefensible on those grounds. But other intrusions seemed aimed at giving the new information tycoons a taste of their own medicine. This was part of the logic of outing Thiel. And it applied particularly to Mark Zuckerberg, whose Facebook was exposing people's lives to the public eye even as he himself, as Valleywag had discovered, maintained a secret Facebook account under the name Zuckerberg.

In July of 2010, Nick hired a paparazzo to follow Zuckerberg around for a weekend. The photographer drove through Palo Alto on Zucker-berg's trail, taking pictures of him outside a bar and at a Stanford event. He took pictures of his house and his girlfriend and his friends. There wasn't really much there. "The most interesting thing about Zucker-berg's life may well be how ordinary it is for such a well-off 26-year-old," noted Ryan Tate, the writer of the resulting Gawker article.

But Tate concluded with trademark self-righteousness, "Mark Zuck-erberg turned strangers' intimate moments into riches. We turned the tables on the Facebook CEO, lurking outside his house, following him out with his girlfriend and pals, and to Chinese language lessons. . . . For all the power and money in Silicon Valley, tech dons have managed to escape the sort of scrutiny the tabloid press brings to bear on the celebri-ties of Hollywood or the moguls of New York. Until now."

The biggest dick get of all, however, the legendary one, was an actual dick. In 2010, AJ crossed all the lines of conventional journalism to please Nick and get traffic, betraying a source and blowing up the sports internet. It began when a sideline reporter for the Jets, Jenn Sterger, con-fided to AJ that star quarterback Brett Favre had sent her inappropriate images. AJ simply printed what she'd told him off the record, writing that he'd done so "because I'm a dick and it's an incredibly funny story." Eventually, other women would come forward, as would an anonymous source offering the photographs themselves for $12,000. "I'd like to reach into the sack of scuzz money and pay for pictures of Brett Favre's dick, please," AJ told Nick, promising him that this would be Deadspin's equivalent of Drudge's Monica Lewinsky scoop. Nick agreed. The money, to AJ's surprise, fit in a single envelope. On October 7, he published a video that included the picture. "We've seen far too many supposedly family-oriented and upstanding professional athletes whose off-field be-havior contradicts their well-manicured public persona," AJ wrote, a bit of sententious finger wagging that didn't really suit Gawker's nihilistic posture. AJ would later justify the story—reasonably—as exposing work-place harassment, but nothing about the way it was written seemed to make that point. Nick in a more honest moment would admit that much of what Gawker did was just "voyeuristic." The post got nearly six million views.

The Favre story rocked sports media and made AJ a star himself. It also sent him spiraling further out of control. In December of 2011, he went to visit the broadcaster Joe Buck at MetLife Stadium, and slipped into the bathroom to do some coke. "When I went to open the bag, I Woody Allened it; the coke went everywhere," AJ told Potter. He didn't want Buck or his partner, Troy Aikman, to know what was going on, "so I cleaned it up by snorting as much as I could. There had to be coke all over my beard and jacket. Joe asked if I wanted to meet Troy, and I was like, 'No thanks.' And I got out of there."

That was AJ at the time. Writers who admired him saw him as a car-ing, hard-driving coach; those who didn't saw him as the embodiment of Gawker's out-of-control, macho, sometimes misogynistic culture. The editor of the porn site *Fleshbot*, Lux Alptraum, thought AJ was the "bro-iest" of the site leads and clashed with him over headlines like "LeBron James Is a Cocksucker." "This is supposed to be a gay-friendly, woman-friendly company, and you have this homophobic, misogynistic head-line blasted on the wall," she complained. Nick sided with AJ: "Nothing has the cut like 'cocksucker.'" It was a long way from the revolution Jez-ebel had been leading, but the early Jezebel team largely avoided the of-fice vibe by working from home.

When AJ took over Deadspin, it was getting about 700,000 unique visitors a month. By 2011, as "The Worldwide Leader in Sextapes," it was up to 2.3 million.

Among the people watching Daulerio's parade of dongs was Andrew Breitbart, who was serving out a kind of internal exile in Los Angeles after the Shirley Sherrod debacle. He'd since made the mistake in January of 2010, with breitbart.com fully established as a kind of funhouse mirror to Gawker Media, of giving up his role as silent assistant who posted links to *The Drudge Report* during the afternoons Matt took off. Drudge responded in April with a ban on links to breitbart.com—a major blow to the website.

But redemption would arrive for Andrew, too, in the form of a famous, cloth-covered erection. The story—which would ultimately take Hillary Clinton down and become central to Breitbart's lore—began on the Saturday afternoon of Memorial Day weekend in 2011 when a Twitter user with the handle @patriotusa76 spotted a strange tweet on Congressman Anthony Weiner's account, and took a screenshot of it. He reshared Weiner's tweet, which had a link to the image, and sent it to a dozen or so bloggers—Andrew Breitbart, Arianna Huffington, and some others. Weiner was a media-friendly figure, a cable news shouter whose email address was widely available to reporters. I had already been doing much of my journalism on Twitter and saw some of the action while I chased my toddlers around my grandparents' house. I emailed Weiner that afternoon to ask what the buzz was about. "The weiner gags never get old, I guess," he replied, a final comment before he, first, claimed he'd been "hacked," and then fell uncharacteristically silent.

The anonymous Twitter user's email was hard to figure out; Andrew and his small team spent Saturday night on a long conference call debating what to do. Halfway through, though, his business partner reminded him of another email: a Texas man had emailed a week earlier, saying he had compromising photographs of the New York congressman. Andrew realized he'd "forgotten a most blatant missing puzzle piece," and that hint, along with Weiner's claim that he'd been hacked, prompted Andrew to publish a piece under the grand byline "publius" with the memorable lede "Hacked or hung?"

A week later, Andrew was on the phone with Meagan Broussard, a Texas woman who was—it emerged—one of many with whom Weiner had exchanged lewd messages. As he paced the sidewalk in front of the offices his new friend Steve Bannon had rented for him, Andrew persuaded her to text him five photographs. They were unmistakably Weiner, and unmistakably sexual. He sprinted upstairs to the office of Breitbart lawyer Joel Pollak, whom he'd brought in to prevent another Shirley Sherrod mess, and gleefully pressed his iPad against Pollak's glass door, laughing.

Andrew raced to get into the spotlight shining on Weiner's fall. When Weiner gathered reporters in a South Brooklyn community center to explain himself, Andrew hijacked the event, holding his own impromptu press conference. But he admitted that his role had been that of a conduit: he didn't have any connection to the original Twitter user who caught Weiner's errant tweet. Still, Andrew worked closely with CNN's Dana Bash and other mainstream reporters to amplify the Weiner story. New York's tabloids feasted on it. Weiner resigned in disgrace.

When Andrew reflected on the episode the next year in his memoir, he boasted that "the victory that has its most obvious roots in our reporting" was the temporary replacement of Weiner by a Republican, Bob Turner. These were pretty small political stakes: Turner was an obscure one-term congressman; Democrats quickly retook the New York City district. But Breitbart's real victory, Andrew felt, wasn't over Democrats. "We had beaten the media again."

That was where Breitbart was different. BuzzFeed, *The Huffington Post*, and Gawker all, in their way, sought to replace—or improve—the old media. That's what they told their investors. That's where the money and attention were, after all. Andrew was up to something different: sustained attacks on what he viewed as an undifferentiated "Democrat-media complex." He fixated on the media's willingness to believe Weiner's claim that he was hacked, and to amplify Weiner's attempts to shoot the messenger—Andrew himself. Meanwhile, Drudge still had not forgiven him for his departure: when the Weiner story broke, Drudge sent his river of traffic to a *Wall Street Journal* story. By then, though, Andrew was beginning to glimpse something new, something even bigger than *The Drudge Report*. The parents and grandparents of those original college kids were now on Facebook, and many of them couldn't get enough right-wing news.

·················

Sold

While Nick sought to expose—sometimes literally—the new tycoons of Silicon Valley, Jonah only grew more interested in
them. They spoke his language. Some of his friends had already raised
tens of millions, or sold their half-baked startups for similar sums.
BuzzFeed, Jonah thought, could join the boom. But while he grew increasingly fascinated with this new world, *The Huffington Post* was
drifting into the arms of a Silicon Valley dinosaur.

Arianna had captured the interest of Tim Armstrong, an ad salesman right out of central casting who had swaggered over from Google to
save AOL, the remnant of the once-great internet company that had
made Kenny's first fortune and would, incredibly, make him another
one. AOL still had traffic, thanks to all the baby boomers who hung on
to their AOL emails, and it even retained a lucrative business in internet
subscriptions, for people who weren't paying attention or hadn't realized
there were faster and more efficient ways to get online. And it had a
handful of blogs from a network that had sprung up to rival Gawker,

including *Engadget*, a Gizmodo rival, and the credulous Silicon Valley tip sheet *TechCrunch*.

Armstrong belonged to a particular category of media executive, familiar to old and new media alike, a born dealmaker who could convince anyone of anything. Like many a great salesperson, he seemed to be able to convince himself of pretty much anything as well. He was a perfect mark for Arianna, whose own reality-distortion field had created an image of *The Huffington Post*—a mecca for young viewers, powered by earnest concern about politics and "citizen journalists" blogging for free—that bore little resemblance to the dark arts KT, Jonah, and Breanna had mastered of gaming Google and getting middle-aged men to click on links that promised photographs of attractive young women.

Armstrong does not appear to have actually understood much about how *The Huffington Post* worked. He was particularly taken by "the importance of recruiting hordes of free bloggers," *Forbes*'s Jeff Bercovici later reported, under the apparent impression that the bloggers were the ones driving most of *The Huffington Post*'s traffic. "It was always, 'Arianna does it. That's what she's built her business on. Why don't we do it, too?'" Armstrong would tell AOL's editors.

His confusion was understandable. Arianna and Kenny had taken some steps to obscure their sources of traffic. At the end of 2009, editors had received a memo banning nudity from the site's front page. "They are KNEECAPPING our traffic," one immediately complained to Breanna in an email; she scrambled to mitigate the problem, suggesting a new option that would display salacious posts on every other page of the site, just not the front.

The maneuvering paid off. The announcement, on February 7, 2011, that AOL was buying *The Huffington Post* for $315 million was electrifying news in SoHo. It meant cash for early *Huffington Post* employees, of course—but it also meant that all that talk about getting rich off Gawker or BuzzFeed or other neighbors (*Business Insider* was a mile north, and IAC across town had just bought the dating site OkCupid) suddenly didn't seem so far-fetched.

Fred Harman and other *Huffington Post* board members didn't really like the deal. Harman thought they could make a billion at an IPO. But Arianna wanted to take the offer, and you couldn't say no to her—her name was on the company. She got cash and, equally important to her, even more power, including a bunch of doomed AOL media properties and the sprawling set of local news websites, Patch. And Kenny and Jonah were ready to sell: each carried a lingering worry that Arianna might, at any moment, pull the project off the rails, or into some other direction all her own.

Kenny had already reaped the political rewards of *The Huffington Post* back in 2008, building a new online base for the Democratic Party and having a hand in electing Barack Obama. Now, the financier was getting paid too. What's more, he got to sit back and appreciate the irony that AOL—a descendant of the company that merged with Time Warner in the great boondoggle of the last bubble—was paying him again.

Jonah had been drifting away from *The Huffington Post*, and by then was spending just one day a week there, less than he spent at BuzzFeed. But he found himself flattened by the deal—depressed. Jonah had been on an incredible ride for a decade, really since the day he sent that Nike email. That stunt had made him a kind of wizard. But then he'd also been able to exercise real power at *The Huffington Post*. It's not often you get to be both the wizard and the king, Jonah's old friend and investor John Johnson told him. He could just go back to wizarding now. If he wanted to work for AOL, they'd probably pay him to muse about the future of the internet. They already had one famous digital futurist, known as Shingy, whom they rolled out to advertisers to spew incomprehensible futurism. Jonah could potentially bring new life to the company's fraying, frantic claim that it still had its hands on the future.

But as the AOL deal ground into gear and the corporate integrators started scheduling meetings about corporate integration, Jonah just vanished. He didn't respond to the emails, didn't show up to the meetings, and made clear he wasn't interested in the sort of contract Arianna was getting, that key executives in big acquisitions get—fat salaries tied to bonuses if the integration goes well. He didn't want AOL to have any hooks in him, to force him to give them advice. He didn't want anything to do with the acquisition. He sold his shares and walked away from the options and the offer of a big salary if he'd stick around.

He had loved building *The Huffington Post*, loved making the traffic grow. Nick had been right in comparing traffic to compound interest. By the time of the sale, the number was huge by his metric of choice: thirty million unique visitors a month to *The Huffington Post* even by the conservative measure ad agencies insisted on, Comscore—an expensive, verified, and updated version of the old Site Meter that had been conceived in 1999 to serve advertisers as a digital version of Nielsen ratings. Jonah liked being at the center of the cultural action, too, being attacked by *The New York Times* or invoked by Obama.

To Jonah, the change was stark: "Everyone was watching us and trying to learn from us and compete with us and having meetings about how they could sue us, and then all of a sudden it was sold and I have nothing to do with it."

Jonah hadn't done it for the money, but now he had a pile of money, which he didn't entirely know what to do with and didn't like thinking about. He and Andrea bought a new Honda Odyssey and a house on a lake north of the city. He could invest in his friends' ideas too. Garrett Camp was raising money for a car-sharing company called Uber; Jonah thought it was cool and pitched in about $10,000, a decision that would ultimately make twice as much as his share of *The Huffington Post.*

All Jonah really had now was BuzzFeed; his second family was suddenly his first. But BuzzFeed showed no signs of going anywhere. Not much traffic, and no clear story to tell. For all the talk of social media, search had until then been BuzzFeed's main source of traffic. The most-viewed post of 2010 was a list of screenshots from the site Chatroulette, in which strangers met, talked, and sometimes took off their clothes; most of the traffic to it came from people googling "chatroulette." Just a month earlier, the big search hit had been "The 11 Best/Worst Vagina Tattoos of All Time [NSFW]." Google again—this is not a post you share with your friends—though the editors also noted a steady trickle of traffic from Facebook. Almost all of it came from mobile phones in South Korea, go figure.

Starting at the end of 2009, not long after Johanesen designed BuzzFeed's new format for lists, the small team had started to see signs that escape from Google dependency was possible. Matt Stopera, a recent graduate of NYU who had begun as an intern, making posts between getting coffee and taking out the trash, had written a series of lists at the end of 2009—"The 30 Most Memorable Mugshots," "The 50 Funniest Headlines," "The 40 Funniest Celebrity Candids"—that had proven exactly the sort of thing people liked to send their friends. As with much of what BuzzFeed did, it wasn't immediately obvious how this was different from the lists that Anna Holmes had been dutifully making at *Glamour.* But they were different: BuzzFeed was built for sharing, and the output of the vast internet's meme makers, curated by one of its editors, would always beat a tired magazine editor's limited imagination. Stopera put together the second-biggest post of 2010, another breakthrough:

"The 100 Best Signs at the Rally to Restore Sanity and/or Fear." That October 30 rally, led by comedians Jon Stewart and Stephen Colbert, had not succeeded in its goal of drowning out the resurgent Tea Party in a thick wave of sarcasm. But the list was full of good jokes, and sharing it was a way to signal your politics—and your sense of humor—to your friends. Most of the 895,297 people who clicked on the post came from Facebook. The News Feed was changing, and the same Americans who had made Facebook a natural organizing site for Barack Obama were now using it to defend the president.

But when Jonah left *The Huffington Post*, Google was still BuzzFeed's main source of traffic, and Jon Steinberg was still struggling to see how he'd build BuzzFeed into a business. In Steinberg's first full year, 2011, the company was on track for just $4 million in revenue—nice to have, but not something that would get attention amid a new generation of hot startups like the eyeglasses company Warby Parker or the office-space company WeWork. The BuzzFeed office was quiet; nobody was working late. And the board meetings were pretty weird too. Kenny, Will Porteous, and Hearst Ventures executive Scott English would sit around the table on Spring Street and Jonah would talk for a while, and then Kenny would say, "I have no idea what you're doing," and they'd all leave cheerfully.

Then, basically the minute Jonah was able to turn his full attention to BuzzFeed, it collapsed.

The problems began at the end of June 2011 when suddenly, out of nowhere, Google went from providing millions of views—about half of BuzzFeed's monthly traffic, then about twenty-five million monthly unique visitors—to zero. Just zero. After all the tweaks Andy Yaco-Mink had done, all the optimization, and all of the tricks they'd figured out to draw in Google traffic—Lamb had even created a user named "sextape"—it all went away.

Google had wiped out websites before. Back in February, the company announced, in the standard wooden language of tech, that Google had just "launched a pretty big algorithmic improvement to our ranking—a change that noticeably impacts 11.8% of our queries." The update crushed a generation of spammy sites that had floated to the top of Google rankings with spammy responses to a ludicrous range of possible searches—from "How to Pick Blueberries in Iowa" to "Ideas for Organizing Scrunchies"—and torched one of the first big internet media companies, Demand Media, another of Fred Harman's successful investments. Buzz-Feed had survived that purge, but now it had fallen off a cliff, and Jonah couldn't figure out why. He specialized in understanding where the Silicon Valley guys were coming from; he had deliberately aligned his content with their needs. And now Google was killing him.

With Google traffic gone, the editors scrambled to tap fully into social media—then composed of Twitter, a random feed of curiosities called StumbleUpon, Reddit, and most of all Facebook. Many of them had learned, from Jonah, an analytical approach: he taught them to think about why people would share something—not just because they enjoyed it, but because the act of sharing would bring them closer to their friends, or say something about themselves. Nobody understood this better than Jack Shepherd, the community manager, whom Jonah had hired away from the animal rights group PETA. Shepherd specialized in simple, direct images of—for instance—a person rescuing a baby goat from drowning. These were categorized on Reddit, where BuzzFeed editors frequently turned for their memes, as "restoring your faith in humanity." Shepherd liked to brag that for a time, the second-most successful post in the history of BuzzFeed was a simple, inspiring list of images that would, in fact, make you feel better about your fellow human beings. Its success showed the way in which social media brought out people's best impulses, the ones they were proud to share with their friends; it gave hope that BuzzFeed and its ilk would pull the internet out of secrecy of a search bar in which middle-aged men were typing "Rihanna topless," and into the light of Facebook, where you were more likely to share the posts that made you look like a good person, the kind who would rescue a goat yourself. (Of course, that list had been the second-most popular; Jack often glossed over the most popular post, a list of "fails"—people falling off escalators and walking into glass doors.)

The king of traffic in 2011 was Stopera, who didn't share Shepherd and Jonah's analytical approach to social media. He simply got it intuitively, reveled in it. He'd been living deep in pop culture since his teens. When he was sixteen, he made it to the MTV show *Fanography* in 2009 because of his profound love of Britney Spears. Stopera had arrived in the city from an idyllic suburban childhood outside Albany, New York, in which the handsome gay kid who loved Britney could be popular and happy in high school. While his colleagues debated the human psychology that promoted specific behavior on social media, he simply scoured the internet for objects that interested him, as he leaned way back in a big chair, nearly eye level with the desk. Then he offered BuzzFeed headlines in the language of urgency and emotion: "32 Pictures You Need to See before You Die" . . . "40 Things That Will Make You Feel Old." Who was "you"? Well—the traditional reader, of course. But the lists were also a prewritten card to your friends, made for sharing, and a path to getting traffic that didn't rely on Google.

Even as BuzzFeed was deepening its connection to social media, Jonah solved the Google mystery. On August 23, an investor forwarded Jonah's panicked pleas to Matt Cutts, who ran search at Google. Late that night, Cutts took a look under the hood. "Matt Cutts wrote back!!!" Jonah emailed his team excitedly. "It's times like [this] that I wish I wasn't the only one awake at 1am." It turned out that Mark Wilkie, the developer, had created a domain called BuzzFed, with a single *e*, and was using it to host embedded content. The tricky-looking similar domain triggered Google's new screens for malware and knocked the site out of the search engine. Five days later, all the Google traffic came roaring back. September 14 was "the biggest traffic day ever, by all metrics!" one of Jonah's new hires, a data scientist, wrote him triumphantly.

Suddenly the site was setting new records every few weeks. BuzzFeed's best traffic day yet came on December 5, 2011. The post, one of Stopera's, was a simple list titled "The 45 Most Powerful Images of 2011," bringing readers back through a series of emotional public moments: Riots in London. An earthquake in Japan. Barack Obama announcing the death of Osama bin Laden. The post had received more than three million views in three days when Jonah mused to a reporter that "the future is going to be about combining informational content with social and emotional content."

There was other good news. Jon Steinberg's relentlessness had begun to pay off. He sold MTV on a marketing campaign for the relaunch of the nineties show *Beavis and Butt-Head* that involved changing the name of the site to *ButtFeed*. He was talking to Toyota about a campaign that would sell its hybrid car with a post titled "The 20 Coolest Hybrid Animals."

The money was starting to come in. The traffic was back. This, suddenly, was acceleration. BuzzFeed was no longer a skunkworks for *The Huffington Post*; it could be, Kenny and Jonah saw clearly, a competitor. Kenny, used to telling the younger man what to do, told Jonah that they needed to seize the moment and make the site something more than a hobby. "I was looking at the site and decided that *BuzzFeed* needed news to broaden its appeal and not just be a bunch of—I'm being polite here—less important pieces of content," Kenny said.

To Kenny, news was the path to get out of the dreck of the internet, the unrefined-oil views nobody would pay for, and present your traffic to advertisers and investors as something more marketable. The answer, in particular, would be to mimic the success of *The Huffington Post* in 2008 and get in on the 2012 presidential campaign, in which Obama appeared to be fighting for his life against a surprisingly resilient right-wing Tea Party. Kenny thought he knew who should do the job: Peter Kaplan, who had been the editor of the *New York Observer* since 1994, and was a genius at getting the attention of the people he referred to as the "power elite." He and Kenny hailed from the same tribe of New York media types, dating back to Kenny's brief career as a reporter for *New York* magazine, and Kenny had tried getting him to come over to *The Huffington Post* before. But Kaplan had told him he "couldn't get past the fact that the page evaporated every day." Kaplan had quit the *Observer* in 2009 after clashing with the paper's new owner, a rich kid from New Jersey named Jared Kushner, who fancied himself a real business guy and wanted to cut costs. Kaplan was languishing in an obscure corner of Condé Nast, editing a men's fashion title that didn't even have a website. His hire alone would put BuzzFeed on the map. So Kenny called him, thinking he might be reconsidering his print-only obscurity. Instead, he demurred.

However, Kaplan told Kenny he'd once known a kid who had impressed him five years earlier at the *Observer*, where the kid had started the first local New York political blog. That was me, though Kaplan cautioned his friend that I was now working for a Washington outlet called *Politico*, and he wasn't sure if I was still any good. Kenny emailed me on a Thursday in late October under the cryptic subject line "idea for you." When I called him, he told me his friend Jonah, whom I'd barely even heard of, had a "publishing venture" we should talk about. I googled Jonah, thought BuzzFeed was weird, and agreed without much enthusiasm. The next Tuesday at Lure, I sat across the table from Kenny's tall, skinny, wild-haired friend Jonah.

....

News Feeds

People knew who Jonah was by then, even if I didn't. He was the traffic guru, the genius behind the *Huffington Post* exit, though nobody quite understood how. He was seen as part geologist, part dowser, and his record of striking digital oil meant that the moneymen were paying attention. White guys in blazers kept greeting Jonah as we sat at a table toward the back of the wood-lined dining room. I was wearing a blazer and jeans, too, the uniform of the moment, but I was conscious that everyone else's uniform seemed a bit more expensive and better cut.

At that point, I suppose that sitting across from me was a little like sitting across a table from Twitter. I was thirty-four, and I'd been blogging about politics since 2004, when it felt groundbreaking. My brain had been pretty well rewired. I spent my distracted days only half listening to the people I was talking to, or the politicians I was covering. What was happening on Twitter often felt more real than the person in front of me. But in moments of lucidity, between bites, I told Jonah about politics, about the rush I've always gotten from breaking news, and how I'd seen Twitter replace individual blogs like mine as the place people followed the news through the day. I kept interrupting the conversation to check my BlackBerry for tips about Texas governor Rick Perry's surging presidential campaign. As usual, I was slightly more interested in the food than you're supposed to be at a business lunch, and finished my lobster roll as Jonah was just getting started on his fish.

Jonah's pitch included a haze of terms I didn't quite understand— "social web" and "viral lift" and "media company." There was one line, though, that stuck with me: the "bored at work network." *Politico* had been groundbreaking, too, in its time, part of a generation that included the tech site *The Verge* and the commentary site *Vox*, blending the technology of blogging with the professional tools of journalism. But *Politico* was aimed at insiders, and its motto had been "Win the morning," with a 6:00 a.m. blast to set the agenda for influential readers. I was bargaining with my small children for another hour's sleep late into the evenings, and realized there was no way I'd be winning the morning. So I'd focused on winning the midafternoon, when office workers hit refresh on my blog at *Politico*. I'd persuaded a *Politico* techie to embed a bit of tracking software on my site so I wouldn't have to wait for clunky updates from headquarters, and I watched it jealously, pleased when I had forty thousand views a day and thrilled when Drudge put me over one hundred thousand. But since the Obamacare battle of 2010, that traffic had plateaued. And I could see that all my sources, all my readers, even my crazy and abusive commenters, had moved on to Twitter, where I was spending more and more time too.

I tried to explain some of this to Jonah, but I felt we parted in a state of mutual incomprehension. When I got home I emailed him a perfunctory note, saying I was "vicariously excited about where you're headed" but that I liked my job and wasn't interested.

I hadn't really been paying attention, and didn't get how serious Jonah was. To be fair, he didn't entirely know where getting into news and politics was going to take him, either, but he accepted Kenny's view that it was crucial. So he moved on quickly, immediately calling up a former *Huffington Post* editor, Nico Pitney, about the job. That evening, I mentioned to my wife, also in digital media, that I'd had a weird, interesting conversation with this guy Jonah, who seemed smart but, obviously, I'd turned him down. She translated his talk about the social web into a language I could understand—big stories, and scoops, spreading around the internet—and told me I was an idiot. Then I called Peter Kaplan, who told me I'd be crazy not to do it, and who explained something crucial to me: Every presidential campaign cycle is defined by a new media outlet. If I played it right, BuzzFeed could define this one. I panicked, which helpfully generated a rare moment of focus. On Saturday, I sent Ken and Jonah a 1,670 word memo that began with my hope that "I didn't convince Jonah that he and I just don't speak the same language, though I can't blame you if I did."

Then I made the case: "BuzzFeed has the structure and the tone of a website that could be central to people's lives. But it's built on sharing everything BUT the big stuff—each item at its core is a bankshot off the culture, a running joke or a joke on a joke. It feeds off and drives the Internet's undercurrents, but it doesn't ripple on the surface.

"The biggest story of 2012 will be the presidential campaign, and it provides a perfect opportunity to elbow oneself into the main narrative. As Peter understood it, that's what you want to do," I wrote.

I looked at my blog that day, and saw a template for what could go on BuzzFeed. With a fresh eye, I saw clearly that it was a mere repository for things I hoped would go viral on Twitter. The little scoops that insiders would share and the articles with more cultural resonance, all chewed up into Twitter-size, context-free fragments. I'd written one post called "The New CW: Obama's Going to Lose." I also mentioned to Kenny and Jonah that I was good at getting myself into the middle of what I described as a kind of spirited online space. I'd written "a profile of the Washington Post blogger who's trying to kill Rick Perry; that in turn prompted an attack on her from a prominent right-wing blogger; which prompted the Post writer to call him an anti-Semite—all playing out on our site." All fun and games, it seemed to me at the time. I promised Jonah that "I could sell the people who move the information—campaigns, operatives, opposition researchers, media types, random obsessives—on the powerful idea that BuzzFeed is a place that's worth their while."

Jonah read it and talked to Kenny and, he told me years later, cheered up a bit. The cure for his sense of directionlessness, it turned out, was politics. He'd loved the relevance and proximity to power that he'd felt at *The Huffington Post*, and he missed it; this was one of the many things he liked better than money. A few days later we went on a walk around Prospect Park, and he offered me the job. We were negotiating the details when Sam Lessin emailed him with what would turn out to be a tempting alternative to hiring me and starting a news organization. All the email said was that Mark Zuckerberg would be in town.

Lessin had met Zuckerberg at Harvard, then moved to New York after graduating and become part of the Silicon Alley scene. He'd created a file-sharing service called Drop.io, and in the fall of 2010, Zuckerberg paid a premium to buy it and bring his old friend aboard. The next year, Zuckerberg suggested the two friends travel to New York together to meet anyone there Lessin thought he should know—and maybe buy their companies with increasingly valuable, though still not public, Facebook shares. Zuckerberg had already learned that he needed to be looking outward and over his shoulder at all times, that he needed to copy and to buy rivals to maintain Facebook's relentless growth. The two rented a suite at the painfully hip Ace Hotel, whose dim lobby coffee bar was the scene of hushed conversation among tech types, and Sam sent out invites to the founders of a handful of hot New York startups, including BuzzFeed. On November 9, Jonah showed up at the Ace.

Jonah told Zuckerberg that he'd been thinking more and more about what he called "social content"—the media that people share on social networks. He'd been forced to when Google screwed him, but by then Jonah had already looked around the corner and seen the big shift from search to social, and he'd begun to make that story his narrative. It was a story that, not coincidentally, shifted the spotlight from *The Huffington Post* to BuzzFeed. And it was something that Zuckerberg had been thinking about, too, if from the opposite side of the two-way mirror. Jonah had loved Zuckerberg's point, the BuzzFeed founder wrote in a Facebook message a few days later, that "routing content on the FB newsfeed is the inverse problem of distributing content at buzzfeed."

Then Zuckerberg floated another idea: that Facebook buy Jonah's company. Jonah responded in the longest Facebook message he'd ever sent, 1,300 words, with a counterproposal.

"I have been working on understanding why content goes viral, why people share, and how media intersects with social networks for almost 10 years. After we talked last week, I realize you are thinking about exactly the same problem from the platform side," Jonah wrote. He had not met Zuckerberg, he said, with the intention of selling the company— he already had a term sheet for $15 million in new investment. "I also just sold Huffington Post so I don't need money and never cared much about money in the first place," Jonah added.

But, he said, he was tempted by the prospect of playing with Facebook's scale, and wanted to indulge in the "thought experiment."

"My current obsession at BuzzFeed is taking informational content and packaging it with emotion and wit so it spreads on Facebook and other social platforms," Jonah wrote. And, he told Zuckerberg, "you want every publisher to think this way. It is a big shift that would disrupt the publishing business and shift the focus of publishers from Google to Facebook."

So he proposed keeping BuzzFeed intact, as the experimental lab of his dreams. It would "never get absorbed" by the larger company, but would instead pull the publishing industry Facebook's way, and "shift the publisher mindshare from a Google/keyword worldview to a Facebook/social worldview."

Jonah proposed moving to Palo Alto to oversee Facebook's News Feed even as he continued to try his ideas out on BuzzFeed. He'd bring in Duncan Watts, the six degrees of separation expert, as Facebook's "chief sociologist." They'd work together with Jonah's old MIT friend Cameron Marlow, who was already in the process of creating Facebook's data science team, and "take the best from data science and machine learning, sociology and behavioral economics, and build enhanced publisher relationships" to make News Feed—the ever-changing column of content that still rules most people's experience of Facebook—"live up to its name."

Jonah had other ideas too. He thought Facebook could track incoming and outgoing traffic to the rest of the web more deeply. And he wanted to "develop an emotional classification system as a feature for News Feed to replace the verticals and keywords that have historically organized content at newspapers and on Google," something like the "WIN" and "LOL" buttons on the top of BuzzFeed's home page.

"If you think this is interesting enough to go beyond a thought experiment, we should set expectations in advance since I have investors who need at least a decent return," Jonah concluded. But, he suggested, if Mark was interested, he'd put off signing his term sheet.

When Jonah flew to San Francisco a few weeks later, he met Mark in a fishbowl conference room along with Mark's deputy, Chris Cox, and

Facebook's head of corporate development—the deal guy. It became clear that Mark was interested in hiring Jonah—not in funding some wacky lab in New York.

Zuckerberg had heard pitches like this before. "Focus is really important," he told Jonah. Also, he said, it didn't really make any sense for Facebook to own a content company. Still, the conversation got weirder. Zuckerberg countered that he would buy out BuzzFeed's shareholders to the tune of the $12 million they'd invested—but he'd let them keep BuzzFeed if Facebook got Jonah, who could hire a new CEO before he went to Facebook and picked up a pile of pre-IPO stock.

Jonah turned Zuckerberg down genially, ending the negotiation with a joke. He said that he believed that acquiring BuzzFeed would, singlehandedly, make Facebook, then worth $100 billion, 10 percent more valuable. Naturally, Jonah said, BuzzFeed should be valued at $10 billion in a stock swap. But Jonah offered to be generous, and take just half of that sum, adding that once he made the deal and became a Facebook shareholder, he'd want Zuckerberg to guarantee he'd never make a deal like that again.

At that point Zuckerberg got Jonah's nerd humor. Jonah flew back to New York, where BuzzFeed was moving into a bright new office on the eleventh floor of an old printing building on West Twenty-First Street and Sixth Avenue. Previous tenants had to lift the presses out of the window with a crane to make way for the internet company. On December 13, 2011, after Jonah had accepted the new round of investment, he messaged Mark to close the loop.

"BuzzFeed is building the definitive social content site and we look forward to being a great FB partner," he wrote, adding that he'd be happy "to continue to informally contribute ideas to the News Feed effort. I truly believe News Feed could become the best source of engaging content the world has ever seen.

"And let me know next time you are in New York," Jonah concluded. "We can party. And by 'party' I mean drink a beer and talk about ideas."

A few days later I came by BuzzFeed's new office and found Jonah unpacking his boxes in the huge open room. He was quizzically turning over a pair of gifts from Zuckerberg: a water bottle in the distinctive Facebook blue, and a $50 gift certificate to be spent on the charity of his choice.

....

The Scoop

A few weeks after Jonah chose journalistic ambition for BuzzFeed over a lucrative exit with Facebook, I invited him and Chris Johanesen over to my place for New Year's Eve 2012, a big house a bit farther into Brooklyn than you usually go, full of my neighbors.

At midnight, he and Johanesen and I sat together on a big couch, and I hit publish on my first post, titled "Welcome to BuzzFeed Politics," in which I promised "the first true social news organization." I wrote anonymously, however, because my employer, *Politico*, had let me out of my contract on the condition that I not have any bylines on this weird new website. They didn't seem to realize that my Twitter feed was by then far more important to the political class than a byline.

Then I went to check the page: it was nearly illegible, the lines almost on top of each other. BuzzFeed had never before published a full paragraph. While I panicked, Johanesen tweaked the code; by morning, BuzzFeed was safe for words. And while the words my little team and I wrote then were mostly pretty forgettable—how much do you want to hear about the most boring presidential campaign in living memory, starring Mitt Romney?—the wind was at our back.

We set out to be the news organization of record for the new social web. We treated Twitter, not our own website, as our front page. We drove all our energy into breaking stories that would spread on that platform, not worrying about our own home page. As older news organizations wrung their hands about whether they should allow journalists to waste their paid time and energy typing on someone else's platform, we dived into it gleefully. I told my reporters, a group of hungry kids excited at the opportunity to compete with their pompous elders, that I didn't want a story that didn't live on Twitter. One reporter, Zeke Miller, was simply the fastest tweeter on the draw, which was actually enough to get attention back then, copying and pasting a press release headline before anyone else. I'd hired another, Rosie Gray, on the strength of her Occupy Wall Street coverage when she was an intern for *The Village Voice*. Initially she came on to cover Ron Paul's right-wing populism, which seemed vaguely related. When he washed out in Iowa, I called her up and told her that she'd now be covering Rick Santorum.

We had money to spend—a bank account full of newly deposited venture capital—and so Rosie was traveling the country in a way Gawker's writers could rarely afford. She pulled over by the side of a New Hampshire road to look Santorum up on Wikipedia, then hurled herself into his campaign, breaking a series of stories, racking up the retweets. Another young reporter—Zeke was the only one of those three who had finished college—was Andrew Kaczynski, who had a genius for exploiting the time-flattening quality of internet video, and was constantly turning up old clips of Mitt Romney saying exactly the opposite of his current position—catnip, again, for Twitter. My fourth political hire, McKay Coppins, the only Mormon on the campaign trail, was willing to grapple with questions of identity—like Mormon underwear—that made secular journalists nervous. Matt Stopera, the intern turned list-making genius, traveled Iowa taking pictures and making lists of things he observed. The editor of the conservative magazine *National Review* called me to praise our "photo-essays," which made us all laugh. But our vibe had impressed the political elites, who were always attuned to the new ways of communicating that they knew they should pretend to understand. And it attracted a cluster of outsiders, people interested in seeing us succeed at the expense of the stodgy old media institutions. When John McCain was ready to endorse Mitt Romney, a quirky source called me up—a combative misfit who would later wind up in Donald Trump's cabinet—because he wanted BuzzFeed to have the scoop.

Jon Steinberg, now BuzzFeed's president, saw immediate value in the scoop—this was legitimacy, and legitimacy could help translate traffic into money. No more explaining memes to ad buyers for the phone company—even as most of the traffic did, in fact, continue to come from the lists of memes whose reach grew with Facebook's. In 2012, our traffic went from thirty million to eighty million unique views a month. Revenue exploded from $4 million in 2011 to $17 million in 2012. This was the kind of growth that was impressive even in Silicon Valley, and the kind that truly scared a mainstream media—*The New York Times* and *The Washington Post* and CNN—struggling to hold on to customers' attention on a fast-changing internet, and to make any money at all. Other elements of Jonah's vision were beginning to pay off too. His bizarre belief that platforms like YouTube would pay BuzzFeed for content one day seemed to be coming true. Jon was negotiating a $10 million deal with YouTube to finance the creation of BuzzFeed's new video division, headed by Jonah's old friend Ze Frank, who had been one of the creators of video blogging.

Jonah loved the new dynamic, and he loved being back in the mix. Neither he nor I really knew what a publisher was supposed to do, but I had a vague idea that it involved sitting somberly at the head of the table at meetings with politicians. When I invited Maryland governor Martin O'Malley to our bright offices on West Twenty-First Street, Jonah sat silently while reporters peppered O'Malley with questions about his presidential campaign. Finally, there was a gap in the conversation, and Jonah asked, "Do you believe in destiny?" The politician was nonplussed. "I mean, do you think that you're destined to be president?" Jonah was trying to get into his head; the reporters, and O'Malley, thought he was nuts. Jonah realized that he couldn't play the roles of both CEO and prankster at the same time. It had been fun to prank Ashton Kutcher—but it was also a little odd that the thirty-five-year-old chief executive was the one pulling the prank, at the head of the pirate raiding party, as well as the one steering the ship. In fact, BuzzFeed had started to shed vestiges of the old days. Just before my hire was announced, I'd noticed a post composed of ripped-off *Playboy* centerfolds and, in a panic, asked Scott Lamb to delete it. There were other things the team didn't like to talk about, like our early reliance on a pseudonymous blogger who basically stole posts from other websites.

When I looked into Jonah's fishbowl of an office in those days, he was often staring at his computer, dragging images into our colorful content management system himself. He was looking for tricks that could keep BuzzFeed growing, assuming its advertising revenue would track its traffic. He didn't write under his own name often anymore, though. In those early days, BuzzFeed's writers had a handful of pseudonyms, or "switch users," for the different experiments they didn't want to be associated with—Damian Savage and Sigmund Piebald Mastersmash, among others—or for the shameless traffic grabs that went under the username "sextape." Jonah liked to operate another switch user: Lily-Boo. Her avatar itself was the average of a set of American women's faces, hair back in a ponytail, looking blandly at the camera. Her interest was in "things that make you say awwwwwwww." For instance, "32 Pictures That Will Make You Say Awwwwwwww." And "20 Cats That Will Make You Giggle." And "14 Puppies That Could Use a Little Help."

Jonah was mining for traffic, as he had been for a decade. Nobody was better at it, nobody saw more clearly the feedback loop between the signals people sent you on social media and the combination of data and creativity that would allow you to feed their own preferences back to them. But over the four years since Wenda Harris Millard's "pork bellies" speech, publishers' fears had begun to be realized. In 2012, some publishers began noticing that CPMs—long, strangely flat—had begun to decline. One factor was the growing scale that giant tech platforms, in particular, could deliver to advertisers—an increase in supply. The other was the growing sophistication of Google's DoubleClick, Facebook's in-house ad tech, and low-profile companies that delivered advertising that could track individuals around the web. Even as the traffic to BuzzFeed, Gawker Media, and other adept digital publishers grew, their operators began to feel that they were running on an accelerating treadmill, needing ever more traffic to keep the same dollars flowing in.

....

LilyBoo

Nick and Jonah still saw each other around sometimes. At the end of 2011, they'd both attended Duncan Watts's fortieth birthday party. Jonah, always an aspiring stand-up, had attempted an outrageous roast, which included one extended joke suggesting Duncan was a racist and another that he was in the closet. Some of their friends were into it, but others squirmed. Watts's parents, in from Australia, were speechless. The only Black man there was Nick's new boyfriend, an actor named Derrence Washington whom he'd met after spending a weekend with mutual friends in Hudson, New York. Nick was particularly appalled by Jonah's attempt at humor.

By the fall of 2012, BuzzFeed had become a serious problem for Gawker, stealing attention, writers, and readers. Jonah was no longer one of those interesting weirdos Nick liked to collect; he was a rival. And Nick's weapon of choice against any rival was exposure. On October 3, in a tweet that made his distaste for Jonah and BuzzFeed clear, Nick wrote that his own opinions "may have been colored by @peretti's 'best man' speech at Duncan Watts' 40th birthday. Excruciating."

"You are right about that speech! Dark humor gone terribly wrong!!" Jonah replied. Nick's tweet, what it contained and what it left out, felt like the classic Gawker threat—of notoriety. A Gawker reporter, J. K. Trotter, followed up months later to say he would be writing about a garbled and racist-sounding version of the speech, and Jonah replied with an extended apology for joining the "very sad tradition of roasting a heterosexual guy with a gay joke," but asking why Nick had "added a racial element."

"If I don't respond to Gawker, you will just publish lies and mischaracterizations that some people will believe. If I do respond, I am sharing more details of a private event from my friend's birthday party," Jonah wrote plaintively, cc'ing Nick and Duncan Watts.

Nick replied with arch amusement. "Oh dear, you took JK's bait. I'm surprised. Without a response from you, there would have been no story.

"I never felt your speech was homophobic or racist; just incredibly awkward," Nick added. "And it's only useful to trot out when you're being a dick on Twitter."

The story was never published. But after that, Jonah always seemed to be looking over his shoulder a little for Nick.

But Nick's real objection to Jonah wasn't his stand-up routine. It was that Jonah's omnivorous appetite for traffic, and his ability to both mine Facebook for views and earn elite praise for news, threatened to overtake Gawker's position at the forefront of new media. And Nick couldn't afford to compete. He'd maintained his distaste for venture capital during this new media boom, whereas Jonah suddenly had a giant war chest and was using it to hire away current and former Gawker stars like Doree Shafrir, Matt Buchanan, Whitney Jefferson, and John Herrman. Just before he'd hired me, Jonah had simply read Gawker's public traffic leaderboards and acted accordingly; he'd hired two writers at the top of them.

Nick, a purist at heart about the connection between searing exposés and traffic, also hated the mechanical way Jonah thought about the substance. Nick thought traffic was a sign of quality; Jonah simply thought it was a resource to be exploited, by whatever tactics—serious or silly, strange or brilliant, cheap or expensive—that came to hand. Where Nick had wanted AJ Daulerio's brutal revelations, Jonah wanted journalism, sure. But he also wanted LilyBoo.

To Jonah, and to financiers fixated on the idea of a new science of content, LilyBoo was the dream: machines, with a little human help, feeding culture back to itself, scaling to infinity. To Nick, this was pretty much the worst nightmare, an automated feed of algorithmic cuteness, harvesting traffic indiscriminately, anonymously shaped by the CEO himself. If you looked closely, sometimes the voice was a little robotic. "Just trying to think of ways to multiply cuteness," read the caption to a list of "50 Toddlers Who Are Best Friends with Their Dogs." As Lily-Boo's bio read, she was "obsessed with the maximally cute." Jonah thought he might have in fact figured out how to maximize cuteness. He had begun spending time on a new social media platform, Pinterest, where people posted and "pinned" images. Jonah had Wilkie write a simple script that took any tag page on the site—dogs, say—and reorganized it by the number of pins. This would, in theory, generate a pure list of pictures sure to make you say awwwww.

So there I was, out in the open office a few yards away, screaming at sources on my cell phone, while my boss sat quietly in the light of his giant screen, rearranging lists of puppies. And the photo lists invariably got traffic. "The True Meaning of Friendship" even broke 250,000 views and won LilyBoo a "viral" badge, which was the way BuzzFeed rewarded community contributors. In this process one could identify the purest vision of the future that BuzzFeed was selling investors and advertisers: that we could take algorithmic measure of social media, skim off the best of it, and feed it back to itself in an endless loop. A lot of technology, a bit of human intervention—in this case, the CEO's own fingerprints— and you had a kind of digital perpetual motion. Accompanying journalism, amped and torqued for the social web, could help convince advertisers this was a serious alternative to the media as they knew it.

And yet LilyBoo never quite cut through. There was something sterile about simply, clinically, feeding people's own social media posts back to them. Matt Stopera's raw, intuitive emotions were the ones that really powered the site's traffic to new heights each month. They were all heart— often a kind of nascent millennial nostalgia. "This is what Ferguson from 'Clarissa Explains It All' looks like today," Matt wrote under the headline "48 Things That Will Make You Feel Old." "She's 30. And married." That one was shared 72,000 times on Facebook. His "13 Simple Steps to Get You through a Rough Day" was a list of funny pictures and silly activities whose central attraction was that you'd want to share it with a friend, and 209,000 people did. Occasionally, Stopera would even get a political hit— if it evoked enough feeling. There was, for instance, the day a blogger spotted an exhausted, bloated Rick Santorum reclining poolside in Puerto Rico. Stopera uploaded the photo to BuzzFeed with a short caption, and Wilkie struggled to keep our site online as liberals on Facebook feasted on the image. LilyBoo never scaled those heights, and we quietly retired the anonymous "switch accounts." But we'd learned powerful lessons from those early, unconstrained experiments about what exactly people would share on social media. And as the platform grew faster than its rivals and we grew with it, BuzzFeed was soon almost entirely powered by the widening river of traffic that was Facebook. And people on Facebook didn't want the truth: they wanted to be entertained. What could be less threatening, back then, than Facebook, where all anyone wanted to share was a few simple steps to get you through a rough day?

. . .

When BuzzFeed's traffic matched his own in 2012, Nick put on a brave face, predicting that BuzzFeed's move to hire journalists would backfire. "Peretti's craving for the quick viral fix will not be satisfied by the nourishing fare," he wrote in a comment on Gawker, predicting that BuzzFeed would "collapse under the weight of its contradictions." But in fact, for Nick, this new challenge came at a bad time. Just as the internet changed around Gawker, Nick's life was changing in a way even his friends hadn't really imagined was possible. He was in love with Derrence, in a steady, distracting relationship that seemed to soften him even toward the people to whom he'd been a remote, terrifying figure. In 2012, Nick and Derrence moved in together. His staff detected the change. The withholding leader seemed, at some points, to actually like them. He invited Coen to the loft to ask her advice about planning a wedding. He began going to therapy. He started harboring doubts about the ruthlessness of his publications.

Nick kept those doubts about Gawker's mission private. But he also seemed to avert his eyes, or at least to take them off the ball. Meanwhile, AJ Daulerio thought he was doing what Nick wanted. He was getting traffic, he was getting attention. Indeed, even as Nick diverged from the harsh old image many of his early bloggers kept in their minds, some of his employees saw AJ as a kind of favorite son to Nick. The Deadspin dick king was hooked, deeply, on the internet and on what he saw as Nick's vision of it. "He needs the next story like an addict needs their next fix," Nick once said. AJ had described himself and the other editors as "puppies that have been trained to bite—even people who came into the house." When AJ got another job offer in 2012, Nick countered with the ultimate prize: running Gawker itself. AJ embodied the ruthless thirst for exposure that Nick saw as the core of Gawker, and of the internet. And while many of the younger writers saw Nick as a kind of dark, unpredictable father figure, AJ's tough talk was combined with something that seemed particularly vulnerable. His memo to Nick on his plans for Gawker began with the promise that "I will not let this job drive me to more substance abuse and depression. I will not let this job make me see this company as an evil place. I will not let this job drive me to write a 10,000-word essay in the Times Magazine about how awful it was." He also resolved to Nick that "I will not let this job make me hate you."

AJ brought to Gawker his trademark style, which ranged from literary flourishes to sex tapes. He combined the two perfectly on October 4, 2012, after getting his hands on a video featuring the over-the-hill professional wrestling icon Terry Bollea, known universally as Hulk Hogan, having sex with his best friend's wife. AJ's article was a bravura piece of writing, one of the best Gawker ever published. It didn't try to justify the sex tape with some larger moral, as AJ had with Favre. Instead, it merely explained what was going on, first in a big-picture way, and then in detail.

"Because the internet has made it easier for all of us to be shameless voyeurs and deviants, we love to watch famous people have sex," he began, contemplating the possible reasons why. People watch, he explained, simply "because it's something we're not supposed to see," but they "come away satisfied that when famous people have sex, it's closer to the sex we as civilians have from time to time."

In writing the hell out of the Hogan tape story, Daulerio was trying, a friend said, to impress his girlfriend of the time, Cat Marnell, another gifted writer who was self-destructing in public. The title of her memoir would be *How to Murder Your Life*. His thousand-word Hogan narrative has a little Hemingway to it. Hogan "has to go, he leans over and kisses the woman. They joke about him loving and leaving but it's okay. 'Be cool,' he says to the woman on his way out the door. They thank each other for the sex. 'You're awesome,' Hulk says on his way out the door. 'So are you,' she says back in a very sincere way." Cue 5.1 million views.

Still, the Hogan video wasn't particularly memorable. Nobody at Gawker made much of it. Nick couldn't even bring himself to watch. It was "another classic AJ-style post from AJ" another writer, Hamilton Nolan, told the author Brian Abrams a couple years later for an oral history of Gawker. Hogan filed suit a few months after AJ's post, and the suit was making its way through the courts. "If it does bring down our company, it would be a funny way to go out," Nolan mused.

Upworthy

As Nick and Jonah's competition intensified in the beginning of 2012, Andrew Breitbart felt he'd finally found his footing. Anthony Weiner's dick, his downfall, and the election of a Republican to replace him had combined for Andrew to wash away the stain left by the Shirley Sherrod incident. Breitbart had brought a new wave of money into the company too: A low-profile hedge fund billionaire, Robert Mercer, had been taken with this new source of power, and invested $10 million. They'd put some of the cash into a splashy redesign, just like the one Nick Denton had done a year earlier to make the Gawker Media brands look bolder and less bloggy. (This stylish redesign had cost the site valuable page views. Chris Batty, the longtime ad salesman, departed over it.) Just as Nick had done, Andrew would make his blogs—initially just lists of stories, the latest first—into something glossier and more professional, with the biggest story of the day pinned to the top left corner.

Breitbart.com's traffic, which plummeted after Drudge dropped Andrew, was coming back, starting to trickle in from Facebook. Somehow, even while Facebook trumpeted its role in the Obama campaign and its executives considered future careers in Democratic politics, Breitbart's sort of people were on there too. Anger at the media and the Clintons, coverage of Black people committing crimes—for Andrew, it was all very promising.

But Andrew hadn't gotten much healthier since he'd landed in the hospital during the Sherrod crisis. He was just forty-three, but he was fat and stressed, and his life was a mess. He was still riding his Vespa from Brentwood to an office in a dingy warehouse near Santa Monica. Andrew confessed to a friend that while he'd become a conservative rock star—"I could get laid in a geriatric center in flyover country"—he owed $133,000 to the Internal Revenue Service; he was still struggling to navigate the internal politics and secret flows of dark money that powered the right-wing media, including many far smaller and less successful sites.

Andrew would sometimes have a drink by himself to unwind, so there was nothing unusual about his stop on February 29, 2012, at the Brentwood, a restaurant and bar near his house. He arrived a little after 10:00 p.m., alone, for a drink. Another man at the bar, a marketing executive, recognized him and started talking politics, trying to get under Andrew's skin by discussing recent stumbles of Republican Senate candidates. Andrew, toggling between his BlackBerry, his drink, and his new companion, engaged cheerfully, and argued that the liberal media, not the Republicans, was at fault. They parted in good spirits, agreeing to disagree.

Andrew Breitbart collapsed on the sidewalk soon afterward. He was rushed to the hospital and pronounced dead at 12:19 a.m. on Thursday, March 1, 2012. Friends at the funeral couldn't help noticing that Matt Drudge, wearing sunglasses throughout the ceremony, looked rested and almost absurdly fit, his biceps bulging out from beneath the sleeves of a black T-shirt.

Jonah had always liked telling stories about Andrew, whom he'd seen as a colorful sideshow whose attempts to take credit for *The Huffington Post* were endearingly goofy, and he wanted BuzzFeed to cover his passing. But Jonah was a slow writer, so he waved me into his office to help, and we sat in white padded chairs while he told me what he remembered. We decided to keep it positive, given the timing, and focused the headline on Andrew's role in starting *The Huffington Post*. Andrew had proposed "a phone number where celebrities could call in and leave voice blogs that would automatically appear on the site," Jonah reminisced. "He wanted that built before launch, and launch was four days away." Jonah told me other details, about Andrew's obsession with Drudge, and his complaints that he'd have to work overtime when Drudge took a week or two off to party at gay nightclubs in Europe. But we left those out. The guy had just died. We published the interview within the hour, and sure enough, Drudge linked it and the traffic rolled in.

In our view Andrew had been a footnote. His site wasn't getting enough traffic to matter—a bit more than a million views a month according to Comscore, which advertisers relied on as a trusted scoreboard of traffic on the web. He'd promised Breitbart would be the *Huffington Post* of the right, but it was getting less than one twentieth of the traffic, stuck way down on the rankings with every other right-wing site on the internet. This was one more sign that the new internet media belonged to progressives. At BuzzFeed, we were looking over our shoulders at a different kind of competitor, one that promised to more closely meld the two great and growing powers of Facebook: its reach, and its progressive political bent. The company was called Upworthy, and its co-founder Eli Pariser was, in a way, to the United States what the young engineer Oscar Morales had been to Colombia. Upworthy launched, by coincidence, the day Andrew Breitbart died.

Eli had started far earlier. On September 11, 2001, he was a shy, left-wing twenty-year-old from Maine who had just graduated from Bard

College at Simon's Rock, an institution made for weird and precocious kids like him. He started a petition to press for a thoughtful, multilateral response to the attacks; it got half a million signatures, and, at twenty-three, he wound up with a job running MoveOn.org, the leading US online political organization. He led its controversial protests against the Iraq War—including an advertisement saying a popular general, David Petraeus, had "betrayed" the United States. In 2008, he used MoveOn's massive email list largely in service of electing Barack Obama.

Eli was among the first to see what was changing. While I watched Twitter suck the energy and audience out of my blog at *Politico*, Eli was looking at Facebook, which was on a trajectory, even by 2011, to dwarf the rest of the internet. To Eli, that meant that the people who used to forward your petition via email now posted links and videos and funneled their outrage into comments. After the 2008 election, he had stopped running MoveOn to write a book, *The Filter Bubble*, where he warned presciently that the subtle personalization pioneered by Facebook and other platforms would "serve up a kind of invisible autopropaganda, indoctrinating us with our own ideas, amplifying our desire for things that are familiar and leaving us oblivious to the dangers lurking in the dark territory of the unknown."

But Eli wasn't interested in being just a pundit. He wanted to get back into the work of politics. In November of 2011, he saw an opportunity to test out how MoveOn could turn filter bubbles into a source of progressive power. As Iowa debated same-sex marriage, a teenager named Zach Wahls gave a powerful speech about growing up with two moms. At Eli's direction, MoveOn packaged the video with a headline made for Facebook: "Two Lesbians Raised a Baby and This Is What They Got." The video got twenty million views. And Eli and Peter Koechley, a former managing editor of *The Onion* who had joined MoveOn, decided to start a business.

Eli met Jonah and BuzzFeed's managing editor, Scott Lamb, in a teahouse in Chinatown the BuzzFeed crew used for confidential meetings, because as far as they could tell nobody there spoke English. Eli asked them how they thought about going viral. Though he was asking for advice, Eli already had a track record and a reputation that put Upworthy on the map. In 2012, he raised $4 million from a group that included Chris Hughes, the Facebook co-founder who'd worked for Obama, and Jonah's original investor in BuzzFeed, John Johnson. The site seemed to justify that investment immediately, receiving nine million views by the middle of 2012—an astonishing start, the sort of traffic numbers people worked years for. The formula was simple: a YouTube video embedded on a page, and a headline to make you click: "Bully Calls News Anchor Fat, News Anchor Destroys Him on Live TV" drew more than four million views. "Mitt Romney Accidentally Confronts a Gay Veteran; Awesomeness Ensues" got nearly three million.

Fast Company called Upworthy "a soulful Buzzfeed," and it was true that there was something about its purity that made us nervous. While we had been trying to deliver straight news and politics in a mix with the silliest and strangest parts of internet culture, Eli was unabashedly using LilyBoo's tactics to package political content. It seemed to be the merger of information and emotion that Jonah had been searching for. I wondered if he regretted hiring me to produce harder news.

Upworthy was almost too good at working Facebook. Like BuzzFeed, it had technical tools that could compare a number of different headlines and tell editors almost instantly which worked best. The ones the site became famous for were often of a style known as the "curiosity gap." For instance: "She Has a Horrifying Story to Tell. Except It Isn't Actually True. Except It Actually Is True." Click! Here is an intriguing tidbit, the headline sometimes said, and you won't believe what happened next! By 2014, *New York* magazine was calling Upworthy "one of the fastest-growing media sites in internet history."

But Upworthy's technical proficiency at maximizing traffic returns was also a vulnerability, and it left Upworthy open to attack from inside Facebook. Jonah had begun to make a habit of cultivating the mid-senior-level Facebook employees who ran its key product, News Feed. He invited them by BuzzFeed's familiar-feeling offices when they were in New York, and stopped by to say hi when he was in the Bay Area. Over coffee in San Francisco, and in spontaneous direct messages on Twitter, Jonah could offer them the one thing Facebook didn't have: insight into how traffic was moving around its rival networks, Twitter and Pinterest. What's more, unlike most in media, he seemed to speak their language, without clumsy simplification from the pompous jargon of journalism. "It was easier to talk to him without having to translate than it was to talk to most media executives," according to a top Facebook executive. They knew Jonah was pushing them, trying to persuade them to shape their service in a way that would help BuzzFeed—but it was nice to talk to someone who thought this new medium could make the world better, who saw you as an ally, not an alien.

Jonah had invested in his relationships with Facebook, and they were paying off, because Facebook was now unquestionably the world's most important source of traffic. Websites across the industry showed a massive spike beginning in August of 2013, as Facebook referrals spiked 69 percent by October. "Can Mark Zuckerberg save the publishing industry?" BuzzFeed's Charlie Warzel wondered. Upworthy seemed unstoppable, rising to a peak of eighty-seven million monthly views in November of 2013.

That month a top News Feed engineer stopped by BuzzFeed, and after he left, Jonah wrote to him about what he saw as a persistent problem in Facebook's feed, the one Upworthy was particularly famous for exploiting. "Right now there is an incentive for publishers to write incomplete headlines to get people to click, aka 'click bait' aka 'the curiosity gap,'" Jonah wrote. "But those headlines fill News Feed with text devoid of information, unlike descriptive headlines that provide value even to users who don't click them. Although this gets more people to the story and many of those people might share the story, the 90%+ who never click the story get no value at all."

Jonah's belief that these headlines were essentially spam led him to instruct me—to the disappointment of some of my traffic-hungry writers—to ban them from BuzzFeed. As he wrote in the email, while other sites might write a headline like "You Won't Believe What Disneyland Forced All Employees to Do in 1965," BuzzFeed's headline was "Disneyland's 1965 Employee Handbook Was Just as Strict as You'd Imagine."

"If you don't click the story you still get the basic point that Disney was strict and conservative in the 60s," Jonah pointed out. "Is there a good way to measure this discrepancy in value? It is something a human editor can do easily, especially one focused on building long term trust with a reader, but feels trickier to automate."

Jonah forwarded me the exchange, adding, "It is really fun collaborating with Facebook's team on how News Feed should work." When Facebook figured out how to purge clickbait headlines, Upworthy's traffic took the hit.

Eli occupied a strange position. He had built his company on top of Facebook's algorithms, but he was also a Facebook critic. His own startup had proved out his dark theory about the filter bubble. Facebook kept trying to refute his argument: their own research, they said, showed that the information you saw on the site was dictated by whom you chose to be friends with—not by Facebook's algorithms.

But Facebook's research contained a curious detail, one of the company's own analysts confided in Eli: relatively small right-wing websites seemed to be getting far more "engagement" by Facebook's metrics than huge liberal ones, like Upworthy, or *The Huffington Post*, or BuzzFeed.

If the progressives were getting all the traffic, Eli asked, what did this "engagement" figure mean? The researcher confessed to him that the company was puzzled by it, too, by the people sharing and resharing posts from clunky old conspiracy websites like *WorldNetDaily* and obscure lists of links at breitbart.com. "There's this pretty much epistemically closed group of people who are super-sharers," he was told. "It's this alternate universe on Facebook that's behaving differently than anyone else."

It wasn't the only sign of a cultural turn. On discussion boards devoted to video games, a newly overt anti-feminist sentiment was brewing. Some of the figures of the early internet were being drawn into that circle. Tracie Egan first took her old friend Gavin McInnes's use of the N-word as ironic rather than racist, but she fell out with him when he began using the word full-throatedly in 2012, she later recalled. And the new clusters of sharing that the researcher had described to Eli were among the first signals that Facebook wasn't quite what the liberal utopians of Silicon Valley and SoHo thought it was, and that a different kind of politics could displace the optimism of Morales and Obama. Facebook's audience had become older, now reaching far beyond the young college-educated elites. And Facebook, it turned out, didn't much like Upworthy, with its irresistible headlines and compelling videos whose function was, mostly, to trick you into leaving Facebook. Upworthy depended on Facebook, but to the platform, it was little more than a bug. A series of decisions—killing those headlines, and encouraging users to watch videos directly inside Facebook instead—would begin to choke off traffic to Eli's project. Those curious clusters of intense engagement, of older, whiter, more right-wing Americans spending more and more time liking and sharing the same articles, and clicking on advertisements as they spent hours on the site—that was what Facebook was going for, that was the future Mark Zuckerberg chose. Andrew Breitbart was dead. But the future he'd imagined was only starting to come to life.

....

Benny

At BuzzFeed, we didn't realize how deeply the rivers of traffic were dividing yet. We thought we could have them all—right and left, silly and serious. So when Benny Johnson first got in touch, I liked the idea.

"Just wanted to introduce myself," read the message that came in over Gchat on the morning of Friday, April 20, 2012. "I'm Benny at the Blaze. Big fan." Then he sent over his most recent traffic hit: "What Did The Blaze Find at the NRA Convention? A Bra Holster, a .22 Belt-Buckle, and a Lady Zombie."

"That's a total BuzzFeed post!" I replied.

I was sitting in my sunny new newsroom that morning, at a long white table just outside Jonah's glassed-in office. This new chat intrigued me. The people building the new media—from Jonah to Arianna, to the Gawker crew, to bloggers like Ezra Klein and me—had always viewed right-wing efforts at online media with a mix of curiosity and pity, seeing *The Drudge Report* as the quirky exception that proved the rule and stifled competitors. Breitbart.com, in particular, had seemed, back in the early 2010s, to represent a strange attempt to force the past—racism, nostalgia, backlash—into the vessel of the future, the internet. But the Blaze, a right-wing website whose proprietor, Scott Baker, had broken off from Breitbart's nascent video operation, looked familiar, and promising in its mix of news and memes: a bit like a right-wing BuzzFeed. So I arranged with Benny Johnson to meet on the floor of the sprawling media center of the Republican National Convention in Tampa, Florida, in 2012. BuzzFeed was the hot young thing of that year's political season, and we attracted *New York Times* luminaries, including its executive editor, Jill Abramson, and signature columnist, Maureen Dowd, to a party at the aquarium, where women dressed as mermaids swam with the fish. Benny was handsome, clean-shaven, and earnest, and he felt like something new, a conservative writer who spoke the language of memes that young people used to communicate on social media. I couldn't help but find it flattering when he told me he'd been religiously copying our work for their site.

The Blaze's figurehead was Glenn Beck, a Fox News host who had won massive ratings for his blackboard of deranged conspiracies about Barack Obama before the network pushed him out in 2011. Now Beck was trying to go direct to his consumers, and the Blaze would be one of his outlets. Its vibe was midwestern. Its tone was less angry, more superficially wholesome than Breitbart's. And Benny was driving a lot of its traffic.

BuzzFeed's editors had learned through trial and error that social media was organized in large part around identities. Write compellingly about what it was like to be born in the 1990s, or to be an Iranian from New Jersey, or a Catholic girl, or to grow up with East Asian parents, and thousands of people would share the post with the magic words "this is me." Their friends would click for a glimpse of insight. The traffic was guaranteed, and the posts extended BuzzFeed's tendrils into new territories.

To reach a broader audience, we needed people who could write about varied identities. That pushed BuzzFeed, whose small staff was nearly all white in its early days, to become among the most ethnically diverse of the new media companies. But we were still missing a big piece of American identity. We didn't have any proud young conservatives, people who could write about what it was like to grow up with guns, say, or to appreciate how the Bush family respected veterans. Benny represented, to me, an untapped new well of traffic, a new identity to plumb. And so I didn't look much beyond that NRA post, which took the BuzzFeed formula—a list of fun, emotionally resonant images—to gun culture. There was no reason that Tea Partiers couldn't see themselves in BuzzFeed, I reasoned, and share elements of their culture—guns, cars, Bibles—just as our progressive audience was doing. I realize now that I allowed my eyes to skate over some of Benny's other hits: for instance, his recurring focus on the obscure New Black Panther Party, and race-baiting headlines like "Don't Miss the Connection: Obama 'Delivered' to Office by Black Panthers, Holder 'Owes Them Some Favors.'" And I certainly didn't run his work through the plagiarism-detection software that had yet to become popular.

I wasn't really worried about whether Benny would fit in. I should have been. It's one thing to expect professional journalists of different backgrounds to come together around the hunt for truth, and to, ideally, bring their different backgrounds into play to do it better. But what if you hire people explicitly in order to project and explain their identities? And what happens if selective information, selective truths, become central to a political identity? I hadn't thought it through. I mistook Benny, instead, for a new instance of an old tradition, conservative journalists who joined mainstream organizations. They could bring with them a new perspective, along with a connection to an audience and to sources that the coastally educated journalists in those newsrooms lacked. In return, they got inside access to the big media organizations the right has always demonized, and which—while often smugly liberal—rarely resembled the left-wing conspiracies they imagined. There was nothing about the new style of social media journalism that suggested it would make it harder than before for conservatives and liberal journalists to discipline themselves to focus on a core of shared facts. I thought perhaps Benny could be the David Brooks or George Will of the meme generation, a bridge between BuzzFeed's reflexive progressivism and the other half of the country, and a check on our own biases. I sent our Washington bureau chief, a towering, tattooed ex-bouncer and veteran Capitol Hill reporter named John Stanton, to meet him. They sat for two and a half hours of what Benny enthusiastically told me was "the best interview of [his] short life," while Stanton told Benny how much fun it was to work for BuzzFeed, and Benny counted how many skulls his prospective boss was wearing (two rings, three on his belt buckle, one tattoo, and one on a necklace).

After it all blew up, though, I'd realize that I had the whole idea backward. Benny didn't represent that old tradition; he would gravitate instead toward something new, a conservative movement more concerned about aesthetics than policy, motivated by nostalgia and culture more than by the overt subject matter of politics. When I really started trying to figure out how I'd misunderstood the situation, I began in Iowa City.

Benjamin Arthur Johnson had arrived at the campus of the University of Iowa in the fall of 2005 fully formed. He wore a blue blazer, khaki pants, and deck shoes, and he smoked a corncob pipe—a kind of "meme of a Republican," said another student active in campus politics, Michael Charles, who thought when he first encountered Benny that he was the "douchiest douchebag I had met in my whole life." Benny's brother,

Zach, had run for student body vice president his freshman year. Zach's ticket was defeated after the student newspaper discovered he'd been soliciting contributions over the permitted amount from outside right-wing donors, with a promise to "embolden conservatives" on campus.

Iowa is the first stop in American presidential campaigns and a proving ground for national politics, and to be on the sprawling university campus in 2007 was to see democracy up close. There was Senator Chris Dodd having lunch with a student leader in the cafeteria; there was Joe Biden, standing alone in the Memorial Union. Mitt Romney would take you to lunch at the campus Subway. After Johnson's brother tried and failed to turn campus politics into something more national, more ideological, though, it settled back into a more parochial set of concerns. After Zach Johnson graduated, Benny Johnson's friends ran, too, losing the presidential race but winning control of the student senate, and they appointed Benny to run the senate communications. At first, the president of the student government, Barrett Anderson, found him outgoing if a bit over-the-top; then Benny simply stopped showing up to meetings.

"He literally never came to work ever," recalled Charles, who was the student organization liaison. "His job was to get comms out about what the student government was doing, and he just didn't do that ever." At the end of the summer, Anderson was so frustrated that he signed off on paperwork stripping Johnson of the role.

The half dozen former students I spoke to, to a one, said they'd been following Johnson's subsequent public career with disgust. After Johnson washed out of student government, he turned his charm on campus Republicans. Before he graduated, Benny was elected chairman of the Iowa Federation of College Republicans, and he appointed a friend and classmate as his executive director.

Johnson says he moved to Germany after college. He later liked to say that he'd worked for the gun company Sig Sauer, though I couldn't find any record of that, and his spokesman later said the company was Wagner GMBH, which specializes in spray guns for painting surfaces. He once described a competition in which chemists tried to make a distillation representing the colors of their countries' flags.

"The Germans could make them really easily," he reminisced when he came back to Iowa as a BuzzFeed star to give a talk in 2013. "I ended up making an American flag one just by coloring it in with marker."

Benny liked to say then that he was a scientist, and that his approach to media represented a kind of analytical mad science. His degree, he said in that 2013 talk, was in organic chemistry. But according to his university, he actually had majored in psychology. And his old friends saw something else: a flimflam salesman with a short attention span and a love of shortcuts, someone who loved the theater of politics and couldn't be bothered to do the work.

"Ben is one of the most ambitious people I've ever met. He's also smart, charming, and handsome," his friend Matthew Bechstein, who was active in gay Republican politics after college, told me. "I don't believe the question is how Ben found his way into politics. When you have all the qualities of a bullshit salesman—politics finds you."

Bechstein had a point. Politics has always been in large part bullshit, salesmanship, flimflam, aesthetics. What's more, Johnson had arrived at just the right time, as a new generation of politicians began to realize the power of the new media and new platforms. While Andrew Breitbart raged against Hollywood and the mainstream media, Benny focused on mastering Facebook, first at the Blaze and then working for me at BuzzFeed.

In those early days at BuzzFeed, we didn't pay much attention to job titles (or pay scales, or much in the way of organizational structure), and most writers and reporters didn't care what they were called. Benny, though, chose a very specific title for himself: "viral politics editor." He positioned himself at the intersection of the kind of analytical approach to content that Jonah had pioneered with experiments like LilyBoo, and my own fixation with political journalism. And while Benny's roots were on the right, his core obsession wasn't that different from anyone else's at BuzzFeed: he wanted traffic. His new colleagues were skeptical of him—Media Matters had released a dossier on Benny's various right-wing views when I hired him—and when he came to New York from his Washington home, Benny was often the only one besides me wearing a blazer. But he had a gift for traffic, and at first he seemed drawn mostly to the pageantry of power: he delighted the internet with visual accounts of interns sprinting to deliver Supreme Court verdicts, or of the Dunkin' Donuts in the grim Capitol basement. He won his colleagues over quickly enough, when they went out after work to a gay bar on West Twenty-Fourth Street, XES Lounge, that had the cheapest drinks in the neighborhood, and he bought a couple of rounds of shots. He'd done his homework, too, and praised the work of each new person he met.

There was, at BuzzFeed, no shame in copying other people's work. The spirit was experimental. One writer would see some new way to present images—"restore your faith in humanity," say—become popular on Reddit, and make a post on BuzzFeed of images that could do that. If it worked, their colleagues would copy it. Benny's work often involved imposing BuzzFeed's framing on American politics—once using the movie *Jurassic Park* to explain the conflict in Syria. In a tense internal meeting, his colleagues complained that it called their attempts at serious journalism into question. I defended it as a valuable experiment while Benny sat quietly, smirking a little.

I sometimes wonder now if Benny was headed inevitably toward the kind of right-wing populism that Donald Trump came to embody. Looking back at his work, I can see him probing for an audience. There were people who hated Obama. There were people who loved guns. There were people who revered American institutions like the Supreme Court, as well as the old Waspy charm of George H. W. Bush's eccentric choices in socks. Benny was following the traffic where it led him, optimizing himself.

In February of 2013, he hit a rich vein that drew a particular rise out of conservatives: The hypocrisy of Democrats and the liberal media. In a post called "7 Things Democrats Would Have Freaked Out about If Bush Had Done Them," he mocked Democrats' silence on things like drone strikes in Afghanistan. And because BuzzFeed's culture encouraged riffing, experimentation, and improvement, it was no surprise to see Matt Stopera's little brother, Dave, do a different riff on the theme with a colleague Tanner Greenring. But Dave's did something new: it broke Facebook. The post was titled "26 Ways President Obama Has Completely Ruined the Country," and it was a joke, drawing on a meme of the moment in which the president was to blame for everything, from grills that were too slippery for the burgers to stay on to cookies too large to be dipped in milk. Readers on Facebook hated it. Conservatives clicked the link expecting a satisfying hate read and felt tricked. Liberals saw the headline and loathed it automatically. Members of both groups reported the piece as spam, tripping Facebook's spam alert system and disabling the post from appearing on its site. The reports against BuzzFeed went from fewer than 100 a day to 1,839 one day that week. Facebook threatened to "disable publishing" BuzzFeed links, and publisher Dao Nguyen's team scrambled to find an explanation, checking hacker boards to see if someone else was using our Facebook identity to cause trouble.

One of the theories was that people were just marking a normal post as spam because they didn't agree with it, but that seemed exceedingly unlikely to Nguyen.

But that was, it turned out, what had happened, though the anger and confusion on Facebook seemed like a minor tear in the matrix, easily mended. By that Christmas, Benny was back in New York for our lavish Christmas party at Webster Hall, where we'd hired Matt Stopera's favorite indie pop star, Betty Who, to perform. Televisions hanging over one of the venue's many bars broadcast a loop of Beyoncé serving a pizza, and we had a booth where employees could make GIFs of themselves. Two writers for Gawker slipped in, tried to make conversation, and found that the public feud between their founders and their brands—snark versus smarm, as Gawker would later put it—made the Gawker writers as unwelcome at the BuzzFeed party as "a suspected pedophile . . . at Christmas brunch," as they later wrote, adding, "Those who knew the identities of the writers visibly stiffened in their presence; one slowly backed away into a crowd while talking, as if attempting to escape from a lunatic."

Finally, our unflappable PR person, Ashley McCollum, confronted them, and did her best to project an optimistic, confident vibe.

"I'm impressed you got in. You should stay!" That did it. They left. The writers missed the scenes BuzzFeed's staff would be talking about the next day, Benny dancing on a floor slick with beer with the mostly liberal young men and women he worked with.

Benny was always the target of progressives on Twitter who saw him as a dangerous protofascist. When a couple of anonymous Twitter accounts began pointing out that some of his posts had language borrowed from Wikipedia, I first defended him. I saw it as part of my job as editor; I also thought that Benny's critics were picking up on minor errors because they didn't like his politics. And BuzzFeed's spirit had always involved remixing the best of the internet, sometimes in those early days by ripping it directly off Reddit. Benny, I declared, was "one of the web's deeply original writers, as is clear from his body of work."

As Twitter critics turned up more issues with Benny's posts, two of our top editors, Katherine Miller and Shani Hilton, and I spent a long night at the office going through his work. What we found wasn't so much malicious as lazy, a matter of copying and pasting from Wikipedia merely to save time in producing content that, unlike much of BuzzFeed, had crossed the hazy line into news and so was being held to a higher standard. We reviewed and corrected more than forty instances of plagiarism, adding an apologetic statement to each article. Benny wasn't answering the phone, so John Stanton headed out into the Washington night to try to find him and fire him in person. (The Blaze, seeing the fuss, also revisited the work Johnson had done for them, and quietly added updates and disclaimers to several posts noting they'd been plagiarized.)

I felt burned and realized that I'd missed something, though I didn't quite know what it was. Later, I'd recognize in Benny something we'd come to associate with the president who was elected three years later. The thirst for attention, the willingness to say absolutely anything to go viral, and the attraction to uniforms and rituals of power. Benny kicked around in the media industry awhile longer, getting fired for allegedly being lazy or erratic or for taking credit for others' work. Meanwhile, the world was turning his way.

23

Disney

By the end of 2013, BuzzFeed was having it all. Our traffic hit 130 million unique visitors a month, riding Facebook's relentless growth. Some of our competitors had begun to imitate everything we did, which mostly amounted to making lists. Others promised to do the same thing we were, but without the embarrassing memes. In Silicon Valley, an ambitious Goldman Sachs banker named Carlos Watson persuaded an old friend, Laurene Powell Jobs, to finance a website called Ozy that would aim to be a smarter, slicker, more socially conscious BuzzFeed.

And in that frothy moment, it seemed to make sense for America's best media company, and its safest brand, to buy us.

Disney, to the degree it had been aware of BuzzFeed at all, had noticed its rather generous interpretation of fair use of Disney's copyrights in items like "Which Disney Princess Are You?" But Disney was also scrambling to figure out how it fit into a rapidly changing digital world, and in the spring of 2013, Ben Sherwood, the former wunderkind producer turned president of ABC News, which Disney owned, sat with the company's chief executive, Bob Iger, at the Coral Tree Café in Brentwood and asked him if he'd ever heard of BuzzFeed. Iger said he had, but hadn't really looked deeply into it. Sherwood explained that ABC News, in his view, had fallen dangerously out of sync with the times, as corporate media lumbered toward what would be referred to in conference room PowerPoints as "digital transformation." What the place really needed, he said, was a DNA transfer. If Disney bought BuzzFeed, the entertainment giant could massively increase the internet company's value by juicing its ad sales—and meanwhile, BuzzFeed would BuzzFeedify ABC News's website and reverse its aging audience demographics. Iger liked what he saw, and he knew he could get in touch with Kenny, who'd nearly done the *Huffington Post* deal with him. Iger's deal guy, Kevin Mayer, a rangy, gregarious executive whom many saw as the next CEO, liked it too. Disney needed a way to deliver its shows on the internet and to circumvent the movie theaters and television stations that represented the dying twentieth century.

Jonah huddled with Kenny and, on September 30, emailed him a long list of the things that would make him want to do the deal—at a price, he proposed, of $600 million. "I want to chase Yahoo and MSN in scale and the NYT in quality," Jonah wrote. He proposed developing a "new cast of online only Disney characters in collaboration with Disney team . . . One of them should be gay, all of them should be inspiring, have good values, and a contemporary, positive style." Plus, he would insist on "continued editorial independence for Ben Smith." He and I were in the middle of recruiting a star investigative editor, Mark Schoofs, from the nonprofit *ProPublica*, and he had an inkling of how hard it would be to make money in that line of work, so he proposed asking for $5 million a year for investigative journalism. Through the fall of 2013, Iger talked to Jonah and Kenny as Disney accountants and strategists quietly examined BuzzFeed's books, and on October 24, we were invited to the House of Mouse.

We traveled to Los Angeles with a pretext: BuzzFeed was opening a cavernous new office, in a former soap factory on Wilshire Boulevard. But the real point of the trip was the meeting at Disney's studios in Burbank, a set of old Hollywood buildings designed by Walt himself. Iger met us at the top of the elevator in the softly lit executive floor. He was alone, relaxed, wearing a sweater and acting like an uncle who was thrilled you'd made it in time for Thanksgiving dinner. Jonah was wearing a button-down shirt with three shades of brown checks, crisp but not tucked in. The event had the false informality of all contemporary business meetings. Iger had just gotten back from Washington, he mentioned, and was so grateful we'd been able to make time for him. (He didn't mention he'd been meeting with President Obama.) I sat on one side of the long table with Jonah, Jon Steinberg, and Ze Frank, Jonah's old internet friend who had started BuzzFeed's fast-growing video arm. A half dozen Disney executives sat on the other. Bob and Jonah each delivered long speeches laying out the companies' value to each other. Jonah had been making a study of Iger, and had come to understand that the role of a CEO at that level was twofold: Iger was a banker, deciding where to allocate resources, and a politician, finessing personal relationships and a public message. I watched Jonah imitate Iger, then watched Iger mirror Jonah's own speech back to him, structuring his discussion of Disney's plans to match Jonah's monologue on BuzzFeed's aspirations. To Jonah, this was Disney's most compelling aspect—the chance to study a true master and to learn from him, to be one of thirteen people reporting directly to the most successful CEO in modern media.

We drove back from the lot to Palihotel, a slick-looking but inexpensive spot on Melrose, where Jonah's room had a balcony over an alley. Steinberg had finagled a prescription for legal marijuana, then a novelty, and while we smoked, Jonah solicited our input. I told him that we were building something great at BuzzFeed, that we were just getting started, that Disney's corporate culture would stifle us. Ze had already told him the same. Jon was shocked we'd consider saying no. He'd left the meeting with Iger on a high, believing that his longtime dream was coming true. Steinberg had loved Disney since he was a fifteen-year-old intern there: he had spent the best summer of his life working on the Aladdin virtual reality attraction, and he still took his family to the theme parks every year. From the perspective of a media company, an offer from Disney was like getting into Harvard, Steinberg said. And from the perspective of a venture-backed startup, the deal was a no-brainer too. Jon's father was a top Manhattan real estate broker, and he'd taught his son the industry wisdom that the first offer you get is probably the best one. Steinberg got down on his knees on the balcony to plead with Jonah to take the deal.

While I receded into a corner, alternately spaced out and laughing hysterically, and while Steinberg begged, Jonah grew even more abstracted than usual. He conducted a kind of Socratic dialogue with Steinberg in which he seemed at times to be talking to himself. He asked why Steinberg really wanted to do the deal, and Steinberg scrambled to give whatever answer would push Jonah toward yes. You just want money, right? Yes, Jon said. But is it really money you want? Or is it status? You don't just want a house—you want it in the right part of the Hamptons, right? Sure, yes, status. Steinberg tried to lead Jonah back toward the wisdom of the deal—but Jonah seemed to be exploring his own motives, wondering what he actually wanted as he towered over Steinberg, laughing. Jonah didn't seem to care about money, and he had a kind of reverse snobbery about the status money would buy. He didn't even like the theme parks, Jonah told his appalled deputy. Steinberg was crushed and furious at me and at Ze; he believed, probably rightly, that if the three of us had been unified, we could have brought Jonah along.

Steinberg and I both stumbled to bed, convinced Jonah would turn the deal down.

But back in New York, when the details came in, it became clear that this was an offer that Jonah, almost, couldn't refuse. Disney was the most admired media company in the world, with a record of well-managed acquisitions like Marvel and Pixar. The price on offer was $450 million with the potential of earning $200 million more, an extraordinary sum for a company that had priced itself at less than half of that just nine months earlier, and whose connection to Disney—a company obsessively protective of its image and its wholesome brands—was just a series of posts like "21 Completely Bizarre Moments in Disney History" (number five: "When Donald Duck promoted condoms during WWII"). Iger was persuasive. Jonah, Steinberg, and Kenny met nightly in Lerer's Upper West Side living room, and Kenny heard them both make their cases—Steinberg's to sell, Jonah's about the risks of being stifled by Disney, and the potential upside he still saw in the company's independence. Kenny knew Jonah would bridle at being pushed too hard, so he tried to nudge his protégé toward saying yes. The deal really was, by any normal standard, a no-brainer. On October 29, Jonah and Kenny flew back to Los Angeles, this time staying in Kenny's preferred hotel, the Chateau Marmont. At nine the next morning, they met Iger and Mayer to go back over the details we'd discussed in the same building five days earlier. Then they all shook hands, and at least some of the men left the room thinking the deal was done. And then, on the flight back, Jonah turned to his seatmate: He didn't think he could do it. Kenny, incredulous and quietly furious, told Jonah to call Iger and end the talks that day.

Jonah thought it would be more honorable to call it off in person, and so he instead called Iger to say he wasn't committed and that he'd like to meet again—and suggested they talk after Jonah's planned speech to

Disney's management retreat in Orlando twelve days later. Jonah was still feeling his old partner Kenny's anger when he traveled to Disney World in Orlando on November 13 to speak to the company. The event was, for some 250 made Disney men and women—the people who get to skip the lines at the theme parks—a nearly sacred gathering, running Thursday to Sunday at the sumptuous Grand Floridian Resort. Iger's smooth public persona dominated the gathering. Executives worked out at 4:00 a.m. in hopes of running into him at the gym and, if they didn't see him, returned at 6:00 a.m. They were the people who ran theme parks in Asia and cruise lines in Europe, and sold content in Latin America and Australia. They signed up for essentially mandatory, and strangely competitive, sporting events, like softball. When Jonah looked down at them from the stage in the grand ballroom, he saw people dressed like their boss, strenuously casual in shorts and collared T-shirts, ready to pretend to be relaxed.

As they gathered, Mayer mentioned to Sherwood that Jonah had asked to meet privately after the speech, shooting his colleague a quizzical look that said, "Weird guy." But if that was how he wanted the signing ceremony to go, that was fine. As they watched Jonah deliver his speech, trepidation grew for the executives who had worked on the deal. While Bob had staged Jonah's speech in a marquee slot to welcome him to the family, the BuzzFeed founder didn't seem to have prepared with any special care. There were no particular references to Disney, to his audience, his future colleagues. Those who had watched his speeches on YouTube recognized recycled jokes—his yarns about the Nike email and Black People Love Us! and his slides of corgis. As Jonah delivered one of his standard, edgy monologues—he liked to ask whether Mormons were better than Jews, and explain that the real difference was about the quality of their distribution networks—an HR executive blanched and told the person sitting next to her that they might have a problem.

Jonah knew he could make himself, his investors, and many of the people who worked for him rich. He knew that the decision was still his to make, and while he was leaning against accepting Disney's offer, he took the stage without quite having decided. But the reception of his speech confirmed his decision. Jonah had never gotten fewer laughs in his life. He had a vision of himself having to explain the internet to these suits for the rest of his career, while they stared blankly back at him and missed his jokes. The thing he had valued from the start when he built a company in his own image was freedom—his own and others', sometimes to a fault. Jonah couldn't see himself as an officer on this tight ship. He thought of something his old friend and investor Chris Dixon once said to him: Do you know how many lame rich guys there are, and how few people who really build something? Jonah just couldn't do it. He walked offstage and into a room with Kevin and Bob. There, he told them apologetically that his heart wasn't in it. The deal was off. There had been a car ready to take him to celebrate; Jonah took it to the airport.

Iger, who could blow up and regain his cool within seconds, was furious that Jonah had walked away from the deal—and equally puzzled that Jonah had accepted the speaking invitation first.

"Fuck him, he loses, that company will never be worth what it would have been worth with us," he said to another executive. But there was no looking back. Four months later, Disney announced it would buy Maker Studios, which helped YouTube stars like the gamer PewDiePie sell advertising, for roughly the same $500 million it had considered spending on BuzzFeed.

For Kenny, Jonah's theatrical decision marked the first break with his protégé. Jon was heartbroken. He thought Jonah was out of his mind, and realized simultaneously that BuzzFeed was Jonah's company. The next thing Jon did, he vowed, would be entirely his own. He started racking up appearances on CNBC, studying how business news got made.

Ze and I were relieved by Jonah's decision, which meant we could go back to making videos and breaking news. We fully believed that the winds of history were at our backs, and that we'd look down at the pittance Disney offered us one day and laugh. And Ze and I weren't the only ones who admired Jonah's balls. In Silicon Valley, that self-effacing boldness and egotism were catnip. And the charts of traffic and revenue pointed ever upward. Mark Zuckerberg, legendarily, had turned down a $1 billion offer from Yahoo! in 2006, defying many of his advisers. Jonah could now go and tell his Disney story to the same people, show off his traffic, take their money, and keep growing.

....

The Dress

Facebook grew and grew. By 2014, 58 percent of Americans were using the platform. BuzzFeed thrived under its wing, rewarding Jonah's confidence in turning down the big money from Disney. The clearest vindication came in the form of traffic. We hit the biggest Facebook gusher yet early in 2014, the numbers dwarfing what we'd been trying to sell Bob Iger the year before. Our numbers led us straight to Silicon Valley, where we could trade them for access to its deep pool of that other unnatural resource, money. At first, it was hard to understand how we'd done it.

The BuzzFeed post was so simple: a quiz asking "What State Do You Actually Belong In?" It was the latest in a rush of quizzes that were, for reasons not totally clear at the time, getting enormous amounts of traffic from Facebook. The format was as old as women's magazines like the ones Anna Holmes used to work for—"What's Your Secret Sexual Personality?" And the substance had nothing to do with the increasingly ambitious journalism we were starting to pull off. But the technology to do it simply and shareably on the web was, in that moment, new, and ours. The questions were not, let's say, scientific: "Which animal do you feel best represents you?" it asked. "What's your party anthem?"

We gathered, astounded, to watch the numbers build on Google Analytics, the giant company's dominant entry into the field that Jonah had helped invent, and that Chartbeat had dominated before Google got into the game. Traffic to the states quiz built to around 200,000 people on the site at the same time—about twice as many people as we'd see across all of BuzzFeed most days. Our Amazon-hosted servers held.

We knew the quiz was working. We weren't sure why. Then Nguyen, who ran BuzzFeed's analytics, noticed something: there was a bug in the quiz. If your answers to the random, silly questions produced a tie between two results, the quiz defaulted to the one lower down in the alphabet. This meant a lot of people got Wyoming. More people, we calculated, than the 582,000 people who actually live in Wyoming. Many of them took to Facebook to complain about it. "Is that still a state?" one reader asked. "I hate the freezing weather. That's why I am in California.☹," said another. "How the hell did I get Wyoming?" asked a third. And so on.

All the results were even less precise than our usual efforts to vaguely associate your pizza preference with your personality type. We couldn't have cared less if the quiz actually matched you to your dream state—it was something to do while you were bored at work, and then it turned into something to argue about online. But if we saw good-natured complaints on our Facebook page, Facebook saw something else: engagement. It didn't really matter what people were saying. What mattered was that they were talking at all, spending more time on the platform, feeling and reacting.

Jonah was, as usual, the one who brought this insight back to the office, by now a sprawling open space upstairs from a Home Depot on West Twenty-Third Street. (He'd heard from other startup founders an axiom of real estate, that you should hop from short-term lease to short-term lease, paying a premium to avoid being tied down, so that you could hire like crazy or lay off half your staff without cumbersome real estate liability.) Jonah was still one of the few media figures whom Facebook's executives could talk to informally—who spoke their language. He'd message occasionally with Mark Zuckerberg and Chris Cox, and when the engineers who ran News Feed came to town, they might wind up drinking and chatting with Jonah at the end of some more formal evening.

The Facebook crew knew Jonah was working them, for information and to shape their thinking in a way that would match his vision for the internet. But they didn't mind it. They were tired of translating their own point of view—about audiences and content and measuring what people really liked—to people who spoke the old media's language, of viewers and readers, and the journalistic and aesthetic standards that determined what they *ought* to like. What's more, Jonah had also proven willing to warn Facebook when its algorithm was inadvertently promoting spammy formats that wouldn't wear well with its users, to flag bugs rather than taking advantage of them, as he had with those "curiosity gap" headlines on which Upworthy had lived and died. Jonah warned Facebook of short-term tricks media companies were using to game its system, and he warned his employees not to play those games. And in return, he got insight into how Facebook was thinking, and why all those people who were definitely, certainly not moving to Wyoming had added up to the most successful post in BuzzFeed's history so far.

The particular piece of insight he brought back from a conversation with a Facebook staffer in 2014 was a simple piece of math: 1 comment = 4 likes. The company's algorithm had shifted to prioritize "engagement," rather than giving a simple thumbs-up. We'd entered a new world, one that Facebook and its critics alike would sometimes conceal behind mystifying technical language, but which boiled down to two things:

metrics based on how much people were sharing, clicking, and talking about a piece of content; and an algorithm that promoted the pieces that drew that engagement—not just to engaged individuals' friends, but to everyone on the vast network. The details would change over time, but the formula wouldn't—and a new global wave of engaging right-wing politicians would be ready for it.

There weren't a lot of ways to look under Facebook's hood if you weren't messaging with Zuck. Way back in 2012, the site had an open API that allowed you to browse public Facebook posts through back doors like "Openbook." Now, in 2014, you could still search Twitter to see what people were talking about, and you could rearrange Pinterest to show you cute dogs to your heart's content. But Facebook, which had also purchased Instagram in 2012, had systematically shut most of those doors, and it guarded its users' data, the heart of its massive advertising business, fiercely.

Nick watched with a mixture of jealousy and disgust. A journalist profiling Jonah had asked Nick in March of 2014 why he didn't like the BuzzFeed founder, and Nick replied that "it's not jonah himself I hate, but this stage of internet media for which he is so perfectly optimized. I see an image of his cynical smirk—*made you click!*—every time a stupid buzzfeed listicle pops on Facebook." Nick at least understood the game. Most media CEOs viewed Facebook with incomprehension, or anger. It had built a better advertising product than they ever had, and ripped their core business out from under them. Then when they tried to talk to Zuckerberg, they met a robot who was half-idealism, half–naked ambition—and who didn't seem to speak their language, of news and civic virtue, at all. That's part of why Zuckerberg and his team liked Jonah. And it's part of why Jonah found himself, two months after a buggy quiz blew up Facebook, explaining to Marc Andreessen why he'd turned down Disney's money.

It was June 23, 2014, just before noon, and I was sitting next to Jonah at the long conference table on Sand Hill Road, home of the famous Silicon Valley office park housing a set of prominent venture capital offices. We were at the Andreessen Horowitz partners meeting, dominated by Andreessen himself, who stood six foot five and had a pointy bald head like an egg (the default avatar on Twitter) and loomed over the table. Some of the partners attended virtually using the crude robots that were popular at the time: iPad heads on top of a stick with a wheeled base.

Our story naturally appealed to Andreessen. The venture capitalist, who had created the first modern web browser, Netscape, and then cofounded Andreessen Horowitz, had been an early investor in Facebook. He was almost alone among Zuckerberg's investors in urging the founder to turn down Yahoo!'s billion-dollar offer. "Mark and I really bonded in that period, because I told him, 'Don't sell, don't sell, don't sell!'" Andreessen told the *New Yorker* when the magazine traveled out to profile him, dubbing him "Tomorrow's Advance Man." Andreessen was, in some sense, the opposite of Iger, the ultimate smooth, big-media politician. Andreessen was a self-styled nerd king, shy and aggressive by turns, a believer in the power of cutting argument, not gentle diplomacy. He was in part responsible for the scale, ambition, and self-image of Silicon Valley, and as 2014 began, we became part of it.

Jonah had prepped us on the strategy: We needed to come in confident, smart, a little intellectual, ready to argue. None of the usual humility. Andreessen was known for harshly challenging founders, but this was a different situation: BuzzFeed was hot, and he knew we were meeting with others on Sand Hill Road, that we'd have other offers. BuzzFeed's traffic and revenue numbers clearly pointed to its becoming a "unicorn"— a billion-dollar-plus company that would make investors rich.

Jonah explained to Andreessen across the long table at his office on

Sand Hill Road why the company would be worth far more than the $450 million Disney had offered. BuzzFeed, he said, was learning to do what he'd been trying with LilyBoo—quantify human emotion on social media and feed it back to an audience with a combination of art and science, then capture the nearly infinite scale and perpetual motion the new media offered. With the simple quizzes that Facebook favored, we were growing faster than ever, and we had a friendly, symbiotic relationship with the company that almost every other media company lacked. It went unsaid that they'd be an obvious buyer of BuzzFeed one day—the VCs could, we assumed, check that out with Zuckerberg. How news reporting fit into the picture was a little hazy, but—Valleywag aside—it was still an era when journalists turned investors like Andreessen into heroes, and one of Andreessen Horowitz's strengths was its mastery of the hype cycle. I got the sense that the investors believed—though it was never formally stated—that BuzzFeed would be one more friendly platform for founders.

Because Andreessen was a man of big bets, he made this one. His firm led an investment round of $50 million that August, valuing BuzzFeed at $850 million and bragging in a press release that the company was already profitable. Behind the scenes, though, these new investors told Jonah to stop worrying about profits. The name of the game was growth, and he should expand as fast as he could, in every direction available, while he still had the momentum. Traffic was the only metric.

Soon after the investment came another surge of vindication. This was February 26, 2015—"The Internet's Greatest Day," BuzzFeed's Charlie Warzel called it, and perhaps also the last good day on the internet, as some people now see it. The day began with a national frenzy over two llamas that escaped from an Arizona retirement home and ran wild for nearly three hours through the streets of Sun City, Arizona, pursued by hapless humans and capturing the interest of millions. Then, near the end of the workday at BuzzFeed's offices over the Home Depot, Cates Holderness got a message. "BuzzFeed, please help," it read.

Cates was one of the old guard at BuzzFeed, hired way back in 2011 when the company was just pulling in people who loved the internet and didn't even really think of themselves as working in media. Cates, in fact, had been working at a boarding and grooming kennel in North Carolina, reading Peggy and Matt on BuzzFeed and sharing the best of their work on her Facebook page.

That afternoon, a Scottish folk singer named Caitlin McNeill had messaged Cates through Tumblr, where she managed the BuzzFeed account, with her urgent request about a wedding she'd played. "I posted a picture of this dress," she wrote of the crappy, badly lit photograph taken by a friend's mother. "Some people see it blue and some people see it white can you explain because we are goING CRAZY." Cates looked at the photograph, plainly of a blue-and-black dress, and thought the email was weird, inexplicable, but eventually asked the people sitting next to her what color they thought it was. One said "blue and black" and one said "white and gold" and they started yelling at each other, each convinced the other was crazy. Pretty soon she had twenty people standing behind her desk incredulously debating the point. So Cates posted the image to BuzzFeed under the heading "What Colors Are This Dress?" and left work. When her train, the F, emerged from the tunnel under the East River a few minutes later, her phone was flooded with alerts. She tried to open them, and it crashed. She restarted it, and it crashed again. She hurried to a friend's house to figure out what was going on. I was reading a fairy tale to my young son when I realized what was happening. I put the book down to frantically assign more stories to capture what I knew would be a flood of traffic spilling over from Cates's post, which would go on to receive more than thirty-seven million views. One reporter called McNeill in the middle of the night in Scotland, which led to "The Dress Is Blue And Black, Says the Girl Who Saw It In Person." Our science editor dialed scientists after bedtime to churn out another piece, "Why Are People Seeing Different Colors In That Damn Dress?"

What was going on, it emerged, was the last, greatest, totally harmless moment of global internet culture. The Dress was divisive, in the purest sense, dividing (according to a BuzzFeed poll with nearly four million votes) the two thirds of people who saw white and gold from the third who saw blue and black. Facebook's engineers had been perfecting its engagement metrics since the debate, a year earlier, over who was destined to move to Wyoming. And the Dress was universal—a form of media that didn't even require literacy to land. It didn't spread, like most memes, along a rising viral curve, passed hand to hand. It spread, instead, algorithmically, as Facebook showed the Dress to users whose friends had not yet shared it, confidently predicting that they would find it just as engaging. Within a couple of hours, our traffic rose to seven hundred thousand people simultaneously, seven times our usual peaks. That sent our engineers scrambling to add servers to BuzzFeed's back end; it was a number not reached before or since by a BuzzFeed post on the web. A couple of hours after it was posted, on the other side of the world, Cates's boss, Scott Lamb, was giving a morning speech at a media conference in Jakarta. All of the questions he fielded were about the Dress.

The Dress was an unmitigated triumph for BuzzFeed and for Jonah—the kind of social content he'd hoped would define us. I toasted a blushing Cates with champagne in the middle of the office. Jonah bragged about it to advertisers. What a score—and also, what a nice thing. Maybe this is what the world would be like in the future—people across nations and cultures all talking about the same fun thing at the same time, with Facebook and BuzzFeed uniting them.

Jonah learned that he'd misunderstood Facebook's point of view when Chris Cox introduced him to Adam Mosseri at a party on the sprawling roof garden of the building Frank Gehry had designed for Facebook in Menlo Park. Mosseri, a tall and unusually open Facebook executive, was in charge of News Feed. His decisions could make or break publishers. "How often do you think things should go viral like the Dress?" Mosseri asked. Jonah was surprised by the question—and by the idea that the frequency of things going viral was up to Mosseri's team. The conversation made clear to Jonah that Facebook was worried about something new: losing control. To them, the Dress hadn't been a goofy triumph: it had been a kind of a bug, something that scared them. The Dress itself was harmless, but the next meme to colonize the entire platform within minutes might not be, and this one had moved too fast for the team in Menlo Park to control.

Many of Facebook's critics were glad to see the platform make this realization: it marked the beginning of a decade in which Facebook would start to realize its own power and try to control it, even if the company's efforts always seemed to be too little, too late. Jonah saw it differently. He still believed in the power of the global conversation to bring out people's best instincts—to joke around harmlessly, to act charitably and brag about it. The people who really saw the danger in virality, he liked to remark, were the leaders of the Chinese Communist Party, who had discovered that they could stop a social movement from starting without totally wiping it out—just by deleting some of its content, enough to stop it from achieving escape velocity. In Mosseri's worried tone, Jonah detected the same threat of censorship. And he saw more clearly than most that the alternative to a wide-open viral internet wasn't necessarily a return to the placid old media world. It would be an algorithm that recommended content to individuals according to a narrower set of guidelines. Facebook's solution wasn't to abandon its algorithms, which could predict what you'd like and show it to you: it was to tighten the scope in which those algorithms worked. Going forward, Facebook would do a better job of keeping people in their lanes and in their bubbles. We at BuzzFeed might have seen the Dress as the beginning of a new kind of global culture, but in fact nothing quite like it was ever allowed to happen again.

....

$850 Million

The beginning of the end of Gawker was clear in retrospect. By 2014, Nick's rivals, led by Jonah, were amassing huge amounts of venture capital money. His enemies, burning with rage from the exposure he'd subjected them to, were secretly plotting to destroy him. But that was also the year Nick, for the first time, seemed to truly lose his edge. The problem was that Nick was happy. Nick was getting married.

He invited the Gawker generations, from Elizabeth Spiers to AJ Daulerio, to the lavish ceremony on May 31, 2014, at the American Museum of Natural History—a little like they were family. Nick had guests check their cell phones at the door, however, so they could "give their full attention to each other." The vows were simple and sentimental. "I was always expected to be successful, but I never really believed I would be happy," Nick told his groom. "I want to make my own family with you."

Afterward, *The New York Times* tried to apply to the affair a wedding scoring system Gawker previously had invented, and gave it a 9: "Works in media: +1, Oxford graduate: +3, Member of couple over 35: -1,

Groom is a board member of a company: +2, Someone famous comes to the wedding and is mentioned: +2, Couple featured in "Vows" column: +2." But when the reporter asked Nick about this cold measurement, he replied, "How about points for whether the people love each other?" The comment suggested to the reporter that Nick's "emotional transformation was nearly complete."

This was disorienting, naturally, for Gawker editors. One of them, Max Read, found that "he was still hard to talk to, just not in a scary way." They'd have lunch, Nick would ask about Max's girlfriend and then confide in his employee about gay "bottom shame."

While Nick mellowed, his friends and his editors worried. It wasn't just that Nick was getting too nice, getting a little squeamish about the work, about the blunt recognition that "the internet has made it easier for all of us to be shameless voyeurs and deviants," as AJ had articulated when he published the Hogan sex tape. Nick also didn't seem as worried as they thought he should be about an odd fact: Hulk Hogan's lawsuit just wouldn't go away. When they brought it up, Nick told them to stop being so paranoid.

And yet AJ thought it was suspicious. There had been dozens of similar legal threats against Gawker over the decade—even Fred Durst had threatened to sue—but most had evaporated in the face of two countermeasures: the continued public humiliation that Gawker could levy against its enemies, and America's uniquely strong First Amendment protections for unpopular speech. Suing a media company was expensive, too, because big damages were so rare that the kind of ambulance chasers who worked on commission tended to avoid the field. The aggrieved target typically had to pay by the hour. And yet Hogan's expensive legal team had pressed ahead through a series of procedural setbacks. A federal judge rejected Bollea's request to force Gawker to take the video off the internet back in 2012. But Bollea had wangled his way into state court in 2013 by changing who exactly he was suing—he'd settled with the guy who filmed the sex tape (Bubba the Love Sponge). Bollea's lawyers were staying in expensive hotels in Florida, even though their client didn't seem to have much money himself. It didn't make sense.

And there were other inexplicable features of the case that made the more conspiracy-minded members of the Gawker circle, AJ most of all, nervous. For one thing, Bollea's lawyers had, in 2014, dropped a single charge from their case—the one that Gawker's insurance would have covered. That's a strange move for someone looking to get paid; it only makes sense to do if you're trying to destroy your target. "It always felt off. It always felt there was something else happening," AJ said later. And when he learned that the suit was actually going to trial, he knew "something bad is going to happen."

AJ wasn't in much of a position to focus on Nick anymore, though. He was leaving to start something new. He thought he had gotten too big for Gawker, though he still revered his old boss, still wanted to impress him. "I wanted to preserve my relationship with Nick Denton, and I thought the best way to do that was to leave on my own terms," AJ later wrote. Nick sent him off with praise, calling him "the most successful editor of Gawker.com," despite AJ's having prioritized more than just traffic. "Even though AJ took the pressure off writers to deliver traffic with every piece, the site now draws 10m visitors a month," Nick wrote.

AJ's new site was called *Ratter*, for which he had anxiously sought, and gotten, Nick's blessing. Not just that: Nick had invested $500,000 in *Ratter*, on the condition that AJ publish it on Kinja, which, though not a tech company in its own right, was finally up and running as the publishing and commenting platform for Nick's sites. Still, *Ratter*'s presence among his content sources indulged Nick's fantasy of building platforms, not just blogs. AJ had wanted Nick's money, but his run of dicks had made AJ such a hot hand that he probably didn't need it. He raised over $1 million more from leading internet media financiers, including from an old rival of Nick's, Jason Calacanis, who had sold another early blog network to AOL. The future *Shark Tank* host Mark Cuban was in, as was the fund of the creator of Facebook's News Feed, Dave Morin.

Ratter was all swagger and mischief. AJ imagined it as local news—but not "fucking boring" like everyone else. "The goal is to break news and make a huge splash as quickly as possible," he said. The model for *Ratter* was Gawker's exposé of the mayor of Toronto, Rob Ford, a Trumpy figure whom they caught, literally, smoking crack. There had to be a story like that in every city, right?

AJ hired a skeleton staff of four to cover Los Angeles, New York, and San Francisco. In the booming tech capital, AJ became fixated upon the thing nobody would talk about: human feces in the street. He had his editor, Will Kane, photograph and post a "turd of the day," complete with a description of its location, color, and odor. This seemed promising to AJ, even if it wasn't getting many clicks.

In some ways you'd rather be at *Ratter*, where you knew what your boss wanted—he wanted what Gawker used to be—than actually at Gawker, where writers had begun to worry that their boss was getting soft. On January 2, 2015, Leah Finnegan, a writer who embodied Nick's ability to bring out both the best and the worst in his staff, wrote a story making fun of the actress Zoe Saldana for naming her children Cy and Bowie. The headline was "Zoe Saldana Gives Birth to Hipster Scum." Nick responded directly to Finnegan in the comments section: "You'll regret writing that headline."

Ratter finally got its breakthrough—a dick, of course—a month later: a picture of the penis of pop star Justin Bieber. Daulerio published the image proudly, under the headline "The Case for Reparations for Justin Bieber's Dick." But a few days and two lawyers' letters later, he wrote a churlish retraction. The dick had not been Bieber's, he grudgingly admitted, before concluding, "My advice for young journalists is this: Never underestimate the power of the d."

AJ's addictions were getting worse too. At *Ratter*, he'd vanish for a day at a time from his small and somewhat bewildered team. And when he was there, he could be erratic. AJ became fixated, almost as soon as the sites launched, with moving them off Kinja, because he worried they were being seen as just another Gawker Media blog. He got obsessed with acquiring the rights to the music of an oddball R & B singer who called himself Swamp Dogg, convinced that owning a piece of albums like *The White Man Made Me Do It* would transform *Ratter* from a blog into a full-scale media company.

And he could never quite get Nick out of his mind. "Let's also take this moment to reiterate that although Ratter.com uses Kinja as a publishing tool, it is in no way affiliated with Gawker Media, LLC," he wrote in the retraction of the Bieber story. "I know it's tough to distinguish that fact sometimes, due to my previous employment at Gawker."

Still, Kane and his colleagues believed that AJ was charismatic enough, brilliant enough when he focused. Resolved to be more generous than Nick, AJ even gave his employees equity; Will had one quarter of a percent of the company, and he would sometimes multiply that by BuzzFeed's valuation—$850 million in 2014—to see how rich he might become if *Ratter* became the next new media hit.

But AJ never got a steady stream of traffic, or money, with *Ratter*. He fired his small staff in May 2015, and closed the site.

There didn't seem to be space on the internet anymore for the unfiltered and indiscriminate exposure, the sex tapes, that had powered AJ's early success. It certainly wasn't working on Facebook. And the new politics of backlash and media criticism—all the things Jezebel had, years earlier, helped spark—descended on Gawker that July 17, when the blog publicly humiliated the chief financial officer of Condé Nast, an unknown figure, for trying to hire a gay escort. "Given the chance, Gawker will always report on married c-suite executives of major media companies fucking around on their wives," Gawker's editor Max Read tweeted as other journalists expressed revulsion. Nick, breaking with Gawker's long tradition, held a vote of the company's corporate managers and had the post taken down.

"In the early days of the internet," Nick wrote, the mission of putting true facts on the internet regardless of personal cost "would have been enough. I cannot blame our editors and writers for pursuing that original mission.

"But the media environment has changed, our readers have changed, and I have changed," he wrote. "In light of Gawker's past rhetoric about our fearlessness and independence, this can be seen as a capitulation. And perhaps, to some extent, it is. But it is motivated by a sincere effort to build a strong independent media company, and to evolve with the audience we serve."

Nick was right about the changed environment. The young bloggers who had been cheeky outsiders a decade earlier were now feared and powerful insiders, whether they acknowledged it or not. The new media, no longer new, was winning. They competed for traffic and influence with *The New York Times,* and they could do just as much damage—even if they didn't care to acknowledge it.

But his editors were furious, confused, and betrayed. They issued a unanimous statement denouncing Nick for taking the decision out of their hands. The story outing a cheating, closeted husband was "solidly in line with what Gawker has asked its writers and editors to do for years," a top editor wrote. That was true. But the internet was changing, and Nick was trying—and failing—to persuade his ragged band to keep up.

Dinosaurs

On June 10, 2015, as Gawker began to lose its footing and BuzzFeed was in the last few months of its pure, unworried rise, Jonah traveled a mile north to the headquarters of *The New York Times*. He was there on a familiar, pleasant task: he was a mammal explaining to the dinosaurs how he'd evolved past them, why he was winning. He was always happy to share BuzzFeed's secrets. It didn't seem likely that the dinosaurs would evolve as they had in the movie *Jurassic Park* and learn to open doors.

Jonah turned up to address the board of directors of the *Times* in a hoodie, playing to type, in the gleaming fifteenth-floor conference room of a new building that many still thought the company couldn't afford. The *Times* thought it needed a high-tech new space, a claim that became a bit of a joke when Snapchat took over the lease on the old building on West Forty-First Street, the one for which Times Square is named. The *Times* was already renting out floors to other companies to make up revenue. The man behind their slow and painfully deliberate transition to the internet, publisher Arthur Sulzberger Jr., presided, along with the CEO he'd brought in to speed things up, Mark Thompson.

Jonah's interviewer was Cliff Levy, an ambitious editor who had won two Pulitzers and returned to oversee the creation of a news app. That always made Jonah laugh—that the only way you could build a new app at the *Times* was if you had not one, but two, Pulitzers. They sat in raised chairs, as Levy asked Jonah about what he'd built at BuzzFeed. Do millennials really consume content differently? Levy asked. Was news just a loss leader?

Then Levy turned to Arthur. "Bear with me for a second," he said. He asked Jonah to imagine "that you were named executive editor of the *Times* tomorrow." What would be the first three things he'd do?

It was a perfect softball to the nerd king. First, Jonah said, he'd ask the board for a raise. Then he'd go into his office and shut the door. And then he'd cry.

That got the anticipated laugh. After all, everyone shared the basic assumption in the summer of 2015 that BuzzFeed was riding the rising tide, and that the *Times* was flailing to grab hold of the new medium. But Jonah had misread the room. They were more confident than he realized. The story of the *Times* would be that of how the dinosaurs had begun to learn to open doors; that newspaper, too, would shape the new internet.

There is a rule in the Sulzberger family that you have to work somewhere else for five years before you can come home to the *Times*. David Perpich wasn't planning to work there at all. But Perpich, a little-known figure outside the *Times*, would go on to play a central role in one of the most surprising stories of the 2010s: the revival of moribund legacy media, and of the *Times* in particular, against the onslaught from the BuzzFeeds and Gawkers of the world. He was an unlikely figure in that turnaround, but also a natural one in an institution dominated for a century by a single family.

Before he was anything else, Perpich was a certain kind of 1990s white kid, raised in the Washington suburbs and obsessed, mostly, with hip-hop. He knew his grandfather, Arthur O. Sulzberger Sr., the courtly publisher of the *Times* until 1992, as an old man who gardened in a sweat suit and taught the kids how to catch frogs. Perpich's young cousins, Sam Dolnick, who lived around the corner in Chevy Chase, and Arthur up in New York, looked up to David, who could beat them at two-on-one basketball. At Duke, he wrote his senior essay on Death Row Records. After working for a couple of failed startups, something approaching his dream job arrived in 2002 when an acquaintance of David's recruited Jam Master Jay, the legendary DJ from Run-D.M.C., to help build something called Scratch DJ Academy. David, slender and superficially a little quiet but deceptively good with people, got in on the ground floor. His specialty was guerilla marketing. He paid DJs to refer to the school in their MySpace profiles, and bought bus ads with a picture of a turntable and the slogan "F@$k piano lessons."

When that project started to get repetitive for David in the summer of 2005, he left for Harvard Business School, then followed the well-worn path from there to the consulting firm Booz & Company, planning a career in the music industry.

Perpich had worked in Booz's media practice before moving on to the more lucrative sector of consumer packaged goods, and he had spent hours puzzling over the difficult economics of online business, the massive scale you needed to make any money on advertising. He was in his childhood bedroom in Bethesda over the Thanksgiving break in 2008 when he read an item on an obscure trade blog called *Eat, Sleep, Publish* about how the *Financial Times* was building a new kind of business by allowing readers to consume a set number of free articles, and then charging them for further access. The blog item was skeptical of the "false dichotomy" between readers who pay for content and those who don't. So Perpich forwarded it to an older cousin, Michael Golden, who had once been a rival for the *Times* throne and remained vice chairman of the company.

"I truly believe this is the model of the future and I think the Times could pull off some version of this," he told Golden. It was "the right compromise—a subscription model built for the dynamics of the web."

"Hopefully you can share it with whoever thinks about these things over there," he wrote.

Though Perpich didn't really know it, everyone was thinking about these things at the *Times* in the fall of 2008. The economy was clearly on the brink of a brutal downturn, and the advertising numbers weren't adding up. The *Times* needed to bet on a new business.

Perpich's email wasn't just a random dispatch from yet another consultant. The thing about *The New York Times* is that it is really a family business, which seemed to Jonah like yet another ridiculous anachronism. This is what Gay Talese discovered in his defining history of the *Times, The Kingdom and the Power*: that the urbane executive editors who seem to run the place in fact serve at the pleasure of their low-profile bosses, and that the crucial decisions about the place's past and future are made by the heirs of Adolph Ochs, who bought the paper in 1896. In 1992, his great-grandson Arthur Ochs Sulzberger Jr.—a fair, cheerful man who was often portrayed in the difficult early aughts as a lightweight, but who in retrospect got the big things right—became publisher. Crucially, he'd repeatedly faced down executives who, in the 1990s, wanted first to slow-walk the internet and then to spin it off into a separate company. He overruled them, and hired Martin Nisenholtz to put the newspaper online anyway.

Two decades later, Arthur Ochs Sulzberger Jr. was still publisher, and David was the son of his beloved older sister. When young David started showing an interest in the *Times*, the people running the company paid attention. Perpich would play a central role in the *Times*'s revival in the second decade of the twenty-first century, but to understand that story, you have to understand how vulnerable the news organization looked in the fall of 2008. That's not easy. As I write this book, *The New York Times* is the most successful news business in the world, one that has absorbed many of the stars of Gawker and BuzzFeed and their digital rivals. But at the end of the first decade of the twenty-first century, the *Times* was something of a laughingstock. When the Mexican billionaire Carlos Slim lent $250 million to the newspaper in 2009, *The Atlantic* was speculating about the possibility that "*The New York Times* goes out of business—like, this May." Meanwhile, the blogosphere more or less *existed* to mock columnists like Thomas Friedman. *The Huffington Post* constantly pantsed the paper by aggregating it and stealing its traffic. The newsroom was defensive, harried and mocked by Gawker, and stressed about the internet.

Perpich had unknowingly inserted himself into the most heated fight in the executive suite, where the people who had been running the digital operation had bought fully into the ideology—our ideology, at BuzzFeed and *The Huffington Post* and Gawker—of a free and open internet, and an advertising business built on a giant scale. It hadn't been an easy sell. When Nisenholtz, Sulzberger's first internet advocate, had arrived at the paper in 1995, he wondered if he'd even have a job for long, because top company executives worried that building a website would interfere with the lucrative business of selling the *Times*' archive to LexisNexis. More than a decade on, he was still running the company's website, and his team of specialized editors had to put up with a sense from their colleagues that they were some kind of B team, and that only the front page of the print edition was meaningful.

"Scale was the only thing that mattered," said Vivian Schiller, one of Nisenholtz's deputies at the time. She and the newsroom editor overseeing the website, Jon Landman, had worked to kill the *Times*' first experiment with a paywall, called Times Select, which ran from 2005 to 2007 and charged about fifty dollars a year for access to opinion writing and some other content. Landman assembled spreadsheets showing that putting older articles behind the paywall was tanking the *Times'* valuable search traffic. Now, the paywall zombie they thought they'd killed was back. The arguments between them and business executives led by CEO Janet Robinson often grew fiery. Jill Abramson, who would soon become the first woman to serve as the *Times'* executive editor, remembered just wanting to look away as Landman tore into Robinson about the damage a paywall can do. "It was a bit like witnessing a fight between your parents when you were a kid."

The newsroom also maintained a traditional disdain for the business side of the operation. But in the executive suite, the mood was dire. And as Arthur Sulzberger searched for new revenue, the obvious answer was to begin charging for what they'd been giving away for free. In 2009, he called the top executives and editors into the Eagle Room, a private dining room where he hosted visiting dignitaries, and went around the table, asking each their opinion.

Bill Keller, the handsome former foreign correspondent who was then executive editor, spoke up and sided decisively against his deputies. His views were simple: "We make this really great stuff—we ought to fucking be able to charge for it," though he didn't put it quite that bluntly in the meeting. Landman knew he was losing the argument. Later, he'd realize Keller's side had been right, that Landman was a "colonel fighting the last war."

The task of making readers pay for journalism was assigned to Paul Smurl, another bright-eyed former management consultant who viewed Sulzberger as a mentor. In February of 2010, Sulzberger informed Smurl that he would be assigned a new deputy: David Perpich. It was, as in any family business, a high-risk, high-reward situation for the manager, and one that some *Times* lifers still seek to avoid. But where Arthur Ochs Sulzberger Sr. had been opaque and imperious, his namesake had resolved to be transparent and professional as the next generation competed for his throne. That didn't mean the older generation wasn't paying attention: Abramson wrote that the senior Arthur Sulzberger had told her to groom his son Arthur ("A. G.") and nephew Dolnick equally, and he grew upset at one point when he thought she was favoring A. G.

The younger generation of the family, in turn, was at times painfully self-aware of the politics. Perpich, at this point thirty-two, had initially ruled out working for the *Times* because he wanted to be sure he could make it on his own terms. His time at Booz qualified him for this job, but he also knew that his colleagues would always assume he came in a special, family door, and that he'd have to prove himself. Smurl, Perpich's new boss, knew that he didn't have any choice in taking on the prospective heir. He was a little nervous about it—but he also bet that making an ally in the Sulzberger family could be its own reward. So it was a pleasant surprise when Perpich also turned out to be good at the job—focused, thoughtful, better with people than you'd expect. Working out of side-by-side offices on the eighth floor, they divided up the work, Smurl leading the strategy and the corporate politics and Perpich managing the 150-person team of designers and developers day to day.

Perpich had little interest in the print newspaper business per se. He and the other digital natives pushed to make online subscriptions cheap, to accelerate the company's shift to digital. The advertising department, by contrast, was still bringing in the vast bulk of its money from print, and feared undermining that position. Finally the two sides agreed that they'd hire the consulting firm McKinsey to advise them on what subscription pricing would be most profitable for the cash-strapped *Times*, and stick with that recommendation. Perpich was disappointed at the high and somewhat confusing prices—fifteen dollars every four weeks for articles on the website and a mobile phone app, twenty dollars for the web and iPad app, or thirty-five dollars for an all-access plan. But he kept his head down and focused on the product. Perpich wanted, in particular, to make sure that the paywall felt like part of the *Times* itself, not some garish overlay on the website.

Out on the open internet, we were puzzled by the new product. As the rest of us raced to scale, the *Times* seemed to be withdrawing into its shell, leaving more traffic for everyone else. The internet sages of that era were pretty sure the *Times'* second attempt at a new kind of paid media wouldn't work. "The risks are great and grave," warned the digital media strategist Jeff Jarvis. NYU professor Clay Shirky pronounced himself "skeptical" on the business model and warned that the effect would be to turn journalism that had been an important public good into a kind of exclusive luxury product.

The *Times* put its paywall in place first in Canada, to iron out any bugs, and soon a colleague turned to Perpich to show him, on the screen of his computer, the very first sign-up. About ten days later, on March 28, 2011, it launched in the United States. The team crowded into a conference room, and Sulzberger and other executives came down for a champagne toast. They settled in to wait and watch the numbers roll in. Perpich's reaction: "Holy crap." They were bigger even than the optimists had expected.

Perpich had, by then, impressed Smurl and—just as important—his elder family members. Colleagues started to wonder if, despite the fact that he had never even tried to be a journalist, Perpich wouldn't emerge as Arthur Sulzberger's successor. He was rewarded with a role running the new products group at the *Times*, where he broke with the long-standing tradition of keeping the people who built and designed the *Times* website siloed on the business side, away from journalists. Instead, Perpich assembled teams that included reporters, product managers, and designers, and built successful products like the cooking app. He probably deserves as much credit as anyone for transforming the company from a legacy news organization to a broader digital media company.

However, Perpich also realized that his innovations worked because he had breached the wall that had been keeping the conversation about digital change out of the *Times'* sprawling, proud, and defensive newsroom. The canny British CEO Mark Thompson came to the same realization, understanding that any successful change would have to feel like it came from within the newsroom. In the fall of 2013, Thompson suggested that a committee of journalists meet to brainstorm new digital products. Abramson, feeling threatened by the move, proposed putting Perpich's young cousin A. G.—who had been an enthusiastic bureau chief in Kansas City and was now a deputy metro editor—at the head of it. Perpich was a natural sounding board and confidant. A. G. Sulzberger initially had intended to use the committee to brainstorm new ideas, but after an endless series of coffees in the *Times'* gleaming new cafeteria, he realized there was actually no shortage of ideas. What A. G. heard, mostly, were complaints about how those new ideas were being given little place in the newsroom's baronial culture. A. G. decided to assemble a small group of editors to write an innovation report, and included people like Adam Bryant, an expert on corporate culture, not digital technology. And after a few sessions of spinning ideas for new products with his committee, he announced to his small new team something he'd been considering from the start: that their goal would not be to figure out new products, but to diagnose the digital ills of the *Times'* core product, its daily news report.

In the first week of December of 2013, A. G. typed out seven pages of notes for the executives to whom he referred, in sharing the memo with his team, as "the bosses." "As we examined our paper and examined the media landscape around us, we came to a pretty striking and I think hugely important realization," he told Thompson and Abramson, according to the notes. "BuzzFeed is not succeeding because of lists or Huffington Post because of cat photos or Guardian because of leaked documents. They are succeeding because of—in order—a killer social strategy, successful search optimization and community building, and a shift towards a more expansive view of the role of a journalist as a public expert."

Kenny Lerer himself had told the committee, A. G. said, that "he would trade their content for ours in a heartbeat," and added, "I'm just amazed you aren't doing more with it."

A. G. would polish those notes into a document called *Innovation*. The laconic, skeptical Abramson asked him to print her out a copy before a business trip to China, a futile attempt to persuade its government to allow a Chinese-language *Times* to reach its citizens. She read the report on the plane, and when she did, she freaked out. It described a newsroom that was broadly clueless about the web. "Many desks lack editors who even know how to evaluate digital work," the report read. The discussion of leaders resisting digital innovation was "code for me," she thought. It was a "personal disaster." She scribbled furiously throughout the flight, and landed thinking her days at the *Times* were numbered. When she and a few colleagues finally met with A. G. Sulzberger's committee to discuss it, she began by pretending she'd drunk the Kool-Aid, but couldn't keep up the mask. Who really wrote this? she asked Sulzberger. Abramson was so bad at putting on a happy face that one senior colleague wondered if she wasn't committing "suicide by cop," attacking her bosses' plan for the future of her own newspaper until they were forced to fire her newspaper.

Abramson later scrambled to embrace the report, but her initial coolness had weakened her hand with the family. When she tried to bring in an ally to a top management job in May, it backfired, and she was pushed out in favor of her deputy, Dean Baquet. The report remained almost entirely secret, even inside the paper. But the next day a source faxed me, at BuzzFeed, ninety-one pages of the ninety-six-page document. We promptly posted it on our website, and I delighted in giving most of the *Times*' staffers their first look at the document—a living illustration of the way in which the digital upstarts were running circles around them.

Top *Times* executives blamed Abramson, furious over her firing, for the leak. The innovation report team thought that A. G. himself had grown impatient and leaked it. The irrational thought even flitted through A. G.'s mind that someone was going to get fired over it, and that might be him. He promised the journalists on his team that he'd fall on his sword and protect them if that's what it came to.

What actually leaked was, to my eyes, as I flitted between Twitter and the black-and-white document, surprisingly banal. Of course the *Times* was behind the digital times. You didn't need a report to know that. There was something hopelessly clunky about its digital products, like a story about an avalanche in Washington State called "Snow Fall," which had generated endless self-congratulations and prize honors, but felt utterly alien to the light and fast-moving style of the internet, disconnected from readers' desires.

What we'd missed was a cliché: culture eats strategy for breakfast. Arthur Sulzberger had shifted the company's strategy when he chose to put the paywall in place. But what Perpich and Dolnick and A. G. Sulzberger spent their time discussing was something different: changing the company culture. "Snow Fall," I later realized, had been important not because it was interesting to readers, but because it persuaded *New York Times* editors that the internet also could aspire to the *Times*' core goal, top-quality journalism. The report's leak—and the fact that the heir apparent had been leading it—finally sent the kind of political and cultural signal that it takes to shift a giant institution.

The young Sulzberger returned to the newsroom nervously after the leak for a series of long conversations with reporters and editors. One of the first people he ran into was David Barstow, a veteran investigative reporter with a stack of Pulitzers who embodied the *Times'* old print values. "I've read every word," Barstow told the nervous Sulzberger, "and when I started I was sure I'd disagree with 85 percent." Sulzberger waited. "You've sold me, and I agree with 85 percent." Barstow found the report powerful because it was so *Times*ian. "The report was just full of great, holy shit reporting. For people like me who are creatures of the old world, this is exactly what we needed." More farsighted old-timers worried about something else: that an influx of people and ideas from the internet, whose allegiance was more to the online conversation than to the *Times*, would radically change the culture, a worry nobody really took seriously at the time.

When Jonah came by the *Times* office, they were still laughing nervously at themselves, still unsure if the changes they'd decided to implement would work. But it was the last moment in which the direction of history seemed clear. That fall, it would become evident that BuzzFeed had begun to crash into the ceiling of the advertising business that was left for publishers after Google and Facebook swallowed most of the business. Jonah would, for the first time, hear his own board push him to cut costs, and resist that suggestion. And just six days after that friendly gathering on Eighth Avenue, and about a mile north, Donald Trump would descend the golden escalator into national politics, American liberals would become desperate to understand what was happening, and the machine Perpich and his colleagues had just built to sell them subscriptions would kick into high gear. The *Times* would master the internet, and be transformed by it, while, in a new cultural moment, BuzzFeed struggled to find its place and Gawker collapsed.

....

Gawker on Trial

As Jonah preened before the *Times*, and even as he and BuzzFeed began to reckon with the limits of what traffic could bring, Nick's world began to fall apart. At first, Nick hadn't bought into the ominous conspiracy theories about Hulk Hogan's lawsuit, treating it instead as yet another chapter in his own self-dramatizing history. And yet this one was different. Nick kept losing. On January 13, 2016, Pinellas-Pasco circuit court judge Pamela Campbell ruled against Gawker's final attempt to dismiss the case. The trial was to begin March 7, in the county seat of Clearwater, Florida.

The AJ Daulerio who arrived in Clearwater had lost some of his swagger. His triumphs at Deadspin and Gawker had gone hand in hand with a decade of all-night drug binges and a kind of hard living that friends at first considered magnetic and then increasingly scary and sad. He still had that great, climactic journalistic run to his name, and his relationship with Nick—he thought—was intact. But he didn't have much else. In August of 2015, after waking up to see a bong, bottles of alcohol, and cocaine on his coffee table, he checked into a detox facility in New

Jersey, only to return ten days later to the alcohol and cocaine and pills. AJ started to get scared. In October, he signed up for Harp Treatment Center in West Palm Beach. Lockhart Steele, his old Gawker colleague, with whom he'd spent late nights doing lines and talking strategy years earlier, took him to the JetBlue terminal at JFK. AJ's career was going nowhere; he was piecing his life back together when the trial began.

The night before the trial, Nick watched the Hogan video for the first time. The squeamishness that had prevented him from watching it back in 2012, he realized, "should have been a warning." Instead, he'd celebrated the traffic. Still, Nick gave no indication that his view of AJ's work, or of their relationship, had changed. They sat together every day for three weeks in the airless Clearwater courtroom. And they took the same stand, in front of a green marble wall, AJ and then Nick, in a case that seemed less and less about the specifics of Hulk Hogan and his best friend's wife, and more and more about how twelve citizens of Pinellas and Pasco Counties felt about what Gawker had been doing all along. Hogan's lawyers were not pursuing Gawker for the charge typically leveled at the media, defamation. The core claim was that the site had invaded Hogan's privacy. In 2012, it might have been hard to identify with the professional wrestler. Back then, most people didn't have their own sex tapes—which were exotic, made by celebrities, and often released on purpose with a nod and a wink. But by 2016, the jury in Clearwater was made up of people with their own iPhones, and perhaps their own nude images they wouldn't want exposed. The explosion of digital images had forced everyone to reckon with the notion of privacy, and to feel they needed to protect it. The idea of publishing someone else's sex tape—a curiosity a decade ago, and a traffic geyser five years ago—had become repellent to ordinary Americans.

Nick tried to explain himself, to make his passion for the truth, whatever it might be, something a regular person could relate to. Slender and graying, his hair cut short, he explained to the Florida jurors that he'd fallen in love with digital media as a child. He'd loved it so much that, as a boy in Budapest, he'd "get the train to Vienna to pick up *Wired* magazine." He couldn't have seemed more foreign if he'd tried.

Nick sat beside AJ without knowing his old editor had already doomed their case. Back in 2013, exhausted from his usual lack of sleep and substance abuse, AJ had sat through hours of a deposition with Bollea's lawyer, Charles Harder. AJ had seemed incredulous that it was necessary, and had dressed more to go out partying than to sit in a conference room. His white shirt was open an extra button at the neck. He snapped when Harder asked him if he could "imagine a situation where a celebrity sex tape would not be newsworthy."

"If they were a child," Daulerio responded.

"Under what age?" Harder asked.

"Four," he said.

Bollea's lawyers liked that exchange so much, they played the recording twice during the trial, and grilled AJ about it on the stand. He'd put on a suit for the trial, and he looked like a kid at a wedding, his collar uncomfortably askew. "If I had the opportunity to insert that I was joking, I should have," he said. Nick, for his part, hadn't seen it coming. The lawyers had told him and AJ not to discuss their testimony with one another. "Look, AJ was AJ—even in his deposition," Nick told me later. "His dark humor didn't work as well as it did on a blog."

Daulerio had spent weeks in rehab in West Palm Beach and was on a bumpy road to sobriety by the time they replayed the video in the courtroom. By now, he was sober in both senses of the word. But the jury was visibly appalled. AJ's joke seemed to stand in for all of Gawker's apparent depravity. One juror even asked if it was possible to sentence someone in a civil suit to community service.

On March 18, 2016, the jury ruled in Bollea's favor, awarding him

$140 million. Nick couldn't make the numbers add up and had to put his sites up for sale. And then Peter Thiel stepped out from behind the curtain. Gawker's real adversary, the one paying the bills and steering Hogan's strange and vindictive strategy, hadn't been Hogan, local Florida boy and flag-waving caricature of Americana. It had been Thiel, remote and nerdy, whose passions included the dream of "seasteading," founding a new civilization on the water that would be beyond not just prying eyes but also national laws and borders. Hiding behind a web of lawyers and hangers-on, Thiel had been feeling out Gawker's weaknesses since 2007; in 2011, he'd started throwing spaghetti at the wall, trying to find and finance legal action that would cripple the media company without getting blood on his own hands. In 2016, he'd finally gotten lucky, as Gawker's recklessness left it wide open to Hogan's claim.

While AJ was at the center of the trial, it had always been, for Thiel, about Nick himself. Owen Thomas's fawning effort to out him was never what bothered Thiel. What had stuck with him had been the Denton comment, the one calling him "strange" and "paranoid," Thiel told the writer Ryan Holiday years later for a book called *Conspiracy*. His vendetta, he said, was "never about the Owen Thomas article. It was the Nick Denton comment." That, Thiel said, had been the real last straw.

Nick didn't buy it. He speculated that the vendetta was really about his coverage of Thiel's investments. Or maybe, Nick thought more fatalistically, about the "techlords" asserting their supremacy, about power acting as power does. But Thiel, Holiday wrote, had simply concluded that Nick was a monster, and believed that "Denton's unending lust for secrets, for attention, his strange insistence that he was a technology entrepreneur and not a journalist, and his need to be feared instead of respected were tells of sociopathy."

In the new American system of wealth and power, Thiel had the capacity to destroy a media company he didn't like, and he'd found a case, and a jury, that echoed his sympathies. And so, finally, on August 16, 2016, the Spanish-language TV company Univision, which had quixotic online ambitions, bought all Nick's sites except Gawker for $135 million. Gawker itself, a nest of legal liability, remained behind. On August 22, 2016, Nick published a characteristically defiant and uncharacteristically sentimental essay on the site's legacy. "Gawker shed an enormous amount of light. It punctured hypocrisy and mocked the ridiculous," he wrote. The site's bitter end "turns out to be the ultimate Gawker story. It shows how things work," he concluded.

In the post, he went out of his way to praise fifteen of the site's stars of the previous fourteen years.

Daulerio, broke and unemployed, read and reread the essay, looking for his name. Nick had been his boss for ten years, his co-defendant in Florida. Daulerio had been a guest at Nick's grand wedding in 2014 at the American Museum of Natural History, and Nick had even invested in *Ratter*. Nick had been "the most important person in my life," AJ wrote four years later, still wrestling with what Nick and Gawker had meant to him. But his old boss mentioned him only in passing, as the "former editor, who wrote the story about Hogan." Being left out of that final post "blew a hole through my chest."

Nick soon settled with Hogan and shuttered Gawker. AJ was left for a time with a $115 million dollar lien against his empty bank account. In rehab, Daulerio had learned to write down things that made him angry and then toss the paper in the trash. Over and over he'd write "Nick Denton" on a piece of paper, crumple it, and throw it away.

For his part, Nick didn't really blame AJ. "It was my traffic bonus system—give the punters what they want—that set AJ's incentives," he reflected later. And he didn't really blame himself, either, didn't agonize about the end of his empire—at least not overtly. Some of Nick's staff wondered quietly if he hadn't wanted to lose the case and end that chapter of his life. The verdict seemed, if anything, to speed up the journey that Nick had begun when he met Derrence. Over the next few years, you could still find him on Gchat; he'd still respond to emails. But he'd had to sell his beloved loft, and many of the people who had known Nick over the years began to wonder where he'd gone. He hadn't moved on to his next thing, or to anything. He'd mostly avoided interviews. And, physically, he'd vanished.

....

Sentiment

Eli Pariser, of MoveOn and Upworthy, had gotten a glimpse of the angry heart of Facebook early on, when he heard about the intense clusters of engagement that sites like breitbart.com produced—though they didn't seem to come yet with any of the original crucial commodity, traffic. Those sites didn't have anything like the Dress. Now Jonah and I got a look in ourselves, after Donald Trump entered the campaign for president, through a small window Facebook opened into its system. Just before the presidential campaign, the company's mild-mannered liaison to an increasingly scared and furious news industry, Jason White, called me up with an interesting offer: Facebook was trying out a new formula for measuring the "sentiment" that users felt toward the candidates who were gearing up to run for president the following year. Facebook would give it to us on a nearly exclusive basis, presumably because its PR team figured that Jonah and I were friendlier to the company, and would have a better understanding of how it actually worked, than many of our rivals.

I wasn't under any illusions about why they were offering us this valuable new stream of data. It was PR for their ad business. Facebook wanted to prove to candidates and campaigns that it was a real player in politics—that going through its platform was a better use of your money than buying television ads. Facebook wasn't just the place for spontaneous youth movements. It was a place you could practice politics, rally passions, raise money, maybe even change minds. Of course, Facebook's pitch matched our agenda, and our beliefs—that social media was the real show, not a sideshow, and that BuzzFeed was on track to replace the struggling *New York Times* for a new generation of readers, not just to supplement it. That didn't seem crazy. Jonah was already raising more money and beginning to talk to NBCUniversal about a round that would value the company at $1.7 billion, about the same as the market capitalization of the *Times*.

So I announced our partnership with fanfare. "We at BuzzFeed News are deeply excited," I wrote, to have "a powerful new window into the largest political conversation in America." I painted a picture of the coming presidential election and proclaimed that "the viral, mass conversation about politics on Facebook and other platforms has finally emerged as a third force"—after television advertising and independent journalism—"in the core business of politics, mass persuasion." This was a new medium for emotion and apparent spontaneity, I wrote, an opportunity to campaign in the language of "an inexpensive new viral populism." And I declared, a bit triumphantly, that Americans would be getting their news from trusted friends, not suspect, one-way old-fashioned media, and that "the way people share will shape the outcome of the presidential election."

I knew I was doing Facebook's advertising sales team a solid here, and I heard later that they'd loved my essay. That was why they were sharing the data with us in the first place. But I believed what I'd written. And what was there to worry about? The early data Facebook shared contained few surprises. Familiar figures like Paul Ryan and Condoleezza Rice received favorable chatter, firebrands like Ted Cruz and Chris Christie saw more mixed conversations. It did seem notable how much more positive the conversations were about Vice President Joe Biden than Secretary of State Hillary Clinton, but I didn't dwell on it.

Through the spring of 2015, we watched the data roll in and wrote about the scraps of insight it offered. Then on March 2, the *Times* broke the news that "Hillary Rodham Clinton exclusively used a personal email account to conduct government business as secretary of state . . . and may have violated federal requirements that officials' correspondence be retained as part of the agency's record." Facebook lit up. On March 1, a normal day, about 151,000 people on the platform had been talking about Hillary Clinton, the data said, 54 percent of them positively. By March 3, the number had spiked to one million, and it stayed there, or higher, through March 6. And in that far larger sample, the 49 percent of negative comments outweighed the 47 percent positive ones.

It wasn't quite like the quiz that told you you should live in Wyoming, but Hillary Clinton had the same kind of Facebook magic. And the emotion she seemed to inspire was primarily negative. The stories about her that stuck were the ones that deepened Americans' anger at an elite that played by different rules than they did. Facebook wasn't a place where you'd figure out the details of what, if anything, was in those emails, or where you'd lend a sympathetic ear to Clinton's explanations that after years of unfair scrutiny by Republicans, she'd wanted a little privacy. But Hillary sure could drive engagement. Another data set in April showed Clinton blowing away even Bernie Sanders by the measure of how many people were talking about her. The problem was that it was mostly unfavorable. But so far, she was the only candidate anyone really seemed to be talking about at all.

That changed on June 16, when Donald Trump began his presidential campaign. His staff had planned remarks, but what dominated media coverage was what he said when he strayed from them: "When Mexico sends its people, they're not sending their best," he said. "They're bringing drugs, they're bringing crime, they're rapists." He dominated the media coverage and immediately shot to the top of the polls. In the Facebook data, we suddenly realized that the other Republicans whose numbers we'd been tracking were barely represented at all, that we were looking at something new. More than ten million Americans were talking about Donald Trump on Facebook in the first week of July. The other hot Republicans—Ben Carson and Ted Cruz—were struggling to reach one million. BuzzFeed's political editor, Katherine Miller, tried to explain what was happening to our readers: "Imagine the Hulk doing a cannonball into a pool and, as a result, all the other people and water in that pool being catapulted from it, so that the only thing left is the Hulk."

And then—it stayed that way. Through the summer and early fall, we stopped writing about the Facebook data because it didn't say anything new. Americans were talking about only two people: Hillary Clinton and Donald Trump. The conversation about Clinton tended to be negative. And nobody could get enough of Donald Trump. In September, a Facebook employee managing the program called Miller to tell her that Facebook were pausing it to upgrade its sentiment analysis, and promised to get back to delivering the data soon. By then, Donald Trump was running wild on the platform. I was a little surprised, but I assumed they'd stopped sending over the news because they found it a little embarrassing: Facebook, whose young employees in Palo Alto prided themselves on being the home of the liberal populism of Oscar Morales and Barack Obama, had been overrun by the angry baby boomers who loved Donald Trump. They were the ones spending hours on Facebook, clicking on the ads that were turning Facebook into one of the world's most lucrative and valuable businesses. (Much later, a Facebook employee told me it had simply been too much trouble to maintain the data, though I'm slightly skeptical that that's the full story.)

While Facebook may have been worried by 2015, it certainly wasn't taking any kind of dramatic action to stop the spread of a new online politics centered on engagement, conflict, and outrage. For all the tweaking, Facebook's engineers had never figured out a way to tamp down the worrying flood of attention that had once fed a spirited debate about the color of a dress—not without giving up users' valuable attention, and the money that came with it. Now screaming matches over race and immigration and sexism appeared in the same numerical patterns. If Facebook had kept sharing its data with us, we would have seen two things that only became public years later in a series of apologies, leaks, and government reports. First, that Donald Trump dominated the platform. His style of provocation, and his attacks on immigration in particular, were exactly the sort of thing that got people talking. His supporters loved it, of course, and shared enthusiastically. But if you hated Trump and everything that he stood for, and expressed as much in a Facebook comment—well, that was engagement, too, a signal to Facebook to spread his message further.

Donald Trump was made for Facebook. So was another type of content: attacks on Hillary Clinton. Among the first to discover that fact were a handful of teenagers in Veles, Macedonia, a small city on the Vardar River, who wanted some spare cash. Their discovery was of a sort of arbitrage: if they could direct Americans, rather than Macedonians, to their websites, they'd be getting paid in dollars, not denars. And even as American publishers had begun to suspect that traffic wasn't quite like oil—a limited commodity that would hold its value—and we were beginning to grumble about trading print dollars for digital pennies, well, digital pennies were still pretty good in Veles. The teenagers created websites like worldpoliticus.com and told people on Facebook exactly what they wanted to hear: for instance, that Hillary Clinton would soon be indicted. "Your Prayers Have Been Answered," declared one headline. Another falsely reported that the pope had endorsed Donald Trump.

They weren't the only ones to reach that insight, of course. After the election, Facebook admitted it had let the operators of a building full of paid trolls in Saint Petersburg, Russia, pay the platform in rubles to promote attacks on Clinton. Trump's own campaign team followed Facebook's advice and ginned up its supporters with the inflammatory messages they'd be most likely to click, to buy a "Make America Great Again" hat and get on the campaign's list of potential donors.

There would, after the 2016 election, be a whole new genre of articles and books explaining how Donald Trump won. Some of them suggested that he, or the Russians, or a shady consulting firm his campaign employed called Cambridge Analytica, had found a way to manipulate Facebook and manipulate us through it. But the Russians had spent a trivial amount of money, just $100,000 all told. An exhaustive British government report found little evidence that Cambridge Analytica could actually deliver on its promises to customers. Trump's own campaign had spent about seven hundred times as much as the Russians on Facebook ads. And Trump's campaign strategy—of riling up his supporters, rather than trying to convert moderates—had indeed meant that he got far more clicks on his advertisements than Clinton. But that had been a matter of political strategy, not a technical trick. Still, the explanation that some clever gimmick had won Trump his campaign suited Facebook well, and in its eagerness to make the forty-fifth president seem like an aberration, Facebook embraced the theory, distributing an internal memo claiming that Trump "got elected because he ran the single best digital ad campaign" the company had ever seen.

A former Facebook employee, Antonio García Martínez, may have hit closer to the truth in an essay he wrote for *Wired*. "A canny marketer with really engaging (or outraging) content can goose their effective purchasing power" in Facebook's advertising engine, he wrote—because people will simply click their ads more. This, he wrote, was why Trump "was a perfect candidate for Facebook."

It's understandable that panicked American Democrats and incredulous journalists were looking for the secret explanation for Trump's victory. But if you zoom out from the United States in the middle of the second decade of the twenty-first century and look more widely, it's hard to credit such theories. Perhaps Trump had some special sauce, or some special help—but then why would India's right-wing populist strongman Narendra Modi similarly have become, as it was said, "King of Facebook"? Or how did Brazil's Jair Bolsonaro come to dominate the platform? What explains the social media power of Rodrigo Duterte in the Philippines, or the surprise, Facebook-powered victory of Brexit in Great Britain? Trump was part of a pattern of confrontational, combative right-wing populism that swept the platform and the world. These leaders' success on Facebook was no more complicated than their success on the mainstream media: they fed controversy and engagement. But while CNN and other mainstream broadcasters eventually began to rein in their own hunger for ratings as they saw Trump exploit their airtime to project a message that painted his enemies—and, ironically, those very television networks—as enemies of the state, Facebook had no comparable mechanism. Facebook measured engagement, and elevated it. It seemed perfectly logical if you were working on the internet then, doing your best to make your own posts generate engagement and go viral. Trump wasn't *doing* anything to game Facebook. He simply *was* what Facebook liked.

A few weeks before the election, I got a lesson on this phenomenon in person from Steve Bannon, who had taken over breitbart.com when

Andrew died, then left it to go chair Donald Trump's campaign. He'd been interested in Jonah since his first glimpse at the business of *The Huffington Post*, so I'd been invited to Trump Tower to exchange notes with him. I walked past the golden escalator and rode an elevator up to an empty conference room to find the chairman alone, and not in any particular rush. Bannon exuded utter confidence, but it didn't feel like a winning campaign. He didn't seem to have much to do. And he told me he was puzzled by BuzzFeed. Breitbart hadn't just chosen Trump, he told me, based on the candidate's political views. Bannon and his crew had seen the energy Trump carried, the engagement he'd driven, and attached themselves to it. BuzzFeed, in Bannon's view, had failed to recognize that Bernie Sanders could generate the same energy, the same engagement. Why hadn't we gone all in for Bernie? he asked me.

Jonah had sometimes asked the same thing. He, too, saw that the energy was on the militant left, and that our staff's sympathies—and his own—mostly leaned the same way. But our journalistic scruples, the impulse toward fairness and away from propaganda, sometimes handcuffed our drive for traffic. Our news operation had gone from being scorned and yoked to the social web to being well regarded among journalists, and even winning the occasional prize—but we were spending more and more money on journalism to maintain the same level of traffic, and though he and I didn't talk about it much, Jonah and I both knew that our existing approach to news depended on the rest of the business remaining strong. But Jonah had bet on me and on that style of news, and so Jonah let me win the occasional skirmishes with our publisher, Dao Nguyen, when he eyed the traffic that a breathless Bernie Sanders fan post might get. I told Bannon that we came from a different journalistic tradition, and we valued it. That answer didn't satisfy any of us much.

After Donald Trump won the Republican nomination, and as he battled it out with Hillary Clinton for the White House, BuzzFeed published another post that stuck in Jonah's mind, one that he thought kind of explained the whole thing. The post was about olives, the salty little snacks that some people love, and some hate. "Let's Talk about How Disgusting Olives Are," read the headline, by a young writer in our new Toronto office. "There are two kinds of people in this world: people who know that olives are gross, and psychopaths."

The post was everything that Facebook favored. It was divisive. It baited you into talking about it. It got up in your face. Over the next few years, it kept popping up in BuzzFeed's statistics, going viral over and over. Its last line read: "Death to olives. 💀"

29

The Dossier

Gawker was gone by January of 2017, but I told my deputy, Shani Hilton, that I could hear its phantom footsteps as I looked at the thirty-five-page document I was hiding on a top shelf in my bedroom in Brooklyn. Washington, DC, and newsrooms around the world, were buzzing about the document, but most Americans had no idea it existed. It was the sort of thing Gawker had been created to publish, and I almost couldn't believe that nobody had put it out yet, that the task might wind up falling to me.

For most of the story of internet media, its origins, characters, and ideologies, I've been a secondary character, at best. I had admired Jessica Coen's Gawker, and back in late 2004 had the modest realization that you could use the same tools—the instant publishing, the obsessive updates—for scoopy political reporting with more new information and less attitude. I started a series of reported political blogs in New York and then, in 2007, got a call from the co-founder of a new website called *Politico* whose founders aimed to blend aggressive insider reporting with Nick Denton's core insight: in the newspaper era, the best stories were sometimes the ones reporters told one another in bars, rather than the ones they printed. Then, in 2012, I was pulled to the cutting edge of the next trend, social media, first by my own obsession with Twitter, and then by Jonah's decision to hire me to help him build a news operation for what was then called the "social web," though neither of us saw clearly where it was going. And so I've popped up here and there in this story, sometimes with my face pressed against the glass of the cooler Gawker universe, sometimes as a middleman in journalists' complicated negotiations with Facebook. But on the internet, everyone gets to be the main character occasionally, and my time came when BuzzFeed News decided to publish a document that would become known as the Dossier.

Although Nick had abruptly exited the scene in the middle of 2016 when he lost the Hulk Hogan lawsuit, I was still carrying quite a bit of his DNA. In particular, I had deeply internalized his view that the job of journalists in the twenty-first century was to reject the patronizing gatekeepers who thought they knew what was best, and simply to print what we had.

I first got wind of the Dossier after a BuzzFeed News reporter, Ken Bensinger, got an unusual invite to a small gathering at a hilltop mansion in Sonoma County, north of San Francisco. He'd been invited on behalf of an old acquaintance, Glenn Simpson, a onetime journalist who had become a kind of private investigator and co-founded the firm Fusion GPS, whose half dozen members were meeting in Sonoma. Ken got lost and showed up late, finding a boisterous, all-male affair: plenty of booze, hunks of meat on the grill, some weed being smoked outside. Simpson drew him into a conversation about a mutual acquaintance, a former British spy named Christopher Steele. Simpson then told Ken something he didn't know: Steele had been working the case of the president-elect, Donald Trump, and he'd assembled evidence that Trump had close ties to the Kremlin—including a claim that the Kremlin had a lurid video of Trump that would come to be known as the "pee tape."

Ken told Simpson's story to our investigations editor Mark Schoofs, who told me about it. Simpson wouldn't give Ken the document, and neither would Steele. It was merely high-grade Washington gossip, irresistible chatter. On December 15, 2016, at BuzzFeed's Christmas party at Brooklyn Bowl, Ken told Jonah that he'd heard something big was coming on Trump.

I heard about the report again over lunch in Brooklyn Heights, when a peculiar character in Hillary Clinton's orbit passed through town. David Brock had been an anti-Clinton journalist in the 1990s. Now he was Hillary's fiercest ally, a genius at raising money for Democratic groups. He showed up at a café on Montague Street a couple of days before Christmas wearing a coat with a lavish fur collar, stashing full shopping bags beside the table. Brock was consumed with the mission of stopping Donald Trump, manic; he was headed, it turned out, for a massive heart attack. He wanted to get the word out about a secret that was circulating among media and political elites, a dossier of allegations about Donald Trump's ties to Russia. David didn't have the document, he said. But he knew *The Washington Post* did, and so did *The New York Times*, as well as a handful of other chosen outlets. Politicians had it, too, he told me, and spies, and as far as I could figure out, so did everyone, it seemed, except the reading public. And me. That, I believed—I'd learned from Nick—made it exactly the sort of thing you should publish. I had learned, too, about the viral power of an object, from an old video of Barack Obama to the Dress, something that readers would fixate on and pass hand to hand. The Dossier was both; the Dossier would be a great story, a journalistic and traffic sensation. And Ken was already close. All he needed was the name that Brock had given me, the name of a confidant of Senator John McCain, David Kramer.

We were hardly the first journalists to get the document—but we may have been the first to get it without promising to keep it secret.

Simpson, whose firm was working for the Democratic National Committee, had months earlier summoned the leading lights of Washington journalism, outlet by outlet, to a tatty hotel off Washington's Dupont Circle. There, Steele calmly shared his shocking suggestion that Donald Trump had been compromised by the Russian government. The journalists came from *The New York Times* and *The New Yorker*, the *Journal*, ABC News, and CNN. Michael Isikoff, who had tangled with Matt Drudge over the Monica Lewinsky story twenty-eight years earlier, got an invite. BuzzFeed did not.

Simpson "loved the cloak-and-dagger world" of espionage, Barry Meier would later write in an unflattering book about the private intelligence industry. He saw himself as a puppet master, and had intended to remain invisible while journalists published the fruits of his and Steele's research. But to Simpson's frustration, those reporters whom he invited to a tatty Washington hotel, the Tabard Inn, couldn't confirm the shocking allegations of the Dossier—that the Russian government might have a video of Donald Trump cavorting with prostitutes in the Ritz-Carlton Moscow, and that one of his top aides had held secret meetings with Russian officials in Prague. The reporters in turn were bound by their clandestine agreement with Simpson not to write about the Dossier itself, its author and promoter, or its path through the American government, even as all those things became equally interesting stories.

By late December, Steele's dossier was in the hands not just of journalists but also of key political leaders like Senate Minority Leader Harry Reid and Senator John McCain. Reid had even written a mysterious letter to FBI director James Comey days before the November election, saying, "It has become clear that you possess explosive information about close ties and coordination between Donald Trump, his top advisors, and the Russian government." He demanded to know why Comey—who had just held a press conference revealing an investigation into Hillary Clinton's emails—would "resist calls to inform the public of this critical information."

Finally, on December 29, David Kramer invited Ken to his office at the McCain Institute. He then did something careful Washington insiders do: he left Ken alone in the room with the document for twenty minutes, without, in Ken's view, giving clear instructions about whether the reporter could make a copy. Ken took a picture of every page, and when Kramer returned, Ken went to a Le Pain Quotidien nearby and read through it on his phone, before sending it on his WhatsApp to Schoofs, who sent it on to me. Kramer later denied he'd allowed Ken to copy it, though we believed the denial was a fig leaf, and Kramer had to revise his own testimony on the point. I printed out the thirty-five-page document that showed Kramer's yellow highlighting and pored over it, looking for details that we could confirm, or knock down. Then I hid my marked-up copy in the back of a closet. We scrambled—as the other news outlets that had the document had done—sending reporters around the world to check out the details; one went to sixty-one Prague hotels to ask if anyone had seen the Trump aide Michael Cohen.

On January 10, I turned to a television in the BuzzFeed newsroom to see CNN's Jake Tapper interviewing his colleagues about a big scoop: "CNN has learned that the nation's top intelligence officials provided information to President-Elect Donald Trump and to President Barack Obama last week about claims of Russian efforts to compromise President-Elect Trump," he declaimed. The briefing, CNN reported, was "based on memos compiled by a former British intelligence operative whose past work US intelligence officials consider credible." And, the network said—ominously, and hazily—they included "allegations that Russian operatives claimed to have compromising personal and financial information about Mr. Trump."

I heard the Gawker footsteps more loudly then. This document was in circulation, affecting the course of public policy, being passed hand to hand among the chattering classes. It had enormous explanatory power when it came to understanding just what had been happening at the highest levels of American government: *that's* what Harry Reid had been talking about, and why John McCain seemed so alarmed. Now that CNN had done the equivalent of waving the document in the air, teasing its "credible" revelations—surely someone, soon, would let regular people in on the secret? I knew what I thought we should do, but asked Hilton, Schoofs, and Miriam Elder, the former *Guardian* Moscow correspondent editing our international coverage, if we should publish it. Years later, Schoofs recalled that I was "determined to be first and convinced to the point of obsessed that somebody else was going to publish it first." I felt the pressure physically. I was, Hilton told me later, "very tense, like a spring." They all agreed the document itself was news.

We stood around Mark's laptop as he typed into the BuzzFeed publishing system that had been built for memes and captions, but could now publish elegant paragraphs in serif fonts. Ken, on speakerphone, warned that we could get sued; I too-curtly told him he wasn't a lawyer, and that I wasn't asking him for legal advice. Then we turned to writing. "A dossier making explosive—but unverified—allegations" had been in wide circulation. The allegations were "specific, unverified, and potentially unverifiable," we wrote. Miriam had been examining the document since the previous day, and had noticed a couple of odd, minor false notes in the discussion of Russian specifics. She took a turn at the laptop. "It is not just unconfirmed: It includes some clear errors," we noted. I sent a copy to our in-house lawyer, Nabiha Syed, for a final review. By 6:20 p.m., we had 350 careful words explaining what we knew, and we decided to put Mark's and Miriam's bylines on it as well as Ken's, with an eye to shielding him from what we knew would be a fierce backlash.

About an hour after Tapper's segment concluded, we published the short article. In the best traditions of the internet, and of Nick Denton's internet in particular, we uploaded the full document as well, as a pdf, free to travel—as I should have known—without the careful disclaimer in the article that linked it. We showed people the strange and intriguing document that elites had tried to keep from them, and we stated plainly what we knew and what we didn't. Then I went to stand in the middle of the newsroom and watch the traffic flow. This was the nicest of the BuzzFeed newsrooms, before or since, designed when traffic seemed equivalent to money and we thought we could afford a whole floor of our own, branded black and red in a deliberate complement to BuzzFeed's cheery red branding. The west end of the long room looked out over Park Avenue South, and on the windowless wall on the east end was a giant screen displaying the traffic to our biggest story. For the next hour, Hilton recalls, my eyes flicked between the big screen, where I watched the Dossier go viral, and my phone, where I watched it dominate Twitter. The tweet that came up the most included a screenshotted excerpt from the Dossier's first memo. It described a "perverted" scene at the Ritz-Carlton Moscow, where Trump allegedly hired "a number of prostitutes to perform a 'golden showers' (urination) show in front of him. The hotel was known to be under FSB control with microphones and concealed cameras in all the main rooms to record anything they wanted to." That excerpt was shared and shared again. Our caveats didn't always accompany it.

The news organizations that had accepted Simpson's invitation to the Tabard Inn were particularly furious. It was somewhat, I believe, because they had been boxed out of covering the real story by their agreements with a source, but also in large part because they genuinely thought what we'd done was wildly irresponsible: floating inflammatory, salacious, and unverified claims about the president-elect of the United States.

The *Times* published an article connecting what we'd done to "fake news," and quoted its executive editor, Dean Baquet, saying, "We, like others, investigated the allegations and haven't corroborated them, and we felt we're not in the business of publishing things we can't stand by." (Soon after that story was published, I got a conciliatory email from Baquet, saying he realized it had been a close call.)

Jake Tapper sent me a furious email that evening saying that publishing the document "makes the story less serious and credible," which was probably true—but if keeping a document secret makes it more credible, you might have a problem. Tapper also said he wished we had, at least, waited until morning to give his news the attention it deserved and ample space from the messy document on which it was based: "Collegiality wise it was you stepping on my dick," he wrote.

I'd expected that backlash, and at first welcomed it. I thought we were on the right side of the decade-old conflict between the transparent new internet and a legacy media whose power came in part from the information they withheld. CNN's report had suggested some omniscient, mysterious intelligence report. The document itself was tangible and weird. Its big-picture claims about Russia's efforts to influence the American conversation through, for instance, amplifying the dissatisfaction of Bernie Sanders supporters with Hillary Clinton, made sense. Some of its specific allegations were lurid and hard—sometimes impossible—to verify. Trump's defenders, who had been facing a shadowy set of anonymous allegations, now had a name and specifics and were able to debunk some of the most outlandish.

And, of course, I loved the traffic. This was a huge revelation, a secret unveiled. My news operation, always jealously eyeing the clicks that came from silly lists and quizzes, finally had its version of the Dress. What made me uncomfortable was the gratitude. Mark's and Miriam's and my phones lit up with text messages from Democrats thanking us for publishing the Dossier—and revealing the depths of Trump's depravity that they already knew to be true. Hillary Clinton had never mastered social media; her supporters had never developed the dense networks of conversations, the memes and conspiracy theories, that powered the Trump movement. But now liberals, forming a nascent "resistance," were starting to build their own powerful narratives on social media that were sometimes more resonant than factual. And Donald Trump's aides, it seemed, were far more eager to focus on disclaiming the lurid allegations in the Dossier than on the messy, and very real, ties between his campaign manager, Paul Manafort, and a pro-Putin oligarch. The notion of a single, vast conspiracy seemed to answer liberals' desperate question of how Donald Trump could have been elected president. Russia clearly had helped. The WikiLeaks hack-and-dump operation was a crucial factor among many in a very close election. You didn't need to believe all the details in the Dossier to know those things.

But perhaps I should have thought a little more about WikiLeaks and anticipated that the people might share the document free of any context. A couple of weeks before the 2016 election, I'd attended a Trump rally in Edison, New Jersey, and on my way in I encountered a solitary Trump supporter chanting, "WikiLeaks! WikiLeaks!" I'd spent quite a bit of time reading through the midlevel campaign chatter, and I asked him which specific documents he thought painted Hillary Clinton in such a bad light. He didn't really know. I realized that I was looking at social media in real life, a man shouting information cast as a symbol of what he already believed about Clintonite corruption, not information meant to convey new knowledge. New reporting related to the Dossier, like when one BuzzFeed News reporter, Anthony Cormier, even persuaded Cohen to let him post a scan of his passport, didn't make a dent.

I watched with increasing discomfort as the Dossier helped lead the sort of educated Democrats who abhorred Trump supporters' crude

rants about mysterious "Clinton body count" murders and child sex
rings in Washington pizza joints into similar patterns of thought. They
read Steele's dossier; they connected the dots. They retweeted threads
about how the plane of a Russian oligarch—previously unknown to
them, now sinister—had made a mysterious stop in North Carolina.
They rallied behind Louise Mensch, a charismatic former British politician who was in New York to work for Rupert Murdoch and trying to
create a right-wing establishment answer to *The Huffington Post* called
Heat Street. It was far too late in the history of the internet, and of conservative American politics, though—her tony brand of conservatism
couldn't compete with breitbart.com and Benny Johnson in their fealty
to the new order of blunt right-wing populism. What Mensch had instead was a clubby British faith in the ability of some kind of deep state to
set things right—expose Donald Trump, *execute* Steve Bannon—whatever
it took.

From the fall of 2016, when she published an early scoop about the
FBI investigating Trump's Russia ties—a good guess or a good tip, nobody ever knew—until the next spring, Mensch seemed, to many liberals, to know what was up. She published an op-ed in *The New York
Times*, and appeared on MSNBC and *Real Time with Bill Maher*. I invited her into our newsroom, where she acted like a character in a movie.
She was glad we were talking, she told me, Mark, and Miriam, because
she might be dead by the end of the month. She made confident claims
about Donald Trump and Russia—though the evidence to prove it to us
was just out of reach. After she left, we sat down to discuss how to pursue
her tips. Miriam was skeptical. Imagine, she said, if this had been an old
guy with wild hair and a white button-down shirt, ranting about conspiracies, rather than a beautiful British politician? Imagine if she'd arrived with two paper bags full of files, not an iPhone? Weren't we just
dealing with a polished new kind of nut?

By April, Mensch was obviously out of control. I asked a BuzzFeed News reporter, Joe Bernstein, for quantification: he found that she had accused two hundred and ten people of being Russian agents. That included thirty-five American politicians and officials, twenty-six journalists, twenty-six organizations and companies, eighteen other Americans, and eighty random Twitter accounts. Sean Hannity and Bernie Sanders were on her McCarthy-style list. After we published those numbers, Mensch stopped getting invited on MSNBC. But on Twitter, she was giving many Democrats something they wanted to believe and to share. We didn't create Mensch and those like her by publishing the Dossier—but our decision certainly fed a deep and appealing belief that the American legal system would expose the conspiracies that were the only possible explanation for Trump's election.

I'd never printed wild claims like Mensch's. We'd been careful, I found myself having to remind people, to say we didn't know whether everything in the Dossier was true when we published it. I defended the decision in public, in a *New York Times* op-ed, and in a deposition, after a Russian man whom Steele had suggested was tied to the hack of the Democratic National Committee sued us. Months after we released the Dossier, Ben Sherwood came by my office at BuzzFeed. We'd met years earlier when he had been the Disney executive pushing the BuzzFeed deal, in the hope that BuzzFeed's social media–driven DNA would revive ABC News. Now he had left Disney to start a family sports platform. I told him that running BuzzFeed had gotten more difficult, with the complexities of management and the realities of digital advertising bearing down on me.

So what did I think now? he asked. Didn't I wish we'd done the Disney deal? "Would we have been able to publish the Dossier?" I asked. "Not in a million years," he told me. Then I told him I was glad we hadn't taken the money.

That was an easy position to take in 2017. It seemed reasonable to argue that publishing the Dossier had been, on balance, good for the country. It had blown wide open a Russia investigation, forced the question of just why Trump seemed so friendly to Vladimir Putin into the public eye. But while the biggest-picture claim—that the Russian government had worked to help Trump—was clearly true, the findings of Robert Mueller's investigation in April of 2019 did not support Steele's report. Indeed, it knocked down crucial elements of the Dossier, like Cohen's visit to Prague. Internet sleuths—followed by the federal prosecutor John Durham—poked holes in Steele's elaborate sourcing, suggesting he'd overstated the quality of his information.

And there had always been a more mundane version of the Trump-Russia story. Trump was the sort of destabilizing right-wing figure that Putin had covertly supported across Europe, and Trump's value wasn't related to a secret deal, but to the overt damage he did. And Trump, BuzzFeed News's Anthony Cormier and Jason Leopold discovered, had a more mundane interest in Russia as well: He had drawn up plans to build the biggest apartment building in Europe on the banks of the Moskva River. The Trump Organization planned to offer the $50 million penthouse to Vladimir Putin as a sweetener.

That real estate project wasn't mentioned anywhere in the Dossier. Yet it seemed to explain the same pattern of behavior, without the lurid sexual allegations or hints of devious espionage. And publishing the Dossier hadn't, in the end, been a dagger to Trump's heart. If anything, it had muddied up the less lurid revelations of his business dealings and his campaign manager's ties to Russia. An FBI agent who investigated Trump, Peter Strzok, later said the Dossier "framed the debate" in a way that ultimately helped Trump: "Here's what's alleged to have happened, and if it happened, boy, it's horrible—we've got a traitor in the White House. But if isn't true, well, then everything is fine."

It had been, Barry Meier wrote, "a media clusterfuck of epic propor-
tions." And the Dossier's overreaching allegation of a vast and perverse
conspiracy would "ultimately benefit Donald Trump."

I accept that conclusion. And yet, true to Nick's values that shaped
my career, I remain defensive of our decision. I find it easiest to explain
not in the grandiose terms of journalism, but the more direct language
of respect for your reader. Don't you, the reader, think you're smart
enough to see a document like that, understand that it is influential but
unverified, without losing your mind? Would you rather people like me
had protected you from seeing it? Tapper was furious at me, but his decision to report on the existence of the Dossier had made our choice
both inevitable and easier to explain. Imagine the alternative, a world in
which the American public knows that there is a secret document making murky allegations that the president has been compromised, a document being investigated by the FBI and briefed to two presidents, and
that everyone who is anyone has seen it—but that they can't. That would,
if anything, produce darker speculation, and more uncertainty. It might
have made the allegations seem more credible than, in the end, they
were. Jonah, too, believed in his bones in the case for sharing with our
audience what the old elites wouldn't let them see, and proved his tough-
ness as a publisher by standing behind us through a difficult series of
lawsuits. After we beat back a major lawsuit over the Dossier, he took me
out for Russian caviar.

We won the suits in part because we'd maintained our journalistic
distance. We argued, successfully, that we were not making these claims
ourselves; we were making the "fair report" of what amounted to a government document. We noted in court that we'd published the Dossier
while holding it at arm's length, noting that we hadn't been able to stand
up or knock down its claims—even if we had inadvertently launched a
million conspiracy theories in the process.

And that's the part of the Dossier's strange career that remains most disturbing to me. It's not simply, as Strzok notes, that the document helped Trump shrug off less extreme allegations about Russian assistance and other malfeasance. The document, like WikiLeaks' Clinton material, became a social media totem for the anti-Trump resistance. The reality of America in the late 2010s had rebutted Nick's and my win-win assurance that people could be trusted with a complex, contradictory set of information, and that journalists should simply print what they had, and revel, guilt-free, in the traffic. Instead, we seemed to be in an impossible, or dangerous, situation: the public had lost trust in institutions while simultaneously demanding those same institutions filter the swirl of claims that surround democracy's biggest decisions.

....

Exile

uzzFeed took Nick's side of the broader argument when we published the Dossier, but Nick was gone, and his feral minions, who would've shared the instinct to reveal everything, had scattered or grown up.

Nick had spent twenty years mining traffic, persuading younger men and women that it was a mirror of the human soul. Then he'd tried to ride the Facebook boom, even as he despised it: for the smarmy, BuzzFeedy nonsense it encouraged, for the venture capital it brought pouring in to his competitors, and for the way it seemed to rule out the possibility that his platform, Kinja, could really compete.

Gawker had fallen behind, too, even before Thiel's deathblow. It slid from the top of the traffic charts, behind *The Huffington Post* and BuzzFeed and others like them. Its contradictions—between Jezebel's feminist truths and the leering misogyny of the old blogosphere, between bloggers' knowing cynicism and the expensively won knowledge of journalists—began to weigh it down. The guilty pleasure of its rage was meant to be consumed privately; anger and snark weren't emotions you wanted to share on Facebook, except perhaps when you were rallying to a partisan political side. Nick, too, stepped back, finding love and weed and surprising his staff in those last years with some personal warmth.

And after the annus horribilis of 2016, when his company collapsed and Donald Trump became president, Nick had quietly slipped away, telling few of his old friends, to Zurich, where the banks keep their secrets and where he'd begun working with a designer and a programmer on what he hoped would be a new project. This one, finally, was firmly in tech, not media. Nick let go of a bit of his image management in Zurich, too, stopped giving interviews of any kind to reporters, with one exception: a curious Swiss journalist named Hannes Grassegger, who had himself played a role in the unraveling Facebook scandals, as the first to report on the wild claims being made by the chief of Cambridge Analytica. The pioneering web designer Oliver Reichenstein, who was working with Nick on the new project, had introduced him to the reporter, and Grassegger was fascinated by the sparks being thrown off America's internet media. He was delighted to learn that Nick—in his view the most prominent exile in Zurich and perhaps the first political refugee of the Trump era—would grant him an interview.

Nick, wearing a gray sweatshirt and sneakers, showed up early to their lunch at Napoli da Gerardo, a frescoed, gilded Italian restaurant near the Sihl River. He'd picked up the habit of punctuality in Zurich, he told Grassegger, along with an appreciation for the country's functioning government services that cut against his libertarian politics. Nick had a card for the national train service. He had turned fifty-one, and found that he loved sunbathing on the deck of the city's nineteenth-century public baths.

That summer, the media sensation was an anonymous document titled "Shitty Media Men," which accused dozens of men of everything from rape to undefined crimes of creepiness. Doree Shafrir, the former Gawker editor who helped start BuzzFeed News with me, had been the first to report on its existence. Nick had pioneered this sort of thing but, viewing it from afar, said he didn't like it. Sounding like the worst critics of the internet he helped build, he said the "competition for attention" had created something that reminded him of the French Revolution— the Terror, the lists, the mob calling for heads.

What he was working on now, Nick said, was the next thing. He'd always liked to communicate in writing, and enjoyed giving interviews via text message to Holiday, the author of *Conspiracy*. What about writing software based on text messages? Then the project started growing more complicated, and ambitious. What about a text-message based social network? This would be a new kind of app for collaborating, which—among other things—guaranteed privacy. The only way to publish anything from it would be by mutual consent. He'd ban anyone who posted a screenshot, and create a world free of trolls, zealots, and spammers, he told Grassegger. It was the kind of technology he'd always wanted to build.

(Nick was, as ever, a product junkie and a tinkerer. When I had coffee with him at Balthazar a few years later, he was still working on the project.)

The day after Christmas of 2017, Nick read a mea culpa by one of the great digital ad guys of his generation, Rick Webb, who was beating himself up over his blindness to the dangers of the new medium. The internet had become a "terrordome," not a utopia, Webb wrote. He'd bought into the 1990s prophecies of a new era of global freedom and connectedness; what he'd gotten was Donald Trump. Webb wasn't sure, knowing now what he'd known then, if he would have helped lead the charge onto the internet back in the 1990s.

Nick then was still tweeting occasionally, about Gawker's legacy or

Peter Thiel's hypocrisy. He seemed to sympathize with Webb's view of their generation's great mistake. The most generous way to see his internet generation, Nick tweeted after reading Webb's statement, was that "we were over-optimistic on the timeline to transparency and the utopia that would inevitably result." Even Nick Denton was disturbed by the forces he'd helped unleash. Looking for a precedent, Nick thought about the last revolution in information technology, which had happened just about two hundred miles north of Zurich, five hundred years earlier. The invention is now viewed as a crucial step in the long march of progress. But, Nick wrote, "between the Gutenberg Press and the Enlightenment came 200 years of religious war."

....

Down Arrow

I n 2016, the year Nick moved to Zurich, Jonah had moved to Los Angeles. He came to be closer to the company's new traffic source. On You-
Tube, BuzzFeed was surfing the attention earned by simple videos that
seemed to recapture the last flashes of a curious, open-minded, uncom-
plicated internet culture. Jonah and Andrea and their twins moved into
a Spanish revival house in Los Feliz, which a local real estate publication
described as "nice but not quite suitable for a high-profile CEO." It was a
short walk from the home of Ze Frank, the volatile and charismatic
figure who ran BuzzFeed's Hollywood video operation, and Ze's new son,
whom he'd named Jonah. And so BuzzFeed's center of gravity moved
west too.

These kinds of videos got an astounding number of views. It began
on YouTube, where BuzzFeed was getting one hundred million views a
month by 2014, but Facebook's insatiable appetite to swallow the internet
prompted the company to launch its own video player in 2015, setting off
a frantic competition to produce content for it. By 2015, Jonah was boast-
ing of a billion views a month. The competition between YouTube and

Facebook for eyeballs propelled BuzzFeed to its peak. On April 8, 2016, two BuzzFeed staffers in white sanitary suits transfixed the world by putting rubber bands around a watermelon in our New York cafeteria on live video, watching the view count grow above 800,000, until the fruit exploded. It also fueled power struggles between my team and Ze's. After an editor in New York began documenting the creation of silly foods—pizza rolls were a big one—in simple, wordless videos, the video makers in Los Angeles began cranking out similar ones, at a scale New York couldn't compete with. Tasty, as they branded the videos, became one of the biggest things on the internet, reaching 1.7 billion video views in September of 2016.

The videos made stars. The most famous were the "Try Guys," four goofy young men who tried out-of-character stunts—wearing heels, taking lie detector tests, or making meat pies in Australia. There was a cast of lower-profile characters—a tribe of LA misfits included a white rapper who went by the sobriquet Baked Alaska, and who had achieved mild fame on the short-video platform Vine by pouring milk on his head. They were trained to do whatever worked on YouTube. Another producer, a Black woman, made a video about stereotypes of Black people that many journalists on Twitter and at BuzzFeed found offensive; in a rare screaming match in one of our executive meetings, Ze defended the creative freedom of the woman who'd made the video, who had found an audience of people who found it compelling—a fact that the traffic reflected, even if elite journalists on Twitter didn't like it. I pushed him to bow to the criticism.

The numbers were enormous, dwarfing the traffic we'd been bragging about on the old internet. And yet, Jonah had begun to notice something alarming, slippery, about the commodity we'd been chasing all along. The more traffic you got, the less YouTube or Facebook paid you for each view. Beginning to feel like real celebrities, the video performers were expecting to be paid as such, but if BuzzFeed were going to oblige, it would be hard to scrape a profit out of the videos. The team in New York was seeing the same thing, as were our competitors across digital media. The company's revenues, which had been tracking BuzzFeed's traffic upward and to the right, threatened to flatten out.

Jonah was slow to recognize that the future he'd foreseen wasn't arriving in quite the manner he predicted. He and Jon Steinberg had, five years earlier, sold the industry on a new kind of "native advertising" built for social media. But BuzzFeed's revenues came in at just $170 million, as it became clear that advertisers weren't renewing the clever, expensive videos or complex, jokey posts that resulted. The company's new president, a hail-fellow-well-met sales executive named Greg Coleman who had once been president of *The Huffington Post*, had raised the idea of selling banner ads as early as 2015, but now retreated in the face of what seemed like BuzzFeed's "religious attachment" to doing something different. But the form of advertising that had been trendy and groundbreaking back in 2011 was now just a lot of work, particularly compared to pressing a button on Facebook. BuzzFeed had been planning to bring in $250 million in 2015; the company ended the year at just $170 million.

Jonah was struggling with the reality that he was accountable for a grim new metric: not traffic, but money. He'd been animated, and had animated those around him, with a belief in BuzzFeed's inevitable rise. Jonah had loved the viral arrow icon, white on a red background, from the moment Chris Johanesen first showed it to him in 2009. It starts at a steep angle and then jogs abruptly to the right and a bit down before resuming its steep upward slope. It had been the badge that appeared on viral content at first; gradually, it became the company's logo, etched in a giant red circle onto the wall of the canteen and the corner of every corporate presentation.

Jonah saw BuzzFeed's course in that arrow: zigzagging, but inevitably pointing upward. He'd detected the rise of social media way back in 2001, and in 2011 he'd filled BuzzFeed's sails with that powerful force. There might be a creak here or a rattle there. But he believed that nothing could really change the company's trajectory once it had begun rising. And for a while, that seemed hard to argue with. Everything he did—Ze's video team in Los Angeles, the newsroom full of journalists, the new BuzzFeed offices from Brazil to France to Japan—seemed just to broaden the sail, to keep us growing faster and faster. Jonah brushed off the occasional warnings. When a board member told him that international growth was harder than it looked, Jonah answered that this was a new era—that Facebook and Google and Pinterest had replaced the old headaches that came with trying to build a global media company, like setting up a printing plant in Paris or hiring drivers in São Paulo. When BuzzFeed's revenue came up $80 million short in 2015—well, that was just the downward tick of the arrow, and $170 million was still a lot of money!

But the arrow was starting to look like a flat line. Even as BuzzFeed reached more and more people on platforms like YouTube and Snapchat, traffic seemed to be losing value at the same rate. It might not have been fool's gold, exactly, but it wasn't solid. The thing with a commodity is that it needs to be limited to have real value. When it came to traffic, there was too much of it out there, and Facebook and Google were too good at selling theirs directly to advertisers. Jonah, who had been chasing traffic for more than a decade, was blindsided by this new reality. And while he and Dao dexterously zigged and zagged to keep money coming in from inexpensive quizzes and lists, the expensive journalism I loved and that made Jonah proud had become more conventional and pricier, further from our early idea of a news service whose front page was the social web. He and I had begun a long series of sometimes passive-aggressive conversations over who ought to be responsible for bringing in money. I resented his suggestion that I, the editor, should pay heed to finances; he expected me to see the need and step into the role. Board members cautioned first in 2015 and then more urgently in 2016 that this was the time for Jonah to start cutting costs—but fiscal responsibility was hardly the spirit of the era's venture-backed rocket ships.

Fortunately for Jonah, even as we at BuzzFeed became dimly aware that traffic's value was becoming unreliable, the slow-moving giants of old media still coveted it. Deciding to enter another round of investments, Jonah returned to NBC, whose CEO—like all media CEOs in that moment—was pleased to be able to show that he owned a piece of the new media boom, at numbers that were still a fraction of what conventional wisdom held was the dying old media business. On November 21, 2016, twelve days after Donald Trump was elected, NBC announced a second investment of $200 million, valuing BuzzFeed at $1.7 billion before the cash came in. It was a "flat round"—the share price hadn't increased since the last investment—which wasn't a great sign for a startup. But it was so far beyond the Disney offer from 2014 that it still seemed to affirm Jonah's decision to turn Iger down. The money was enough for us to keep paying the growing bills—for a staff of about 1,700, a dozen offices, and a culture that tried to keep up with the perks of the tech industry, from a frozen yogurt machine to lavish holiday parties. Above all, the money was supposed to transform BuzzFeed fully into a lucrative video company. In reality, it arrived just in time to prevent the floor from falling out. The money would provide the kind of cushion Nick Denton never had, a cushion that would save the company.

BuzzFeed wasn't the only company grappling with the devaluation of traffic. *The Huffington Post*, once a flagship purchase of a digital advertising company, now belonged to a telecom company, Verizon, which couldn't seem to make the ads it brought in pay for its operations. In January 2017, Eli Pariser sold off what was left of Upworthy. The digital media companies to watch, suddenly, were *The New York Times* and *The Washington Post*, whose chronicles of Donald Trump's excesses converted millions of readers into paying subscribers. Now the new publishers were copying them—*Business Insider* put up its paywall in 2017.

Jonah's confidence still wasn't paying off on BuzzFeed's revenues, even if the new money had bought ample breathing room. The NBC investment was followed quickly by the first layoffs in BuzzFeed's history in the beginning of 2017, a small cut to the business side that served mostly as a sign of weakness. That summer, Jonah shocked the ad industry by announcing that the company would accept banner ads, an obvious admission that BuzzFeed's model, its belief in its own ability to make anything spread virally across an open internet, was no longer working. Now he had to sell the same commodity as everyone else—his audience's mere attention. His dreams of a glamorous, *Mad Men*–style advertising business were turning into pork bellies.

The thing was, Jonah had never doubted the trajectory of the arrow because it all seemed so clear to him. He thought he had irrevocably attached BuzzFeed to the unstoppable power of social media. If Facebook and Twitter and Pinterest rose, so would he. Kenny believed that BuzzFeed would be to the social media giants what MTV's parent company, Viacom, had been to the big cable companies—like Comcast and Time Warner. Internet companies, cable companies—they were distribution; they needed content, and BuzzFeed would sell it to them.

But Facebook wasn't following the rules of that analogy. Facebook wasn't like a cable company—it depended on user-generated content, and seemed to like it that way. And its dominance meant that there were no other social media companies in a position to bid for content. After Facebook bought Instagram, Facebook was pretty much the only player, and Zuckerberg had lost his early interest in acquiring BuzzFeed. For the old media companies like *The New York Times*, the shift was what they'd always expected; they had been trying for years to make money without Facebook. It was a challenge, but it was a challenge they'd seen coming. For BuzzFeed, Facebook's hegemony was an existential threat, and Jonah's board—once happy to leave occasional meetings half comprehending his futurist predictions—was getting restless. Investors like Hearst had been in the company for more than a decade. Kenny was ready to cash in his investment. And as BuzzFeed tried to stay close to its main source of traffic, Facebook, it suddenly seemed like we had a tiger by the tail.

Meaningful Social Engagement

As BuzzFeed tried to squeeze pennies out of its vast Facebook traffic, America's intensifying domestic conflict now was playing out around, and about, the dominant social network. Facebook had, since the 2016 election, been making worthy announcements about misinformation, but they had little effect. BuzzFeed quizzes jostled with racist Trumpist provocations for space in people's feeds. Young people drifted away from the platform while their parents and grandparents used it to yell at one another about politics. Finally, in January of 2018, Mark Zuckerberg made another effort, and announced a "major change to how we build Facebook." The company had gotten "feedback from our community," he wrote, that posts from companies and the media were "crowding out the personal moments that lead us to connect more with each other." He promised new modifications that would help Facebook users connect with family and friends. That would allow them to "feel more connected and less lonely." He acknowledged that "passively reading articles or watching videos—even if they're entertaining or informative— may not be as good" for users' mental health and well-being.

The change would be a new metric, announced by Zuckerberg himself: "meaningful social interactions." Publishers would take a hit, Facebook warned, but it was for the greater good. The Trump news cycles weren't helping anyone. The idea was so clear, even sweet. Jonah saw an opportunity there too. BuzzFeed, unlike other publishers, hadn't boomed in the Trump years. We'd been growing before, when people were sharing lists that reminded them of what it was like to be a nineties kid, or to grow up Persian. They'd used media to connect with people like them, and to give their diverse friends a window into their own experience. Meaningful social interactions, Jonah believed, would favor that kind of content again. And meanwhile, our news division had never taken Bannon's advice, never tried to optimize for passion over truth. While Jonah whispered to Facebook and I set my team enthusiastically to participating in their experiments in video and text, I'd been having my own quiet conversations with one of Rupert Murdoch's loyal retainers, a slender Australian named Robert Thomson, about how to position both of our companies to get Facebook to begin paying us millions of dollars for our news. This was a kind of protection money that Thomson had long been trying to squeeze from the platform, and while I was playing good cop to his bad cop, I was feeling increasing pressure to bring in money to pay my reporters.

This kind of politicized negotiation wasn't exactly the way Jonah had imagined, years earlier, making money from Facebook and YouTube, but the platforms hadn't quite followed the path he expected: They had begun to pay for content, as he had predicted, but they were also seeking to eliminate the middleman by dealing directly with the people they labeled "creators"—a system that had wrecked Maker Studios, the YouTube ad network Disney had bought instead of BuzzFeed. The platforms were essentially turning video stars into Uber drivers, dealing with atomized individuals rather than virtual taxi fleets.

Still, Jonah was right, at first, about the Facebook shift. BuzzFeed's Facebook traffic didn't take the dramatic hit that other publishers did after Zuckerberg's announcement: the algorithm deemed the social interactions we were creating "meaningful." And Ze's focus on YouTube meant that Facebook's cuts to its video views—there would be no more watermelons, any more than there'd be another Dress—weren't catastrophic. But as 2018 wore on, and he watched his writers react to Facebook's incentives, Jonah began to worry. It wasn't so much the traffic—it was where the traffic was going. That summer, he began warning his Facebook contacts that the site wasn't doing what Zuckerberg had promised. In October, Jonah visited Palo Alto to meet the new head of News Feed, another Facebook veteran named John Hegeman. After the meeting, Jonah drafted him a memo laying out in unusually blunt terms what seemed to be going wrong.

The new math of MSI "isn't actually rewarding content that drives meaningful social interactions," he wrote. "When we create meaningful content, it doesn't get rewarded."

He sent over some examples. The classic sweet BuzzFeed stuff still pulled at heartstrings—but "I Tried Riding a Bike with My Corgi" got only 325,000 impressions. Inspiring stories by and about Black and Latino staffers showed a wide mismatch between actual user interest and tabulated view counts. The video "7 Rules to Live by with Regina King" had gotten "17.8k shares (!) but only 580k views?" Jonah wrote. A video about homemade tamales around Latin America, a type that had been a reliable hit on our food vertical Tasty, actually did seem to be producing meaningful social interactions, and connecting people—but barely got any views. Meanwhile, everything from self-care and mental health advice to hard news exposés was tanking.

Perhaps more alarming was what Facebook's audience *was* being fed. "The content that is working isn't our best content," Jonah admitted bluntly. A growing share of our traffic now came from gritty true-crime videos with headlines like "A Man Was Stabbed at a Haunted House" and unsettling posts like "15 Dark and Disturbing Pictures from within an American Frat House." More came from the worrisome category Jonah described in the email as "racially controversial content." An Australian BuzzFeed writer well attuned to Facebook's preferences, for instance, had thrown together a bunch of tweets for a post titled "21 Things That Almost All White People Are Guilty of Saying." A scholar might see the article as part of the internet's deepening focus on identity, and as an interrogation of the notion of whiteness as the unmarked, universal value. But the actual substance of it was a bunch of silly jokes that a white Aussie spending a lot of time on Facebook knew would go viral—"white people love saying 'get these away from me' after eating a few chips" and "white people love saying 'what's the damage' when getting the check." The reaction on Facebook suggested that the meaningful social interactions the post was creating had nothing to do with either the dumb jokes or the cultural analysis. People thought we were calling them racist, or being racist, and their "meaningful" interactions were angry complaints, devolving into screaming matches with one another. The top Facebook comment read, "Wtf is wrong with you BuzzFeed! We are all human beings not your egotistical bullshit of stereotypes you can just categorize! We have hearts and feelings."

The post was "notably our biggest organic FB hit in weeks or months, on the back of, essentially, arguments about whether it is racism," Jonah reported glumly to Hegeman.

Meanwhile, Jonah wrote, "we're seeing other brands create terrible content and get rewarded." He sent Hegeman a list of the worst of the internet, often from British outlets like LADbible and the *Daily Mail*. Some of it was junk science—"happiness makes you fat." Some of it was the sort of dumb, sometimes violent prank once popular on Vine, like a guy duct-taping his girlfriend to a door. Others were just horrifying—articles about the rape of a two week old, or about a person who'd bitten their nails so much that their thumb had been amputated.

Facebook had succeeded in identifying what people would truly, meaningfully interact with, the things they would share and talk about. Their algorithm was holding an ever-more-precise mirror up to Americans' psyches, and intensifying their strongest reactions. But the company's obsession with metrics, with giving people exactly what they would react most strongly to, had produced almost the exact opposite of what Mark Zuckerberg promised—a nation that was alternately angry and horrified, and uniquely preoccupied with fighting on Facebook about race.

What that meant for BuzzFeed, which had followed Facebook to this precipice, was "pressure to make bad content or underperform."

While BuzzFeed wrestled with the new Facebook incentives, other corners of the internet had fewer qualms. *Times* reporter Kevin Roose had begun looking at the pieces of content that were actually dominating Facebook, using a tool called CrowdTangle. The results were almost entirely confrontational right-wing articles. Writers like the Andrew Breitbart's protégé Ben Shapiro, and the former BuzzFeed writer Benny Johnson, were now on top. Elsewhere on the internet, the Los Angeles BuzzFeed employee Baked Alaska had revived the style of dumb stunt that had made him a star on Vine, and by 2018 was roving the streets of Los Angeles, recording a video livestream while speakers broadcast comments from viewers. Within minutes, the speakers were blasting out the N-word.

Facebook employees knew what they'd done. "Our approach has had unhealthy side effects on important slices of public content, such as politics and news," a team of data scientists wrote in a memo that a whistle-blower, Frances Haugen, provided to *The Wall Street Journal*. But top executives couldn't countenance the loss of engagement that might come with actually tamping down on the divisive speech that seemed to attract, in the late 2010s, most of Americans' attention. The company did figure out how to dial back the toxicity of its platform, but it would reserve that for extreme situations—the run-up to elections around the world, for instance—and usually left the tap of anger open, keeping its users glued to the site. Traffic to its app and to advertising was the core of Facebook's business, and executives focused on the bottom line, refusing to do anything that would meaningfully cut into Facebook's revenue. In the end, it was that same emotional substance that paid the bills and powered a decade of unrest. One afternoon in September of 2019, as the *Times*'s Cecilia Kang and Sheera Frenkel wrote, Zuckerberg dropped by the Oval Office to sit across from Trump at the giant old Resolute desk. He told Trump that Facebook's analysts had reviewed the company's data, and that "the president had the highest engagement of any politician on Facebook." Trump's account, with twenty-eight million followers, was winning. The president, they reported, was "visibly pleased."

Benny Johnson was pleased too. That February, he'd joined Turning Point USA, the youth arm of the Trump movement, as its "chief creative officer." It was seven years exactly since he'd been dancing at the Buzz-Feed holiday party at Webster Hall. Now he was a minor-movement rock star, prancing onstage in front of five thousand young activists at a giant convention center in West Palm Beach. They thrilled to his message that "the left can't meme."

I'd been following Benny's career, taking it as a kind of personal emblem of what I hadn't seen coming. In my last months as the editor of BuzzFeed News in 2019, I thought I'd write an article about what I'd gotten wrong, and what I'd learned; I wondered if he'd thought about it too. I emailed him, and we met at the Hawk 'n' Dove, a divey bar on Capitol Hill. Benny was wound tight, still angry that we'd fired him, wearing a gray suit and a bright white shirt. He told me that he thought he'd been singled out, that other BuzzFeed writers had lifted copy from Wikipedia with impunity. I told him I thought he was different because he was writing about the news, not aggregating memes. Then he told me he'd considered suicide after I fired him, "a gun to [his] head," and that only his faith had carried him through. I wasn't sure if I believed him about that either.

He warmed up when he started talking about the media landscape, about how much he was enjoying the showmanship and the hyperpartisan conflicts of the Trump years. He loved, in particular, the young socialist congresswoman from the Bronx, Alexandria Ocasio-Cortez—"a perfect foil," he said. He loved the new world we'd helped create.

"It's as though I had one too many shots of Jameson with John Stanton and woke up five years later," he said, "and everything I dreamed had come true."

Later that summer of 2019, not long after I sat with Benny at the Hawk 'n' Dove, Donald Trump hosted a social media summit at the White House. Benny marveled as he walked through the grand marble Entrance Hall, where he was greeted by a giant *Game of Thrones* meme printed on poster board and, between two marble columns, an enlarged printout of one of the president's tweets: "Many are saying I'm the best 140 character writer in the world."

The guests milled around in wonder. Along with Benny and his boss, the Trump youth movement leader Charlie Kirk, they included pretty much anyone with a big social media following and an unquestioned loyalty to the president. Gateway Pundit, a leading purveyor of false news, was there, as was a guy who wrote under the Twitter pseudonym @carpedonktum and was famous for making an edited video of House Speaker Nancy Pelosi, which generated Democratic outrage and a presidential retweet. So was a pro-Trump singer-songwriter, Joy Villa, in a tight red, white, and blue dress with the word "Freedom" on the skirt, and the Black Trump supporters known as Diamond and Silk, who had recently won an apology from Facebook, which had treated their political claims as dangerous misinformation. They walked among easels carrying enlarged words like "deplatforming" and "demonetization"—the tools that had begun to be used to chase extreme voices off social media—with their definitions. Another enlarged Trump tweet read, "Social media is totally discriminating against Republican and conservative voices." Then they took their seats in the Rose Garden, where Trump delivered a broadside against Facebook and Twitter, which had made all of their careers, for taking mild steps to enforce the platforms' own rules. The guests posted faithfully. The White House calculated that the combined reach of the group was one hundred million people. Benny thought to himself, "The internet is ours."

33

Layoffs

At Donald Trump's White House in 2019, right-wingers were cele-
brating the conversion of traffic not into money, as Jonah and Nick
had imagined, but into raw political power. But Jonah was running a
company now, not a guerilla-marketing stunt. Once he'd thought traffic
was digital gold. Now, it was elusive, and sometimes expensive. Once
BuzzFeed's clever advertisements had gone viral all on their own. But
gradually Facebook had taken a larger and larger cut, and now instituted
rules that pretty much required that publishers pay to have their clients'
ads—unlike editorial posts—promoted on the site. The prices you had to
pay Facebook to send your sponsored content across the web varied with
the season, but always rose around Christmas, and in late 2018 BuzzFeed
suddenly found itself spending millions to distribute the branded posts
and videos that had long been its main source of revenue. By the time the
books had closed on 2018, the company made more than $307 million—
but spent $386 million to make it, for a loss of more than $78 million.
The NBC war chest, raised just two years earlier, was running low.

Investors, who once saw BuzzFeed as the future, were now more interested in the present. Jonah's board was even more restive. As 2018 drew to a close, he finally acknowledged that traffic couldn't carry him out of his predicament, and that he'd have to start cutting.

Jonah had trimmed around the edges before, reorganizing the sales organization and shutting an office in Paris, where BuzzFeed's high-low mix didn't quite seem to cut through. But I'd talked him out of cuts to our American news operation. He'd always wished we could find a less conventional way to do journalism—more memes, fewer things that looked like *New York Times* articles—but he appreciated the attention and prestige it brought, and unambiguously loved the way a newsbreak could upend Donald Trump's presidency or force a business to change its practices. When Trump attacked us over the Dossier and called Buzz-Feed a "failing pile of garbage," Jonah and his commerce whiz kid Ben Kaufman printed T-shirts with those words, and we sold $25,000 of them in a day. When he'd considered cuts before, I played to the joy he took in that kind of combat, to his vanity, and to the concern that a wave of bad press could damage BuzzFeed's image and revenue.

In the fall of 2018, we both knew that this argument had run its course. Jonah delivered the bad news to me in his New York office, which was barely furnished except for the energy bars he kept to counteract his weight loss from a vegan diet, and handed me off to our finance department to work out the details. He was thin, and stressed, though he still kept a quality that I'd always seen as righteous optimism but was beginning to worry was magical thinking. He had an idea that news could find some alternate route to sustainability, perhaps as a nonprofit, though there was no real path to get there. In January, we announced deep cuts, which reflected a recognition that while traffic might flow across international borders, we hadn't been able to make dollars follow. We shut down the news team in Australia, and began talking quietly about whether we could find local buyers for BuzzFeed branches in places like Germany and Brazil.

For my part, I called the editor of *The New York Times*, Dean Baquet, for advice. He'd been through the ups and down of the newspaper industry, eventually quitting a top job at the *Los Angeles Times* rather than gut the place. He told me I should first think about whether the cuts were too greedy, or too severe, to defend. They weren't. We ought, I thought, to be able to run a decent business and a great newsroom on $300 million a year. Then he said that he knew I'd have an impulse to deliver the bad news to everyone myself, and that I'd see that as responsible; it was actually, he told me, egotistical and self-absorbed. I should instead share the unhappy responsibility with the senior managers who'd helped make the painful decisions of whom to lay off. I was stunned he'd seen so clearly into my head, and I took his advice.

I made some of the calls on January 25, 2019, including to John Stanton, the tattooed giant who had established our presence in Washington, DC, a guy I loved and admired. He was shocked, and surprisingly gracious, as were most of the people we laid off, though many of them grew increasingly angry over time as they reflected on the idea that our hopeful talk had masked growing financial problems. Within days, I was hearing that the staff were about to unionize to insulate themselves as best they could against another wave of firings. A few weeks later, I was at the home of Craig Newmark, the billionaire Craigslist founder, helping to preside over a fundraiser for a local news site in New York, when I realized I'd missed a wave of calls. I dialed in to find Jonah and the rest of BuzzFeed's executive team frantically trying to figure out how to navigate employees' demands that their union be recognized. Jonah had already worried publicly that a union would make it harder for BuzzFeed to stay nimble, and would hurt employees more than it would help them; I thought it wouldn't change the situation as much as either he or the organizers thought, but I also knew how deeply they wanted it, and I argued for giving it to them. Jonah finally agreed, on the condition the statement be in my name and clearly note his dissent. The compromise didn't work. Employees saw the union as an issue of their rights and their place in the world, not of mere industrial relations.

"This is a turbulent time in our industry, and we've seen that our company and our management can only do so much to protect us from the broader economic forces shrinking the media landscape," one reporter, Albert Samaha, said in a press release. We fought bitterly for months over exactly how many of them would be in the bargaining unit. And the union fight quickly made Jonah the target of angry, coordinated Twitter campaigns and stunts, like the inflatable rat that staff members briefly rented. (The NewsGuild, unlike better-funded blue-collar unions, couldn't afford a permanent inflatable rat.) This was all new for Jonah. He'd played different roles on the internet: the trickster, the boy genius, the founder. He knew how to shape his image, and he enjoyed how people saw him. Now he was just management, a suit—and an incompetent suit at that. Twitter was full of angry employees. The press, which had varied over the previous few years between rapturous and skeptical, was now downright dismissive. *The New York Times*—whose board had invited Jonah in to tell them the future of media just four years earlier— was now mocking his woes ("Not All Fun and Memes," read one headline) like they'd known it all along. On both sides, there was a bit of the bitterness that came from a deep confusion about what BuzzFeed News was for. I've come to regret encouraging Jonah to see our news division as a worthy enterprise that shouldn't solely be evaluated as a business. Jonah resented what seemed like ingratitude from people whose work he so valued that he was approaching $100 million in losses. But the news employees worked hard and had no interest in being seen as charity cases.

The sharpest source of financial pressure came from Jonah's board. It still included allies, like Will Porteous, the early investor, and Chris Dixon, the Andreessen Horowitz appointee. But Porteous and his firm RRE had now been invested in BuzzFeed far longer than a venture capitalist prefers. Dixon's attention was elsewhere, on the cryptocurrency business, which would turn him into a venture capital superstar. NBC, which had once seen BuzzFeed as its bridge to the future, now believed that the giant media company's future was not the web but a streaming video service, and NBC's representative on our board had begun to worry that it wouldn't be getting its $400 million investment back. Kenny, the board's chairman, was losing faith in Jonah too.

Jonah had been Kenny's protégé, but the investor made no secret that his deepest priority was his family. He'd once told an interviewer he had no problem with nepotism. "What could be better than working with your children?" Kenny asked. Now his son, Ben Lerer, had built a company that drew millions of views to videos on channels like NowThis-News, which specialized in liberal politics, and the Dodo, the largest animal site in the world. Kenny believed that a merger of Ben's and Jonah's companies would make both stronger. It would also be an elegant coda to his career building media companies. The companies opened their books and held detailed talks about how a merger would work. But some BuzzFeed board members felt Kenny had strayed into inappropriate favoritism. And the companies could never agree on a price, or on the crucial detail of who, exactly, would run the merged thing. In the summer of 2019, Kenny resigned from BuzzFeed's board, leaving Jonah to march into our bright boardroom, which faced north on the sixteenth floor of its Park Avenue headquarters, without a powerful ally.

Jonah became focused on a new business objective: finding a way out from under the expectations of investors who felt they'd paid too much or waited too long, and a way to keep the company spinning forward.

BuzzFeed was on track to lose $37 million in 2019—an improvement—but nobody had signed on with Jonah to break even. Investors had seen him as a visionary; now they were beginning to worry that they'd gone along with a kind of magical, deterministic thinking about the digital future. Jonah, in turn, was eager to be rid of a board made up of doubters.

Jonah's desperation took human form in Carlos Watson, the relentless networker with a big smile and an enveloping handshake who had, in 2013, persuaded the richest woman in the world, Laurene Powell Jobs, to finance his high-minded BuzzFeed alternative, Ozy. When Carlos first sold the idea, it had been keyed to the dreams of Silicon Valley billionaires: BuzzFeed, but without the silly memes, the emotion, or the left-wing politics, and with a Black CEO who was a welcome change in a white-dominated industry. This was a website devoted to the things, Watson promised, that millennials really craved—new ideas, technology, and people, all wrapped around centrist politics so capacious that its marquee interviews, which Carlos conducted, included *both* George W. Bush and Alexandria Ocasio-Cortez. Powell Jobs was his first investor, and her name alone brought in all the rest of the money he needed to launch the company with his business partner, a young former Goldman Sachs banker named Samir Rao.

The problem with Ozy was that it never quite found anyone who wanted that content. Perhaps nobody ever would have, but the measures of "meaningful social engagement" that Facebook and the other platforms were using to amplify the most divisive, angriest articles helped ensure that Ozy would get very little traffic. (Once, a chocolate chip cookie recipe went viral, but that wasn't on brand for Carlos, and the site never did it again.) Instead, they faked it, at an escalating pace—which Watson later defended as standard industry practice. Ozy had been purchasing views from online brokers from at least 2014, according to emails I later obtained, but it was a reporter at BuzzFeed News who caught them at it in 2017—they were claiming credit for views that had actually popped up behind a reader's browser, unbeknownst to the supposed reader. Still, Ozy's slick facade and appealingly diverse and moderate politics made it a darling of the advertising industry, and when marketers were pushed to buy ads on Black-owned websites, they often went to Ozy.

Jonah saw through Ozy's traffic schemes. You just had to look at its YouTube pages, on which some videos had just a handful of views, to see what was going on. But he was impressed with Carlos; if he could bring in $40 million in annual revenue selling a fake product, imagine what he could do with a real one! The two men talked terms in the fall of 2019, and Jonah suggested that Carlos join BuzzFeed as a top executive. However, Jonah was never as interested in Ozy's scant offerings or Carlos's sales talents as he was in what Carlos had suggested he could do for him: bring in Laurene Powell Jobs. Ozy could be the solution to all Jonah's problems. In this fantasy, Powell Jobs would buy out the rest of BuzzFeed's board and invest in the company at a valuation inflated enough that it would be easy for BuzzFeed, in turn, to buy Ozy from her. Jonah would be rid of the restless board members, and he'd have a new, Black Jon Steinberg on the board at a moment when media companies were increasingly sensitive to their lack of diversity.

Carlos, as it emerged, had a bad habit of making promises he couldn't keep. With his salesman's talents, he grasped Jonah's situation, his need for the kind of bailout only Powell Jobs could perform. But Powell Jobs's Silicon Valley circle had begun to sour on Carlos years earlier, as word trickled back about the degree to which he was trading on her name and those of other early investors she had brought in, including the Silicon Valley angel investor Ron Conway. Powell Jobs hadn't invested in the company's most recent fundraising round. By November of 2019, it was clear that Carlos couldn't actually deliver his old friend's money, and Jonah lost interest. Carlos would grow increasingly desperate, the fakery increasingly intense. Powell Jobs and Conway began distancing themselves from the company, and Carlos looked for new investors who would buy his story of a flashy new media company finding huge success on the internet. He had Goldman Sachs ready to invest $40 million in 2021 when the investment bank asked to chat with a YouTube executive about Ozy's success. But the success was fictional. To keep the illusion alive, an Ozy executive impersonated the YouTube employee on the conference call. But one of the Goldman bankers caught on to the scam, quietly killing the deal, and alerting YouTube to the deception. YouTube, in turn, called the FBI.

Jonah found a new opening instead. Verizon, which had acquired *The Huffington Post*—now officially *HuffPost*, with Arianna gone—had no interest in running a progressive news site. *HuffPost* was in terrible shape, and Verizon—though it theoretically controlled a huge digital advertising business in the form of Yahoo!—seemed unable to focus on something so tiny, so miniscule, as $30 million in losses for long enough to build a real business around the website. The cell phone industry was booming, but the traffic business was collapsing inward. Indeed, *HuffPost*, from its splashy sale in 2011 to its grim fate eight years later, seemed to embody the false promise of traffic.

On October 18, 2019, the *Financial Times* had reported that Verizon was looking to unload *HuffPost*, and the next day Jonah emailed Verizon's CEO, Hans Vestberg. "Are you really considering selling it? Should I take a look? It has been a while, but I started the company, and have some ideas on how to revitalize the business. Or if you already have a buyer, I could partner with them," he wrote.

Vestberg responded with a single word: "No."

Jonah wasn't deterred. He reopened the conversation with Guru Gowrappan, a former Alibaba executive responsible for the doomed task of managing Verizon's websites. A year later, on November 19, 2020, the companies announced a deal: BuzzFeed would "buy" *HuffPost* from Verizon in an all-stock deal; Verizon would also, remarkably, invest in BuzzFeed. "Verizon is literally paying BuzzFeed to take over Huffington Post," the media writer Peter Kafka noted. It was a humbling collapse for a website that still had thirty-six million unique monthly visitors, according to Comscore's conservative measurements—about half of BuzzFeed's web traffic.

Jonah was delighted to retake his old company. He was also delighted by what he found there. BuzzFeed had, in the lean years, become expert at squeezing every diminishing dollar out of a page view. Verizon, with its vast scale and no-name brands, couldn't be bothered. BuzzFeed laid off a wave of well-compensated old hands and adjusted the advertising systems for a company that needed every penny. The combination cut *HuffPost*'s losses as Verizon had never been able to.

Jonah had one more trick for BuzzFeed and *HuffPost*. As the value of pure traffic had gone down, BuzzFeed and the other online publishers had become increasingly focused on dollars. The new idea was to turn your website into a storefront, first for Amazon and then for its competitors, mainly Walmart. *The New York Times* had bought the review website *Wirecutter* to get into this business, but BuzzFeed's immense traffic allowed Jonah's site to reach readers with appeals to fun, inexpensive products that seemed to bring the feeling of the friendlier parts of the internet into your home.

Jonah returned to the one thing he could control, BuzzFeed's books, and prepared to slash costs with more layoffs, and to redouble his focus on the grim, profitable business of making lists of things people would buy, collecting small fees from Amazon for each purchase. Jonah threw the company into the effort with a desperate urgency. Peggy Wang, his versatile first hire who had been the keeper of BuzzFeed's editorial voice, led the team that became expert in selling everything: cookware, dresses, and Christmas gifts, sex toys, and succulents.

They also sold sneakers. After Amazon popularized online affiliate marketing, as it's known, brand-name retailers jumped in. One of them was Nike, the company Jonah had made his name attacking nineteen years earlier. Few BuzzFeed employees remembered that story, and Jonah was in no position to dwell on the irony. By the fall of 2020, BuzzFeed was overflowing with affiliate-marketing headlines: "Just 20 Things You Can Get On Sale at Nike Right Now"; "15 Pairs of Sneakers On Sale at Nike That'll Have You Clearing Out Space in Your Closet"; "Nike's Having a Big Sneaker Sale in Case You Want New Kicks for 2021"; "~Run~, Don't Walk to Nike Because Their Sale Section Is an Extra 20% Off for Black Friday."

When I suggested this irony to Jonah years a few years later, he rolled his eyes. He'd been fending off jabs about Nikes since he got into the advertising business in 2011. But he liked Nike shoes. The company had long since cleaned up much of its supply chain. It dominated the sneakerhead basketball culture whose fashion Jonah had always felt most comfortable in. But he loathed the pat, ironical remarks, so he always wore New Balances.

Through it all, Jonah had managed to build a business on scale and traffic, with an eye always to making money. He and Dao had made page views valuable, even if they could never find a way to pay the high costs of the newsroom. It could have been depressing, but Jonah laughed it off.

He'd found a new edge in the traffic he'd been building, in the huge brand he'd created in BuzzFeed. And it was these small percentages of sneakers—and sex toys and dresses and gifts—that would make BuzzFeed profitable, finally, in 2020, with a bare $11 million in earnings off $321 million in revenue. *HuffPost* brought in more potential shoppers. Those dollars would set the stage for Jonah to finally get clear of his investors and his doubters, and to take the company public.

34

Baked Alaska

T he internet is ours," Benny had said, and he had a point. Jonah and Nick and their editors—Peggy and Anna and Jessica and AJ and I—thought we were inventing digital media, along with all the journalists and writers and techies around us. And yet the figures who would create the new American Far Right had been flickering around the edges of that picture from the start. There, at BuzzFeed's office in Chinatown, sat Chris Poole, better known as moot—the creator of 4chan. There, hanging out late into the Brooklyn nights with Jezebel's Tracie Egan, was Vice co-founder Gavin McInnes, who went on to start the pro-Trump militia known as the Proud Boys. There was Andrew Breitbart, mentor to Ben Shapiro and a generation of right-wing online figures, co-founding *The Huffington Post*. There was Steve Bannon paying us a visit. There was Benny in BuzzFeed's West Twenty-First Street office, making lists. We'd seen them as the marginal characters in our story; by the time my editor and I were talking this book over in 2022, that picture looked exactly wrong: we seemed to be, he mused, Rosencrantz and Guildenstern in their tragedy.

On January 6, 2021, soon after Trump lost reelection, I was watching the right-wing mob storm the Capitol when I saw another familiar face. His real name was Anthime Joseph Gionet, but he didn't really go by it. When Ze Frank hired him at BuzzFeed in 2015, Gionet told everyone his name was Timothy Treadstone, but everyone called him by his hip-hop sobriquet, Baked Alaska, Baked for short. That was a reference to the amount of weed he smoked, and to the Anchorage childhood that haunted him.

Gionet had grown up in Alaska's biggest city, the youngest biological son of a pair of devout Christians. His father was a pharmacist and his mother a nurse, but their true passion was for missionary work, and they created a group to preach the gospel in the Russian far east. They traveled there so often that Gionet missed a year of school, where he was a memorable figure: charismatic, but with a mean streak. His parents would eventually adopt five children from Russia.

Gionet left his home state for a Christian college near Los Angeles, and then tried to make it in that city's creative scene, becoming a goofy caricature of white American culture, with a bleached mullet and a mustache. His songs included "Grizzly Bear Trappin'," and he delivered lyrics like "I cook moose like TGI Friday's." In 2012, a new social media platform, Vine, launched that seemed designed for his over-the-top style. There, millions of teens watched outrageous stunts and pranks—*Jackass* was the cultural inspiration—and just as BuzzFeed's staff obsessed about going viral on Facebook, Gionet figured out how to crack Vine. Once, he filmed himself knocking some magazines off the shelf at a grocery store in a video that attracted hundreds of thousands of views. Another time, he poured a gallon of milk over his head at a convenience store and reaped similar traffic.

That willingness to do whatever it took to go viral was the quality we were looking for at BuzzFeed in 2015. Ze Frank had come up in the same early internet scene as Jonah, and made his own discoveries about virality when a simple animation he created for a birthday party went everywhere. He later helped invent the tight-shot, quick-cut style of internet video blogging, or vlogging, with his own online show, and he was in the process of conquering YouTube with the same inexpensive, goofy content that had made BuzzFeed so popular on the web.

Narrowly speaking, the provocative Alaskan rapper didn't quite fit in on the small team of, mostly, young women responsible for posting videos to different platforms, who had the pulse of BuzzFeed's mostly female audience. He had the only mullet in the house. Straight white guys were a distinct minority, and those who were there favored beards over mustaches and had ostentatiously liberal politics. But while Gionet was a misfit at BuzzFeed's cavernous studios on Sunset Boulevard, he was part of a band of misfits anyway. The people making internet videos in West Hollywood in 2015 were those who hadn't found a place in the traditional Hollywood categories, in which writer, actor, director, and cinematographer were all distinct professions, and perfectionists sneered at the messy, amateur world of YouTube. In that way, Gionet, who had created his own character and shot and edited his own videos, fit right in. The people he was drawn to felt themselves to be outsiders too. The two people he was closest to at the time were a Black woman and a trans man who thought of him as a sensitive soul. He confided in his friends how haunted he was by his childhood, and by the sense that his parents had pushed him aside for their adopted Russian kids, had made him feel "nonexistent" to them. He seemed uncomfortable in his skin, with his identity. Once, the team took an outing to be in the studio audience at *The Price Is Right*; when someone came out to check the names of guests, Gionet—known to his friends only as Tim Treadstone—bolted rather than show his ID and risk a conversation about who he really was.

BuzzFeed video wasn't a political place, but Gionet's politics seemed to fit at first. As the 2016 election campaign took hold, he put a Bernie Sanders portrait on his desk, two former colleagues said. His loathing for Hillary Clinton wasn't out of place on the left then. But after Hillary Clinton won the nomination, he held on to the grudge, and moved on to wearing MAGA hats around the office. That was the era when sarcasm often masked racism, the era of the "ironic Nazi." His colleagues wondered if this was real or ironic, heartfelt or part of the persona.

The LA crew didn't spend much time on Twitter—that was for news junkies and journalists—so nobody paid much attention to the new friends he was making online. Gionet was always going for the retweets, and he found them across town at Breitbart, where one of Steve Bannon's stars was a British former tech journalist named Milo Yiannopoulos. Milo was a star on college campuses, where he delighted conservative students and outraged the liberals. He was also, his leaked emails would later reveal, in secret contact with overt white nationalists, and worked to slip the ideas of proudly racist websites like American Renaissance into Breitbart's coverage. When Milo retweeted Gionet's scathing commentary about Hillary Clinton, Gionet could get dozens more retweets, hundreds of likes, more and more followers eager for more of the same. Gionet eagerly followed that energy. In April of 2016, he went on vacation and never came back; when he belatedly resigned, he informed his boss that he'd taken a job as the "tour manager" for Yiannopoulos, a darling of the racist and antisemitic "alt-right." Colleagues were momentarily shocked. Then they scrolled through Gionet's Twitter account, where his increasingly vile statements had been getting him more and more retweets from Far Right figures, and realized that they shouldn't have been.

It was, many of them thought, mostly about the retweets. As Gionet's former boss noted, this was "BuzzFeed 101. He was just kind of optimizing." Just as we'd been optimizing videos and posts for Facebook and

Twitter, he'd been doing the same to himself. "His politics have been guided by platform metrics," reflected a top BuzzFeed producer, Andrew Gauthier. Gionet's colleagues had abided by some unspoken boundaries: factual accuracy, liberal social mores, common decency. There was a purity in the way Gionet had abandoned those guardrails and thrown his identity on the mercy of the internet, turned himself into its mirror. He lacked any of the scruples or social ties that can prevent a person from becoming an extremist. Ever since he started pouring milk over his head for the Vine loops, and producing goofy raps for the views, he'd made clear he'd do pretty much anything for attention. And if, for instance, sharing top billing with the overt white supremacist Richard Spencer at a march-slash-riot in Charlottesville that summer would generate attention—well, why not. There, wearing a "Don't Tread on Me" baseball cap, he chanted the white nationalist slogan "You will not replace us" with a column of extremists in white polo shirts carrying torches, whom he called "fam" and "bro." "We're proud to be white," he declared. "Hail victory." He achieved a new kind of fame the next day when he got a shot of chemical irritant to the face and poured milk on his head and eyes, this time for practical reasons, while telling an unseen cameraman, "Keep streaming."

After Trump was elected, Gionet had produced some new songs to honor him—"MAGA Anthem" and "Trump Is My President." But he didn't get an invitation to the White House social media summit. Nor did Milo, whom a BuzzFeed News reporter had caught making Nazi salutes on camera while singing "America the Beautiful." Milo and Bannon had kept their ties to overt white supremacists secret at Breitbart, and even as the White House opened its doors to misinformation peddlers and anonymous Twitter trolls, Yiannopoulos was still too extreme. So was Gionet, whose *Jackass*-style stunts had always been tinged more with violence than with MAGA ideology. He kept looking for new ways to build a following. In 2019, he even tried on becoming an apostate, telling a reporter that he had "recently left the alt-right" and regretted what he'd contributed to "that culture."

"I was just a normal guy who liked memes and I got radicalized," he said then.

When that turnabout didn't get him any attention, he went back to the old Vine standbys: dangerous stunts. They often involved finding excuses to blast people in the face with a chemical irritant that he liked to call "content spray." When, in December of 2019, he was arrested in Scottsdale, Arizona, for spraying Mace into the eyes of a bouncer, an officer reported that Mr. Gionet "informed me that he was a 'influencer' and had a large following on social media," according to a police report.

By then, Gionet had been subject to the evils that had been denounced at Trump's social media summit. He'd been deplatformed—thrown off Twitter and Twitch—and had his YouTube videos demonetized. So he was streaming to DLive, a blockchain-based service, when he entered the Capitol on January 6, 2021. He strode around like he owned the place. "America First is inevitable! Fuck globalists, let's go!" he yelled. At one point he advised other rioters not to damage anything; at another he yelled at a police officer that he was a "fucking oathbreaker, you piece of shit."

Gionet's excitement grew as he watched the number of viewers to his livestream rise. It was easy to relate to—it reminded me of that afternoon in April of 2016 when a couple of my colleagues had transfixed the world by putting rubber bands around a watermelon, watching the view count grow above eight hundred thousand, until the fruit exploded. "We've got over ten thousand people live, watching, let's go!" he said excitedly, standing in the trashed office of a senator from Oregon, Jeff Merkley. "Hit that follow button—I appreciate you guys." His followers excitedly replied, cheering him on to "hang all the congressmen."

At one point, someone off camera warned that President Trump "would be very upset" with the antics of the rioters. "No, he'll be happy," Mr. Gionet responded. "We're fighting for Trump."

Later, when it became clear that Trump would not, or could not, protect the rioters, Gionet went briefly underground, posting frantically from short-lived Twitter accounts that he was in hiding. The FBI caught up to him in Houston nine days later, on January 15. The federal court in Washington, DC, didn't have much sympathy for the rioters, whose actions, the circuit's chief judge said, had been "reprehensible as offenses against morality, civic virtue, and the rule of law." Then they fitted him with an ankle monitor and sent him back to Scottsdale. He was not, it turned out, chastened.

On March 31, the ankle bracelet was off and Gionet, awaiting trial, was streaming again. In one video, he films as police arrive to inform him that there have been complaints that he's harassing people. In another, he picks a fight with a friend, and when the friend slaps the camera out of his hand, Gionet himself calls the police. He leers at an attractive female cop, and does his best to provoke others. And in a video that appears on an unlisted Twitter account, he complains that the federal agents on his case are "fat faggots and dykes," a piece of information he says he's learned from the Nazi publication the Daily Stormer. He says he's been watching a lot of documentaries about violent standoffs between Far Right figures and federal agents at places like Waco and Ruby Ridge.

On June 4, 2021, the federal officer monitoring him before trial dragged him back in front of a federal judge, via videoconference, to demand that he be barred from streaming videos. It was clear from the videos, his pretrial release officer told the court, that he was trying "specifically to agitate, anger, and offend and provoke a violent response to the video during livestream for people to continue to comment." Then Gionet piped up to clarify. "Calling the cops—that's a prank," he explained, before his lawyer cut him off. The judge said he found the videos "inane," but that Gionet had stayed just on this side of the line and hadn't violated the conditions of his release. What's more, Gionet and his lawyer had made a compelling case that streaming on social media was the defendant's job, and had been ever since he started at BuzzFeed six years earlier.

The court couldn't take away a man's ability to feed himself. As Gionet told the judge, "That's my income."

Gionet kept streaming, kept playing cat-and-mouse with social media platforms and courts alike, all through the next year. In January of 2022, a Scottsdale judge sentenced him to thirty days in jail for the attack on the bouncer, after prosecutors called him "lost" and a "danger to society." On May 11, he appeared in federal court to plead guilty on a single misdemeanor charge connected to the attack on the Capitol. But when Gionet told the judge that he was pleading guilty on his lawyers' advice despite believing "I'm innocent," the judge rejected his plea. Finally, Gionet relented and pleaded guilty, and, in January of 2023, a federal judge sentenced him to two months in jail. He had "made a mockery of democracy," Judge Trevor McFadden told the thirty-five-year-old defendant, who had been convinced on the evidence of his own live stream. The judge marveled at how brazen his crimes had been: "You did everything you could to publicize your misconduct."

....

Conclusion

By 2022, the internet had splintered. A new set of right-wing social networks, with names like Rumble and Gab, were channeling the energy that Tim Gionet tapped during the insurrection at the Capitol. Baked Alaska, indeed, was one of the first to join Donald Trump's new network, Truth Social. Meanwhile, *The New York Times* and *Washington Post* were hoping a new surge of interest as Donald Trump reemerged into public life would revive subscription businesses that had flagged in his absence, as Democrats again turned to them to understand what they feared. But the *Times* was still awash in cash, and had taken in a handful of prominent internet media figures—Gawker's Dodai Stewart and Choire Sicha, *Vox*'s Ezra Klein, *Recode*'s Kara Swisher, and me. We had fled there to ride the change in the internet's weather, and to be reluctant trophies for a thriving old media company. Meanwhile, a bottom-line-focused businessman, Bryan Goldberg, had restarted Gawker, whose scabrous veterans at publications like Vice and all across Twitter accused the rest of the media of going too soft on right-wingers.

The downtown New York scene by now was a distant memory. The

2010s were, for many, a regret. Marc Andreessen, in particular, later told others he was remorseful about ever investing in BuzzFeed. He'd come to believe that BuzzFeed News and I had taken a hard line on one of his companies, a failed insurance startup called Zenefits, specifically in order to prove our independence from him. The thought hadn't crossed our minds; we hadn't thought, or realized, he was that important, though by 2022 his and Chris Dixon's massive investments in cryptocurrency had made them both even larger players in American life.

Others who had gotten on the bandwagon a little late had regrets too. Carlos Watson faced investigations by the SEC and FBI for the fakery his company, Ozy, had pulled on its way to becoming the next new media darling—something I'd wound up exposing in the *Times*.

As for Nick, his natural detachment seemed to have intensified with time. When I ran into him having a chilly outdoor pandemic dinner at a West Village restaurant in late 2021, he had grown philosophical about Gawker's fall. "We can blame ourselves, as liberals always do. Or remember that a hard-right billionaire set up a law firm and spent eight figures in order to crucify an outlet that dared to criticize him," he texted me. Nick spent much of the COVID-19 pandemic in SoHo. And he was still working on his app. "Like Andreessen, I think there's a Talmudic internet still to be made," he told me, referring to an internet that would find a way to, technically, achieve the old blogger dream of integrating news and commentary. "So I tinker."

That new internet could be about transparency, too, he believed. But he'd come to think that Gawker's—and my—version of transparency, of the compulsion of leaks and aggressive reporting, actually produced dishonesty and self-censorship. "Where did I end up on transparency?" he texted. "In an unlikely place, actually: sources have to be in control if they're going to say anything interesting. And they have to be safe. Especially now. Transparency has to be coaxed, not forced."

Jonah, almost alone, was still singing the old song. By the beginning of 2021, BuzzFeed had dug its way back toward modest profitability, and Jonah finally saw a way to buy himself out of his corporate predicament, a moment of opportunity. In January of 2021 a new financial instrument called a SPAC was hot. It was short for special purpose acquisition company, a publicly traded shell company that would buy BuzzFeed, dissolve itself, and leave Jonah as the CEO of a public company. The market was frothy, and Jonah had his pick of the SPACs. Kenny's son, Ben, had one. So did a South Africa–born financier named Adam Rothstein, whose SPAC, 890 Fifth Avenue Partners, was named for the headquarters of the Avengers. To Kenny's dismay, Jonah went with Rothstein, who offered him the two things he wanted: control, through a special class of stock, and a new pile of capital to invest. Jonah already had a plan for some of the cash: he would buy Complex, a sneakerhead media company whose website and popular videos betrayed no ambivalence about the worship of Nike, or of commerce in general.

The market was hot; had BuzzFeed moved fast, as others did, it might have made it through with more than $100 million in new capital. But there was a problem. The SPAC valued BuzzFeed at less than the $1.7 billion price tag at which NBCUniversal had invested $400 million. NBC had long since decided that the future of the internet was elsewhere, and had pivoted to a streaming platform called Peacock, but the new plan would cost them money and lose them face. For eight excruciating weeks, Jonah and his board negotiated with NBC to get them to sign off. They finally settled with a slew of conditions, including a personally humiliating concession: If its share price didn't make it to $12.50 by December of 2023, NBC would seize some of Jonah's own shares.

On Friday, June 25, 2021, I met Jonah on Irving Place, around the corner from BuzzFeed's COVID-empty office. He was looking quizzically at his phone. He handed it across the table to me. The email subject line was "Yachting."

"I just read about BuzzFeed's plans to go public," the email began. "We are a 'superyacht' brokerage with a fleet of yachts available to rent or buy globally. If you have any plans to buy or charter a yacht, I would be very happy to help."

"I've been waiting for this moment," Jonah deadpanned.

But while NBC tortured Jonah, BuzzFeed's momentum stalled. SPACs cooled, and the investors realized that the easiest money was to be had by pulling out even before the company became public. As BuzzFeed limped toward the public markets in December, it was clear that the company had missed a lucrative moment, and that SPACs were now ice cold. All but $16 million of the promised sum had dried up. NBC had punished Jonah, but also stood to hamstring its own investment.

Still, Jonah felt nothing but relief on December 6, standing in Nasdaq's digital studio, right upstairs from CNBC. (The main studio had been booked far in advance by someone else.) He'd invited me both as a shareholder and in my new capacity as media columnist for *The New York Times*, and suggested I wear a T-shirt announcing that I couldn't be in photographs due to the conflict of interest regularly noted in my column—the sort of thing he was always trying to get me to do, and that I never did.

There's a line in Tom Stoppard's play *Rosencrantz and Guildenstern Are Dead* that occurred to me after my editor pointed out that perhaps Jonah and I, thinking of ourselves as protagonists, had been passing through someone else's story. "Where we went wrong was getting on a boat," Guildenstern remarks mournfully at the end. "We can move of course, change direction, rattle about, but our movement is contained within a larger one that carries us along as inexorably as the wind and current." Back in 2001, Jonah bet his friend Cameron Marlow that he could control the internet. And perhaps more than any other media figure of his generation—maybe more than anyone save Mark Zuckerberg and Donald Trump—he had sought, and at times managed, to steer the new medium. But the medium couldn't contain the message. "The internet" had become, merely, society itself; the forces that had come to dominate it—populism to the right and the left, most of all—were social forces, not digital ones. The geniuses who succeeded in this era hadn't dominated those forces. They had, like Trump, become their vessels; or, like Zuckerberg, offered them a channel. Jonah had tried to shape them, but the best even a genius can do, most of the time, is usually to see those forces coming and catch their drag.

Cameron never paid Jonah off for their two-dollar bet, though he probably should have. The Watermelon, the Dress, the Dossier—Jonah had certainly replicated the feat that got him into this stuff in the first place, the Nike letter. But the larger idea in that bet was control—the idea that Jonah could command these forces he'd helped unleash. He had tried. BuzzFeed's failings, the painful layoffs that had been the worst moments of Jonah's career in 2017 and 2019 and 2020, had come in part from his utopian ideology, from a kind of magical thinking. He had invested in offices around the globe that would struggle to adapt to a world that was still organized nationally. And after that he'd invested heavily in a news operation on a scale that he believed the platforms would be logically obliged to support, but which they hadn't. Now he'd outmaneuvered rivals like Vice, Vox Media, and even the Lerer family's Group Nine to be first to the public markets—only to watch his stock price fall, as many furious former employees, dogged by a technical issue, could only watch the value of their shares drop. But while the more carefully-run *Vox* made frugal acquisitions, including the Lerer family's Group Nine, BuzzFeed entered a downward spiral. Within months, the SPAC would be seen as an iconic disaster of the late tech bubble, its shares falling to below $1 in early 2023 from $10 a year earlier. That left BuzzFeed with a market capitalization of less than 20 percent of what Disney would have paid for it back in 2014.

Jonah hadn't managed to control the internet or the stock market, but he did maintain control of his company. The SPAC deal established two categories of BuzzFeed stock, one of which controlled all the votes. Jonah would be the only one to hold that stock. It was the same type of arrangement Mark Zuckerberg had. BuzzFeed dryly disclosed in a federal filing that among its risks was Jonah's "concentrated control" and the fact that "Mr. Peretti may have interests that differ from those of the other stockholders and may vote in a way with which the other stockholders disagree." Indeed, NBC wasn't the only investor who believed Jonah had taken a low price in exchange for control. Kenny, in particular, had let his displeasure be known. But most of them were just happy to get a decent return. Jonah still had his company, his purchase on shaping the internet. He'd made it through. And he didn't want to buy a yacht. He was barely, by the standards of media executives, even paying himself a salary: $225,000 plus a bonus in 2020. He wanted to buy more internet companies with his stock. He was again, he felt, on a kind of a mission, on an adventure, another chance to shape a future digital world and win that bet with Cameron Marlow.

I can't help myself from rooting for Jonah, who is one of the few survivors of his era, cannier and more ruthless than he seemed. But I find myself, at the end of this, on Cameron's side of the bet. Jonah and Nick saw more clearly than anyone around them the cultural forces in the new internet, and it took enormous vision and drive to channel them, for a time. But this book has been, for me, a humbling exercise in what I missed, even as I was there. I hadn't realized the degree to which Anna Holmes's Jezebel pointed directly to social media a decade later. I hadn't understood the role of Nick's and Jonah's influences on my own decisions. And I certainly hadn't realized until I began reporting out this book the extent to which right-wing populism always seemed to be sitting just down the white Ikea table from this progressive internet scene, looking over its shoulder, learning its lessons. If Facebook's staff thought Barack Obama was the culmination of what they'd built, it turned out he was just a way station on the road to Donald Trump. Gasoline can create useful energy, but it can also simply burn, and by 2023 it seemed clear that the power of this new social energy had been to destroy any institution, from the media to the political establishment, that it touched. Those of us who work in media, politics, and technology are largely concerned now with figuring out how to hold these failing institutions together or to build new ones that are resistant to the forces we helped unleash.

Acknowledgments

This book, like most reporting, benefited from the generosity of dozens of people who didn't have to talk to me, but did because they wanted the history of this strange period rendered accurately. I am particularly grateful to Jonah Peretti and Nick Denton, who put up with questions that ranged from trivial to cosmic at all hours over a period of more than a year.

I'm also grateful to the people who got me into this mess: Seth Lipsky, who taught me to break news; Tom McGeveran and the late Peter Kaplan at *The New York Observer*, who started me blogging; John Harris, Jim Vande-Hei, and Robert Allbritton, who brought me to *Politico* and then let me go; and of course Kenny and Jonah for betting so heavily on my ideas about news at BuzzFeed. I'll also be eternally grateful to the political reporters who joined that insane, Twitter-centric venture in January of 2012—Andrew Kaczynski, Rosie Gray, Zeke Miller, McKay Coppins, Ruby Cramer, and the late, visionary Michael Hastings; to our colleagues including Scott Lamb, Ryan Broderick, Doree Shafrir, Ashley McCollum, and Katie Notopoulos, who somehow made it work in the earliest days.

My bosses at *The New York Times*—Carolyn Ryan, Jim Windolf, Ellen Pollock, and Dean Baquet—were generous enough to let me write this book (and interview *their boss* for it) while I was on the hook for them, and taught me a lot about the resilience of a great news organization.

The founding team at Semafor—Justin Smith, Garett Wiley, Gina Chua, Rachel Oppenheim, Steve Clemons, and Ojus Jain—put up with my casting a last look backward in the spring of 2022 as we navigated toward an entirely new media era.

Many of my friends and colleagues were sounding boards or sources of the ideas in this book (whether they realized it or not), including Katie Baker, Jim Bankoff, Heidi Blake, Kate Bolger, Andrea Breanna, Dylan Byers, Jessica Coen, Miriam Elder, Janine Gibson, Peter Hamby, Samantha Henig, Shani Hilton, Anna Holmes, Saeed Jones, Ivan Kolpakov, Scott Lamb, Jessica Lessin, Katherine Miller, Janice Min, Brian Morrissey, Casey Newton, Dao Nguyen, Lydia Polgreen, Will Porteous, Katie Robertson, Carole Robinson, Albert Samaha, Lockhart Steele, A. G. Sulzberger, Kara Swisher, Nabiha Syed, Katherine Thomson, Robert Thomson, Peggy Wang, and Sara Yasin.

The incomparable Julie Tate did a spectacular job checking the facts and the ideas. My agents, Keith Urbahn and Matt Latimer, made this process terrifyingly easy, and contributed trenchant ideas along the way. Maggie Haberman, writing her own book in parallel, kept me reasonably sane. The writer Michael Wolff explained to me how to write a book, and assigned and named this one. Scott Moyers, Mia Council, and Helen Rouner gave great advice, patience, and support, and made it an actual book.

My parents, Bob and Dian Smith, gave me ideas and edits. My kids, Hugo, Emma, and Eli, never let me take myself too seriously, and each contributed substantially to my thinking about digital media. Eli also built the pink and green keyboard I typed much of this book on. And I'd never have gotten anywhere professionally, and certainly not written this thing, without Liena Žagare, who always checks my assumptions and sharpens my ideas, and who was my sounding board, first reader, and toughest editor.

Notes

Chapter 1—The Bet

7 **Soon after he graduated:** Jonah Peretti, "Capitalism and Schizophrenia: Contemporary Visual Culture and the Acceleration of Identity Formation/Dissolution," *Negations* (Winter 1996), http://www.datawranglers.com/negations/issues/96w/96w_peretti.html.

8 **Arriving in Cambridge:** Jonah Peretti, "Clay," in *Falling for Science: Objects in Mind*, ed. Sherry Turkle (Cambridge, Mass: MIT Press, 2008), 63.

8 **The other chart:** Jonah Peretti, "Culture Jamming, Memes, Social Networks, and the Emerging Media Ecology: The 'Nike Sweatshop Email' as Object-to-Think-With," http://depts.washington.edu/ccce/polcommcampaigns/peretti.html.

9 **"A broad social and technical":** Peretti, "Culture Jamming, Memes, Social Networks."

Chapter 2—Traffic Control

12 **Those columns included:** Nick Denton, in *My First New York: Early Adventures in the Big City (As Remembered by Actors, Artists, Athletes, Chefs, Comedians, Filmmakers, Mayors, Models, Moguls, Porn Stars, Rockers, Writers, and Others)*, ed. David Haskell and Adam Moss (New York: Ecco Press, 2010).

13 **A later history of Wilton:** Richard Mayne, *In Victory, Magnanimity, in Peace, Goodwill: A History of Wilton Park* (London: Routledge Press, 2003).

13 **The Jewish history:** Catie Lazarus, "Nick Denton on Peter Thiel, Gawker, & Bankruptcy," November 2016, in *Employee of the Month, Slate*, podcast, 35:53, https://open.spotify.com/episode/4yJANagTk33PTHoG27HtXK?si=d8cc70250a134068.

13 **Nick was as a child:** Jay Rayner, "The Brit Dishing the Dirt on America," *The Guardian*, March 8, 2008, https://www.theguardian.com/technology/2008/mar/09/gawker.

14 **Instead, he chose to be:** This was the same impulse that would, half a decade later, drive a generation of journalists to the internet: if you felt like an outsider, and didn't want to climb a ladder that began with fetching coffee in New York or tea in London for unappreciative magazine editors, you could move to Prague or Budapest and prove yourself on the front lines of a huge story. Sometimes, it was the same exact people, from Nick Denton to me to the late nineties online news pioneers Will Welch and Ken Layne. Later, it would be foreign correspondents like Miriam Elder in Moscow who taught other journalists how to use social media platforms like Twitter.

14 **As a cub reporter:** Lazarus, "Nick Denton on Peter Thiel, Gawker, & Bankruptcy."

14 **the article took a turn:** Nick Denton, "Dreams of the Website Wannabes," Medium, September 14, 2016, https://medium.com/nicknotned/dreams-of-the-website-wannabes-87ecfba3602c.

15 **One startup guy:** Brian Abrams, *Gawker: An Oral History* (2015), loc. 44 of 1902, Kindle.

16 *The Guardian* **sniffed:** Amy Vickers, "First Tuesday: A Networking Success Story," *The Guardian*, August 31, 2000, https://www.theguardian.com/media/2000/aug/31/4.

16 **Nick gave the impression:** Abrams, *Gawker,* loc. 44 of 1902, Kindle.

16 **He imagined consumers:** Jason Kottke, "Whatever Happened to Moreover?," Kottke.org, October 22, 2003, http://kottke.org/03/10/moreover.

19 **Strikingly handsome with a dark complexion:** Maximillian Potter, "A.J. Daulerio Is Ready to Tell His (Whole) Gawker Story," *Esquire*, January 5, 2017, https://www.esquire.com/news-politics/a51625/aj-daulerio-interview.

19 **He had one of media's:** Abrams, *Gawker,* loc. 270 of 1902, Kindle.

20 **He illustrated the interview:** A.J. Daulerio, "Between a Rock and a Hard Place: Gawker's Elizabeth Spiers," *The Black Table*, July 10, 2003, https://web.archive.org/web/20070202071737/http://www.blacktable.com/daulerio030710.html.

Chapter 3—Black People Love Us

24 **His last great one:** Lola Ogunnaike, "Noticed; Black-White Harmony: Are You Kidding Me?," *New York Times,* November 17, 2002, https://www.nytimes.com/2002/11/17/style/noticed-black-white-harmony-are-you-kidding-me.html.

26 **Jonah stole the show:** Jonah Peretti, "My Nike Media Adventure," *The Nation,* March 22, 2001, https://www.thenation.com/article/archive/my-nike-media-adventure.

28 **Ultimately, Jonah and Watts:** Michael Shapiro, "Six Degrees of Aggregation," *Columbia Journalism Review,* May/June 2012, https://archives.cjr.org/cover_story/six_degrees_of_aggregation.php.

29 **But the** *Times* **ad:** Duncan Watts and Jonah Peretti," Viral Marketing for the Real World," *Harvard Business Review,* May 2007, https://hbr.org/2007/05/viral-marketing-for-the-real-world.

30 **"FD=The intern in my office":** "The Lost Washingtonienne," *Wonkette*, May 18, 2004, https://www.wonkette.com/the-lost-washingtonienne-wonkette-exclusive-etc-etc.

31 **Further to his detriment:** Ken Layne, "Yes We Can: Wonkette Goes Solo," *Wonkette*, April 14, 2008, https://www.wonkette.com/yes-we-can-wonkette-goes-solo.

32 **She had run for governor:** "Huffington Enters California Gubernatorial Race," CNN, August 7, 2003, https://www.cnn.com/2003/ALLPOLITICS/08/07/huffington .recall/.

32 **Her contact list contained:** Shapiro, "Six Degrees of Aggregation."

32 **When Kenny arrived:** Nina Mertz, "Arianna Huffington's Home Offers Family Charm," *Chicago Tribune*, June 22, 2008, https://www.chicagotribune.com/real -estate/chi-huffington-snoop-0622jun22-story.html.

32 **The room was full:** William D. Cohan, "Huffing and Puffing," *Vanity Fair*, February 2011, https://www.vanityfair.com/news/2011/02/ariana-huffington-201102.

33 **A leading political commentator:** "Drudge Report Sets Tone for National Political Coverage," ABC News, October 1, 2006, https://abcnews.go.com/WNT/story?id= 2514276&page=1.

Chapter 4—Drudge

36 **Matt Drudge was, in fact:** Matt Drudge, "Speech to the National Press Club on Media and the Internet," June 2, 1998, Washington, DC, https://www.americanrheto ric.com/speeches/mattdrugdenationalpressclub.htm.

36 **The two men connected:** "Breitbart Reveals Secret Drudge, Rush History to Hollywood Republicans," DemoCast, August 5, 2011, YouTube, filmed August 3, 2011, at the Hollywood Congress of Republicans meeting, North Hollywood, California, video, 33:45, https://www.youtube.com/watch?v=F9qR0n-KPVI&t=565s.

36 **Matthew Lysiak later reported:** Matthew Lysiak, *The Drudge Revolution: The Untold Story of How Talk Radio, Fox News, and a Gift Shop Clerk with an Internet Connection Took Down the Mainstream Media* (New York: BenBella Books, 2020).

37 **Andrew was awed:** "Breitbart Reveals Secret Drudge, Rush History," DemoCast.

38 **Andrew termed what she:** Rebecca Mead, "Rage Machine," *New Yorker*, May 17, 2010, https://www.newyorker.com/magazine/2010/05/24/rage-machine.

39 **They'd promised the publisher:** Lysiak, *The Drudge Revolution*.

39 **Even in 2005:** Lysiak, *The Drudge Revolution*.

39 **In Andrew's later tellings:** "Lists: What's Your Source for That?," *Reason*, October 2007, https://web.archive.org/web/20080919111403/http://www.reason.com/news /show/122048.html.

39 **Kenny at first saw Andrew:** Felix Salmon, "BuzzFeed's Jonah Peretti Goes Long," Matter, Medium, June 11, 2014, https://medium.com/matter/buzzfeeds-jonah-peretti -goes-long-e98cf13160e7.

40 **"He was terrified":** BuzzFeed Staff, "How Andrew Breitbart Helped Launch Huffington Post," BuzzFeed News, March 1, 2012, https://www.buzzfeednews.com/art icle/buzzfeedpolitics/how-andrew-breitbart-helped-launch-huffington-post.

40 **Andrew went crawling:** Kevin Roderick, "Breitbart Back to Drudge," *LA Observed*, June 22, 2005, http://www.laobserved.com/archive/2005/06/breitbart_back.php.

41 **"I want to help him":** Greg Sandoval, "Breitbart.com Has Drudge to Thank for Its Success," CNET, November 30, 2005, https://www.cnet.com/culture/breitbart-com -has-drudge-to-thank-for-its-success.

41 **In that telling:** Andrew Breitbart, *Righteous Indignation: Excuse Me While I Save the World!* (New York: Grand Central Books, 2012).

43 **"Three years ago":** Breitbart, *Righteous Indignation.*

Chapter 5—Contagious

44 **The Hollywood scoopster:** Sharon Waxman, "The Internet Remembers: Nikki Finke's DOA Verdict on HuffPo," *TheWrap*, February, 8, 2011, https://www.thewrap .com/internet-remembers-nikki-finkes-doa-verdict-huffington-post-24514.

45 **After reaching 1.9 million:** Data provided to the author by Andy Yaco-Mink.

46 **The former finance blogger:** "Gawker Exclusive: The Conde Nast Cafeteria," Gawker, March 24, 2003, https://gawker.com/011699/gawker-exclusive-the-conde -nast-cafeteria.

48 **The metric, of course:** Scott Rettberg, "Report from the Contagious Media Showdown Launch Thing," *Scott Rettberg* (blog), May 21, 2005, https://retts.net/index .php/2005/05/report-from-the-contagious-media-showndown-launch-thing-2.

49 **As an invitation asked:** Antlers, "Contagious Media Panel & Launch Party," *The Secret Life of Antlered Girls* (blog), May 19, 2005, http://antleredlife.blogspot.com /2005/05/contagious-media-panel-launch-party_19.html.

50 **"unlike the cumbersome":** Alex, "Forget-Me-Not Panties," Museum of Hoaxes, May 23, 2005, hoaxes.org/weblog/permalink/forget_me_not_panties.

50 **The site got 122,000:** "Contagious Media Showdown," May 2005, https://web .archive.org/web/20050626030139/http://showdown.contagiousmedia.org.

50 **puzzled Jay Leno:** The "Crying while Eating" clip from *The Tonight Show with Jay Leno* can be accessed here: https://vimeo.com/49733597.

Chapter 6—Valleywag

52 **He was cheap:** Vanessa Grigoriadis, "Everybody Sucks," *New York,* October 12, 2007, https://nymag.com/news/features/39319.

52 **In a world of Brooklyn:** Darren Rowse, "Verisign Buys Moreover," ProBlogger, October 11, 2005, https://problogger.com/verisign-buys-moreover.

54 **It's hard to capture:** Jessica Coen, "Gawker's 123 Reasons to Love New York Right Now," Gawker, December 21, 2005, https://gawker.com/144595/gawkers-123-reasons -to-love-new-york-right-now.

54 *The New York Times* **wrote:** Katharine Q. Seelye, "Memo Passed On; Job Is Lost," *New York Times,* October 25, 2005, https://www.nytimes.com/2005/10/25/business /media/memo-passed-on-job-is-lost.html.

54 **She lived by the hourly:** David Smith, interview by Brad Culbert, Webmasters' Library, accessed July 6, 2022, https://www.webmasterslibrary.com/interviews /readInterview_cid_sitemeter.html, Site Meter was, like so much of the 1990s

internet, a hobby. David Smith created it for his own website, then quickly got over-whelmed by his customers' needs.

55 **That was the spirit:** Data provided to the author by Lockhart Steele.

55 **"Do you understand you've hired":** Brian Abrams, *Gawker: An Oral History* (2015), loc. 677 of 1902. Kindle.

55 **Steele arrived at Franklin Street:** Abrams, Gawker, loc. 677 of 1902. Kindle.

55 **Nick would ask the editor:** Abrams, Gawker, loc. 767 of 1902, Kindle.

55 **Jessica welcomed AJ:** Jessica Coen, "Gawker Media Launches Oddjack," Gawker, June 1, 2015, https://gawker.com/106006%2Fgawker-media-launches-oddjack.

56 **They watched as Nick stood:** Jessica Coen, "Team Party Crash: Gawker Gets the Huffington Post Drunk," Gawker, September 23, 2005, https://gawker.com/127050/team-party-crash-gawker-gets-the-huffington-post-drunk.

56 **Then Huffington kicked off:** Tom Scocca, "The Gawker King," *New York Observer*, October 3, 2005.

57 **"No one can really argue'":** Tom Scocca, "The Gawker King," *New York Observer*, October 3, 2005, https://observer.com/2005/10/the-gawker-king/.

59 **She later learned that:** Rachel Sklar, "How a Night with Arianna Huffington Changed My Life," Medium, May 9, 2014, https://medium.com/thelist/how-a-night-with-arianna-huffington-changed-my-life-d9c3b7ecdc5b.

60 **Coen felt utterly:** "Animal New York Un-hibernates, Hosts Party," AdRants, October 23, 2005, http://www.adrants.com/2005/10/23.

63 **"There's an old saying":** Jessica Coen, "Fred Durst: Touch My Balls and My Ass and Then Sue Gawker," Gawker, March 4, 2005, https://gawker.com/035041/fred-durst-touch-my-balls-and-my-ass-and-then-sue-gawker.

64 **"I never meant the suit":** Mark, "Fred Durst Apologizes for Giving Us a Legal Reacharound," Gawker, March 8, 2005, https://www.gawker.com/035371/fred-durst-apologizes-for-giving-us-a-legal-reacharound.

64 **"Marissa Mayer used to date":** "Editorial: Google's Power Couple," Valleywag, February 2, 2006, https://web.archive.org/web/20060207012737/http://www.valleywag.com/tech/marissa-mayer/editorial-googles-power-couple-152210.php.

65 **One particular target:** Nick Douglas, "We Want to Know If You're Single Mark Zuckerberg so We Can Contact You Maybe," Gawker, September 8, 2006, https://www.gawker.com/199540%2Fwe-want-to-know-if-youre-single-mark-zuckerberg-so-we-can-contact-you-maybe.

65 **"Mark, get some shoes":** Nick Douglas, "Mark Zuckerberg, No One Wants to See Your Toes," Gawker, November 10, 2006, https://www.gawker.com/214115%2Fmark-zuckerberg-no-one-wants-to-see-your-toes.

66 **A week later, right after:** Nick Denton, "Smoking Sarah Lacy," Gawker, November 14, 2006, https://gawker.com/214733/smoking-sarah-lacy.

Chapter 7—Plateau

68 **That slogan, "The Internet Newspaper":** Lerer came up with the slogan, and doesn't think his junior staff knew what they were talking about. The words tied together

past and future, "made a connection between how people were getting their news and how people would get their news," he told me later.

71 **Now Jonah hired him:** Jonah Peretti, "CONTAGIOUS FESTIVAL!!!!!!!!!!," *Huff-Post*, March 1, 2006, https://www.huffpost.com/entry/contagious-festival_b_16577.

71 **The contest, hosted on:** Jonah Peretti, "How to Make Something Contagious," *Huff-Post*, February 7, 2006, https://www.huffpost.com/entry/how-to-make-something -con_b_15229.

72 **The victorious Vance Lehmkuhl:** Vance Lehmkuhl, "Huffington Post Contagious Festival: Winner," Vance Lehmkuhl Visual Portfolio, http://www.v4vance.com.

76 *The Gawker Guide:* Denton's deputy Gaby Darbyshire produced the book, with the help of a young standup comic who was close to the Gawker scene: Jonah's sister Chelsea Peretti.

76 **But instead it exposed:** Caroline McCarthy, "Report: 'Gawker Guide' Doesn't Con-quer Bestseller Lists," CNET, November 1, 2007, https://www.cnet.com/news/report -gawker-guide-doesnt-conquer-bestseller-lists.

76 **The book's failure:** Vanessa Grigoriadis, "Everybody Sucks," *New York*, October 12, 2007, https://nymag.com/news/features/39319. Why *were* we young New York jour-nalists so angry? *New York*'s Vanessa Grigoriadis identified the "rage of the creative underclass" in 2007, and captured the moment in one of the few pieces of commentary from that era that aged really well, noting that the backdrop was a "general decline of newspaper and magazine publishing" and the disappearance of the $200,000 a year publishing job: "Journalists are both haves and have-nots. They're at the feast, but know they don't really belong—they're fighting for table scraps, essentially—and it could all fall apart at any moment. Success is not solid. That's part of the weird fascin-ation with Gawker, part of why it still works, five years on—it's about the anxiety and class rage of New York's creative underclass." Gawker, she wrote, provides a "moral drama about who deserves success and who doesn't." Gawker was the "Manhattan ver-sion of social justice" to Grigoriadis, "a blog about being a writer in New York, with all the competition, envy, and self-hate that goes along with the insecurity of that position."

Chapter 8—Sideboob

79 **explained it bluntly:** BuzzFeed Staff, "The Mullet Strategy," BuzzFeed News, July 27, 2007, https://www.buzzfeednews.com/article/buzz/The_Mullet_Strategy.

Chapter 9—$5 a View

83 **Nick had always been:** Paul Boutin, "Denton to Pay Bloggers Based on Traffic," Gawker, January 1, 2008, https://www.gawker.com/339271/denton-to-pay-bloggers -based-on-traffic.

84 **This was an obsession:** Brian Abrams, *Gawker: An Oral History* (2015), loc. 788 of 1902, Kindle.

85 **On December 19, 2007, Thomas:** Owen Thomas, "Peter Thiel Is Totally Gay, People," Gawker, December 19, 2017, https://www.gawker.com/335894/peter-thiel-is -totally-gay-people.

86 **Thomas could, of course:** Owen Thomas, "Does Nick Denton Wish He Were Peter Thiel?," Gawker, July 11, 2008, https://gawker.com/5024376/does-nick-denton-wish -he-were-peter-thiel.

86 **Thiel was enraged:** Ryan Holiday, *Conspiracy: A True Story of Power, Sex, and a Billionaire's Secret Plot to Destroy a Media Empire* (New York: Penguin, 2018).

86 **The cheerleading tech blog:** Michael Arrington, "When Will We Have Our First Valleywag Suicide?," *TechCrunch*, March 3, 2008, https://techcrunch.com/2008/03 /02/when-will-we-have-our-first-valleywag-suicide.

86 **post about his own boss:** Thomas, "Does Nick Denton Wish He Were Peter Thiel?"

Chapter 10—Girly Gawker

90 **Her ambitions were:** Anna Holmes, "Bragging Rights & Birthdays: 3 Years of Jezebel.com," Jezebel, May 20, 2010, https://jezebel.com/bragging-rights-birthdays -3-years-of-jezebel-com-5543073.

92 **Tracie Egan was a:** [Tracie Egan], "A Lick in the Butt," *One D at a Time* (blog), October 30, 2006, https://web.archive.org/web/20061130153240/http://onedatatime.com.

92 **"In a world where lying":** Anna Holmes, "Faith Hill's 'Redbook' Photoshop Chop," Jezebel, July 17, 2007, https://jezebel.com/faith-hills-redbook-photoshop-chop-why -were-pissed-279203.

94 **Moe was skeptical:** Moe Tkacik, "Kennedy Flo$$bergz 4 Obama!," Jezebel, January 29, 2008, https://jezebel.com/kennedy-flo-bergz-4-obama-350075.

94 **Holmes couldn't help:** Holmes, "Bragging Rights & Birthdays."

95 **"It's pretty natural and obvious":** Anna snorted incredulously when I read her this quote in 2022. It wasn't predestined; it was something she *did*.

95 **When the writers veered:** This was, in retrospect, an early version of being canceled, though Anna recalls "that they had the power to make you upset, but they didn't have the power to cause you to lose your job or your friends." The stakes weren't very high, but it was stressful to go through it several times a day.

97 **As 2007 became 2008:** Joshua Stein, "'Most of the Damage Happened after I Passed Out,'" Gawker, January 2, 2008, https://gawker.com/339399/most-of-the-damage -happened-after-i-passed-out.

98 **"I felt pressured":** Slut Machine [Tracie Egan], "The AVN Convention & Awards: I Came, I Saw, & I Came Some More," Jezebel, January 16, 2009, https://jezebel.com /the-avn-convention-awards-i-came-i-saw-i-came-so-345284.

98 **So she thought she was:** Mindy Tucker, "Shoot the Messenger," With Reservation, June 30, 2008, http://withreservation.com/080630shoot2/reservation-slideshow .php?image=18.

99 **But Winstead couldn't:** Lizz Winstead, "Jezebelism," *HuffPost*, July 12, 2008, https://www.huffpost.com/entry/jezebelism_b_110903.

Chapter 11—Politics

102 **Monica Lewinsky affair:** Callum Borchers, "Arianna Huffington, and How the 'Enabler' Attack on Hillary Clinton First Sprouted," *Washington Post*, May 13, 2016,

https://www.washingtonpost.com/news/the-fix/wp/2016/05/13/when-arianna
-huffington-and-others-first-accused-hillary-clinton-of-being-an-enabler.

102 **Obama sought Kenny:** Jonah's jack-of-all trades function extended, once, to pretending to be Kenny's assistant when the phone rang with Obama's number. Once
Jonah had confirmed it was the senator himself on the phone, not an aide, Kenny
snatched it away.

103 **On business trips:** Paul Berry, interview by Laurie Segall, "Former HuffPo Exec on
Embracing Gender Fluidity," CNN, May 23, 2018, video, 4:41, https://www.cnn
.com/videos/cnnmoney/2018/05/23/paul-berry-gender-fluidity-love-huffington
-post-cnnmoney-orig.cnnmoney.

108 **You'd publish a story:** Max Read, "In the 2010s, BuzzFeed Made the World a Meme:
Jonah Peretti on the Dress, the Dossier, and the Next Pivot to Video," *Intelligencer,
New York*, November 26, 2019, https://nymag.com/intelligencer/2019/11/buzzfeed
-jonah-peretti-2010s.html.

Chapter 12—Digging Obama

109 **But he'd handled:** Amy Schatz, "BO, UR So Gr8," *Wall Street Journal*, May 26, 2007,
https://www.wsj.com/articles/SB118011947223614895.

110 **The platform went from:** Associated Press, "Number of Active Users of Facebook
over the Years," Yahoo Finance, October 23, 2012, https://finance.yahoo.com/news
/number-active-users-facebook-over-years-214600186--finance.html.

111 **Because Facebook wasn't quite:** Heather Havenstein, "My.BarackObama.com Social Network Stays Online after Election," *Computerworld*, November 10, 2008,
https://www.computerworld.com/article/2534052/my-barackobama-com-social
-network-stays-online-after-election.html.

112 **But what inspired the execs:** David Kirkpatrick, *The Facebook Effect: The Inside
Story of the Company That Is Connecting the World* (New York: Simon & Schuster,
2011).

113 **He went to bed:** Kirkpatrick, *The Facebook Effect*.

114 **Cerami had met:** Ari Berman, *Herding Donkeys: The Fight to Rebuild the Democratic Party and Reshape American Politics* (New York: Picador, 2012).

115 **In an email to Twitter's:** Nick Bilton, *Hatching Twitter: A True Story of Money,
Power, Friendship, and Betrayal* (New York: Portfolio, 2014).

115 **He speculated that if Facebook:** Steven Levy, "The Alternative Universe Where
Facebook Bought Twitter," *Wired*, March 6, 2020, https://www.wired.com/story
/the-alternate-universe-where-facebook-bought-twitter.

Chapter 13—$100 Million

117 **"I had looked over":** Joshua Green, *Devil's Bargain: Steve Bannon, Donald Trump,
and the Nationalist Uprising* (New York: Penguin Books, 2017).

120 **On November 4, 2008, Obama:** The top search term on *The Huffington Post* that
day was "Nailin Palin," the name of a porn video.

Chapter 14—Unique Visitors

124 **A prank that:** Jonah Peretti, "Yo Ashton! Thanks for Tweeting!," BuzzFeed, May 8, 2009, https://web.archive.org/web/20090508034302/http://www.buzzfeed.com /jonah/yo-ashton-thanks-for-tweeting.

125 **He called Jonah:** PageSix.com Staff, "Ashton Kutcher a Prank Victim," *New York Post,* May 10, 2009, https://pagesix.com/2009/05/10/ashton-kutcher-a-prank-victim.

126 **Meanwhile, the traffic climbed:** Jonah Peretti, "BuzzFeed Has Over 5 Million Readers!!!," BuzzFeed, December 24, 2009, https://web.archive.org/web/20091225114331 /http://www.buzzfeed.com/jonah/buzzfeed-has-over-5-million-readers.

126 **Jonah "is a bit":** Nick Denton (@nicknotned), "Jonah @Peretti is a bit of a dick. But he's one of the web's few original thinkers – and showed me the danger of the local maximum," Twitter, March 26, 2010, 12:18 p.m., https://twitter.com/nicknotned /status/11097315695.

128 **He led an $8 million:** Erick Schonfeld, "RRE Ventures, Ron Conway, and Founder Collective Bet $8 Million on BuzzFeed," *TechCrunch,* May 12, 2010, https://tech crunch.com/2010/05/12/buzzfeed-8-million.

130 **The social network had skyrocketed:** Associated Press, "Number of Active Users at Facebook over the Years," Yahoo News, May 1, 2013, https://news.yahoo.com /number-active-users-facebook-over-230449748.html.

Chapter 15—Breitbart Dot Com

134 **By publishing this video:** "Video Proof: The NAACP Awards Racism-2010," Breitbart News, July 19, 2010, https://www.breitbart.com/politics/2010/07/19/video-proof -the-naacp-awards-racism-2010.

Chapter 16—Dicks

138 **But that site got:** Brian Abrams, *Gawker: An Oral History* (2015), loc. 699 of 1902, Kindle.

138 **There, AJ's addictions:** A.J. Daulerio, "Astoria," *Small Bow* 3, no. 24, https://www .thesmallbow.com/top-newsletters/astoria.

138 **But Leitch quit in June:** Maximillian Potter, "A.J. Daulerio Is Ready to Tell His (Whole) Gawker Story," *Esquire,* January 5, 2017, https://www.esquire.com/news -politics/a51625/aj-daulerio-interview.

138 **AJ, all swagger:** Abrams, *Gawker,* loc. 1405 of 1902, Kindle.

139 **AJ belonged to:** A.J. Daulerio, interview by Aaron Lammer, "A.J. Daulerio, #213," September 28, 2016, in *Longform,* podcast, 1:02:16, https://longform.org/posts /longform-podcast-213-a-j-daulerio.

139 **The writer Maximillian Potter:** A.J. Daulerio, "Patriots Other Young Cheerleader Follows Well-Traveled Path to Stardom," Deadspin, November 3, 2008, https://dead spin.com/patriots-other-young-cheerleader-follows-well-traveled-5075170# viewcomments.

140 **In 2009, the creepier corners:** John Gonzalez, "Trafficking in Sleaze?," *Philadelphia Inquirer,* July 21, 2009, https://www.inquirer.com/philly/hp/sports/20090721 _Gonzo___Trafficking_in_sleaze_.html.

141   **The episode was a grotesque:** Nancy Dillon, "Erin Andrews Endures Brutal Cross Examination as Lawyer Suggests Nude Leak of Video Advanced Sportscaster's Career," *New York Daily News*, March 1, 2016, https://www.nydailynews.com/sports /erin-andrews-questioned-nude-video-helping-career-article-1.2549112.

141   **The next year, AJ published:** Gabriel Sherman, "Gawker Ex-Editor A.J. Daulerio: The Worldwide Leader in Sextapes," *GQ*, January 19, 2011, https://www.gq.com /story/aj-daulerio-deadspin-brett-favre-story.

141   **It looked to many observers:** Michael Sebastian, "Read Gawker's Shocking Response to a Video of a Young Woman Possibly Being Raped," *Cosmopolitan*, March 12, 2016, https:// www.cosmopolitan.com/politics/news/a55146/gawker-editor-sex -tape-aj-daulerio/.

141   **And it applied particularly:** Owen Thomas, "Mark Zuckerberg's Double Life," Gawker, July 9, 2007, https://www.gawker.com/276473/mark-zuckerbergs-double-life.

142   **But Tate concluded with trademark:** Ryan Tate, "Mark Zuckerberg's Age of Privacy Is Over," Gawker, July 28, 2010, https://www.gawker.com/5597100/mark-zuckerbergs -age-of-privacy-is-over.

142   **"I'd like to reach into":** A.J. Daulerio, "Brett Favre's Cellphone Seduction of Jenn Sterger (Update)," Deadspin, October 7, 2010, https://deadspin.com/brett-favres -cellphone-seduction-of-jenn-sterger-upda-5658206.

142   **Deadspin's equivalent of:** Sherman, "Gawker Ex-Editor A.J. Daulerio."

143   **Nick in a more honest:** John Hudson, "Nick Denton's Done Defending Himself," *The Atlantic*, March 8, 2011, https://www.theatlantic.com/culture/archive/2011/03 /nick-denton-done-defending-himself/348665.

143   **The post got nearly:** Ben McGrath, "Brett Favre, Deadspin, and the Streak," *The New Yorker*, October 29, 2010, https://www.newyorker.com/sports/sporting-scene /brett-favre-deadspin-and-the-streak.

143   **The Favre story rocked:** Potter, "A.J. Daulerio Is Ready to Tell His (Whole) Gawker Story."

143   **Writers who admired him:** Abrams, *Gawker*, loc. 1405 of 1902, Kindle.

143   **The editor of the porn site:** Abrams, *Gawker*, loc. 1687 of 1902, Kindle.

143   **it was up to 2.3 million:** Sherman, "Gawker Ex-Editor A.J. Daulerio."

144   **I emailed Weiner:** Jonathan Allen and Ben Smith, "Lewd Photo Was Hack, Weiner Says," *Politico*, May 28, 2011, https://www.politico.com/story/2011/05/lewd-photo -was-hack-weiner-says-055877.

145   **A week later, Andrew was:** Andrew Breitbart, *Righteous Indignation* (New York: Grand Central Books, 2012).

Chapter 17—Sold

147   **AOL still had:** Peter Kafka, "AOL's Amazing, Inexplicable Money Factory," *Recode*, August 6, 2014, https://www.vox.com/2014/8/6/11629584/aols-amazing-inexplicable -money-factory.

148   **He was particularly taken:** Jeff Bercovici, "The Honeymooners," *Forbes*, June 8, 2011, https://www.forbes.com/forbes/2011/0627/features-arianna-huffington-tim -armstrong-aol-honeymooners.html?sh=2d6c3c806050.

149 **But Arianna wanted:** My wife and collaborator, Liena Žagare, sold her network of local news sites to Patch and worked there during 2011, an astonishing year in which the company burned through more than $100 million on a dream that someone may actually figure out at some point, which is building a good business doing local news everywhere.

150 **By the time of the sale:** Jay Yarow, "Huffington Post's Traffic Spiked Last Month—Thank AOL?," *Insider*, April 8, 2011, https://www.businessinsider.com/huffpo-traffic-2011-4.

151 **Matt Stopera, a recent graduate:** Matt Stopera, "The Viral Web in Real Time," BuzzFeed, https://web.archive.org/web/20091216035708/buzzfeed.com/mjs538.

152 **The problems began:** BuzzFeed, "BuzzFeed Raises 15.5 Million," PRWeb, January 9, 2012, https://www.prweb.com/releases/2012/1/prweb9087897.htm.

152 **Google had wiped out websites:** Amit Singhal and Matt Cuts, "Finding More High-Quality Sites in Search," *Google Official Blog*, February 24, 2011, https://googleblog.blogspot.com/2011/02/finding-more-high-quality-sites-in.html.

153 **The update crushed:** Jeff Bercovici, "Congratulations, Demand Media. You're Still Pretty Dumb," *Forbes*, January 26, 2011, https://www.forbes.com/sites/jeffbercovici/2011/01/26/congratulations-demand-media-youre-still-pretty-dumb/?sh=51e053c85198.

154 **When he was sixteen:** Chris Ryan, "Britney Spears' Biggest Fan Shares His Britney Stash," MTV News, December 9, 2009, http://www.mtv.com/news/2294797/britney-spears-biggest-fan-shares-his-britney-stash.

155 **Suddenly the site was setting:** Megan Garber, "How Buzzfeed Got Its Biggest Traffic Day . . . Ever," NiemanLab, December 5, 2011, https://www.niemanlab.org/2011/12/how-buzzfeed-got-its-biggest-traffic-day-ever.

155 **He sold MTV:** Ryan Casey (@goryango), "loving the Beavis and Butthead takeover on Buttfeed uhhh I mean Buzzfeed," Twitter, October 26, 2011, 9:41 a.m., https://twitter.com/GoRyanGo/status/129190898385960961.

156 **But Kaplan had told him:** Nathan Heller, "The Cranky Wisdom of Peter Kaplan," *New Republic*, September 14, 2012, https://newrepublic.com/article/107247/the-cranky-wisdom-peter-kaplan.

Chapter 19—The Scoop

165 **At midnight, he and Johanesen:** BuzzFeed Staff, "Welcome to BuzzFeed Politics," BuzzFeed News, December 31, 2011, https://www.buzzfeednews.com/article/buzzfeedpolitics/welcome-to-buzzfeed-politics.

Chapter 20—LilyBoo

173 **"This is what Ferguson":** Matt Stopera, "48 Things That Will Make You Feel Old," BuzzFeed, November 4, 2012, https://web.archive.org/web/20121104014125/http://www.buzzfeed.com/mjs538/things-that-will-make-you-feel-old.

173 **His "13 Simple Steps":** Matt Stopera, "13 Simple Steps to Get You through a Rough Day," BuzzFeed, April 3, 2012, https://web.archive.org/web/20121104012124/http://www.buzzfeed.com/mjs538/13-simple-steps-to-get-you-through-a-rough-day.

174 **When BuzzFeed's traffic:** Jay Yarow, "Nick Denton Is Crushing BuzzFeed and Jonah Peretti Right Now in Gawker's Comments," *Insider,* April 26, 2012, https://www .businessinsider.com/nick-denton-on-buzzfeed-2012-4.

174 **In 2012, Nick and Derrence:** Max Read, "Did I Kill Gawker?," *Intelligencer, New York,* August 22, 2016, https://nymag.com/intelligencer/2016/08/did-i-kill-gawker.html.

175 **He also resolved:** A.J. Daulerio, "How Things Work," *Small Bow* 2, vol. 46, https:// www.thesmallbow.com/top-newsletters/how-things-work.

175 **"Because the internet":** Maximillian Potter, "A.J. Daulerio Is Ready to Tell His (Whole) Gawker Story," *Esquire,* January 5, 2017, https://www.esquire.com/news -politics/a51625/aj-daulerio-interview.

Chapter 21—Upworthy

177 **A low-profile hedge fund billionaire:** Zachary Mider, "What Kind of Man Spends Millions to Elect Ted Cruz?," *Bloomberg,* January 20, 2016, https://www.bloomberg .com/news/features/2016-01-20/what-kind-of-man-spends-millions-to-elect-ted -cruz-.

178 **But Andrew hadn't gotten much:** Matthew Lysiak, *The Drudge Revolution: The Untold Story of How Talk Radio Fox News, and a Gift Shop Clerk with an Internet Connection Took Down the Mainstream Media* (New York: BenBella Books, 2020).

178 **Another man at the bar:** Matthew Belloni, "Andrew Breitbart Talked Politics in L.A. Bar an Hour before Dying," *Hollywood Reporter,* March 1, 2012, https://www.holly woodreporter.com/news/general-news/andrew-breitbart-dead-la-bar-politics -296386.

178 **Andrew Breitbart collapsed:** Lysiak, *The Drudge Revolution.*

179 **He'd promised Breitbart:** McKay Coppins, "Breitbart's Inheritors Battle over His Legacy," BuzzFeed, October 22, 2012, https://www.buzzfeed.com/mckaycoppins /breitbarts-inheritors-battle-over-his-legacy.

180 **he warned presciently:** Eli Pariser, *The Filter Bubble: How the New Personalized Web Is Changing What We Read and How We Think* (New York: Penguin, 2011).

180 **As Iowa debated:** Angie Aker, "Two Lesbians Raised a Baby and This Is What They Got," MoveOn, November 30, 2011, https://front.moveon.org/two-lesbians-raised -a-baby-and-this-is-what-they-got.

181 *Fast Company* **called:** Anya Kamenetz, "How Upworthy Used Emotional Data to Become the Fastest Growing Media Site of All Time," *Fast Company,* June 7, 2013, https://www.fastcompany.com/3012649/how-upworthy-used-emotional-data -to-become-the-fastest-growing-media-site-of-all-time.

181 **By 2014, New York:** Nitsuh Abebe,"Watching Team Upworthy Work Is Enough to Make You a Cynic. Or Lose Your Cynicism. Or Both. Or Neither," *Intelligencer, New York,* March 23, 2014, https://nymag.com/intelligencer/2014/03/upworthy-team -explains-its-success.html.

182 **"Can Mark Zuckerberg save":** Charlie Warzel, "Facebook Drives Massive New Surge of Traffic to Publishers," BuzzFeed, November 20, 2013, https://www.buzzfeednews .com/article/charliewarzel/out-of-the-blue-facebook-is-now-driving-enormous -traffic-to.

182 **Upworthy seemed unstoppable:** Sam Sanders, "Upworthy Was One of the Hottest Sites Ever. You Won't Believe What Happened Next," *All Things Considered*, NPR, June 20, 2017, https://www.npr.org/sections/alltechconsidered/2017/06/20/533529538/upworthy-was-one-of-the-hottest-sites-ever-you-wont-believe-what-happened-next.

Chapter 22—Benny

189 **Zach's ticket was defeated:** Jason Pulliam, "Funds Letter Sparks Outrage," *Daily Iowan*, March 1, 2006, http://dailyiowan.lib.uiowa.edu/DI/2006/di2006-03-01.pdf.

189 **There was Senator Chris Dodd:** Benny Johnson, interview by David Rubin, "How to Win the Culture Wars with Star Wars Memes," *Rubin Report*, February 9, 2020, video, 1:04:56, https://www.youtube.com/watch?v=MEwNnR5BgWo.

190 **"The Germans could make":** Benny Johnson, "Find Your Inner Scientist: Benny Johnson at TEDxUIowa," December 7, 2013, video, 18:24, https://www.youtube.com/watch?v=hhxShMjw6Xg.

190 **But according to his university:** Email from University of Iowa spokesperson Anne Bassett to the author, May 27, 2021.

193 **Finally, our unflappable PR person:** Caity Weaver, "What GIF Is This?," Gawker, December 13, 2013, https://gawker.com/what-gif-is-this-1482760301.

Chapter 23—Disney

199 **The price on offer was:** Alyson Shontell, "BuzzFeed Is Now Valued at ~$200 Million, but Investors Think It Has Billion-Dollar Potential," *Insider*, January 3, 2013, https://www.businessinsider.com/buzzfeed-is-now-valued-at-200-million-investors-think-its-has-billion-dollar-potential-2013-1.

Chapter 24—The Dress

204 **He'd heard from other startup:** The other reason that startups prefer short leases is so that they can shrink quickly if they need to lay people off. Jonah hadn't yet considered that could be possible.

212 **Going forward, Facebook:** Max Read, "In the 2010s, BuzzFeed Made the World a Meme: Jonah Peretti on the Dress, the Dossier, and the Next Pivot to Video," *Intelligencer, New York*, November 26, 2019, https://nymag.com/intelligencer/2019/11/buzzfeed-jonah-peretti-2010s.html.

Chapter 25—$850 Million

213 **He invited the Gawker generations:** Amy Sohn, "Two Paths to the Same Destination," *New York Times*, June 8, 2014, https://www.nytimes.com/2014/06/08/fashion/weddings/two-paths-to-the-same-destination.html.

214 **This was disorienting:** Max Read, "Did I Kill Gawker?," *Intelligencer, New York*, August 22, 2016, https://nymag.com/intelligencer/2016/08/did-i-kill-gawker.html.

215 **"It always felt off":** *Nobody Speak: Trials of the Free Press*, directed by Brian Knappenberger (Netflix, 2017), https://www.netflix.com/title/80168227.

216   **over $1 million more:** Jeremy Barr, "A.J. Daulerio's 'Ratter' Has Raised More Than a Million," *Capital New York*, January 13, 2015, https://web.archive.org/web /20150212061620/http://www.capitalnewyork.com/article/media/2015/01/8559991 /aj-daulerios-ratter-has-raised-more-million; Lockhart Steele interview July 21, 2021, said 1.7 million.

216   *Ratter* **was all swagger:** John McDermott, "Former Gawker Editor A.J Daulerio on His New Local News Site," *Digiday*, March 28, 2014, https://web.archive.org/web /20150212084134/http://digiday.com/publishers/daulerio-ratter.

Chapter 26—Dinosaurs

221   **He knew his grandfather:** Julia M. Klein, "The NYT's Quiet Strategist," *Duke Magazine*, December 8, 2020, https://alumni.duke.edu/magazine/articles/nyts-quiet-strategist.

222   **Two decades later:** "Children of the Times," *New York*, October 13, 2008, https:// nymag.com/news/articles/08/10/20081013_sulzberger.pdf.

223   **When the Mexican billionaire:** Michael Hirschorn, "End Times," *The Atlantic*, January/February 2009, https://www.theatlantic.com/magazine/archive/2009/01/end -times/307220.

224   **It was, as in any:** When I arrived at the *Times*, one old-timer gave me this piece of advice: "The rule is: don't let anyone in the family find out what your name is."

226   **The internet sages:** Jeff Jarvis, "The Cockeyed Economics of Metering Reading," *BuzzMachine*, January 17, 2010, https://buzzmachine.com/2010/01/17/the-cockeyed -economics-of-metering-reading.

226   **NYU professor Clay Shirky:** Joshua Benton, "Clay Shirky: Let a Thousand Flowers Bloom to Replace Newspapers," NiemanLab, September 23, 2009, https://www.nie manlab.org/2009/09/clay-shirky-let-a-thousand-flowers-bloom-to-replace -newspapers-dont-build-a-paywall-around-a-public-good.

228   **The report remained:** Myles Tanzer, "Exclusive: New York Times Internal Report Painted Dire Digital Picture," BuzzFeed News, May 15, 2014, https://www.buzzfeed news.com/article/mylestanzer/exclusive-times-internal-report-painted-dire -digital-picture.

229   **Top** *Times* **executives blamed:** I can't reveal my source but did get their permission to say that the document came from neither Sulzberger nor Abramson.

229   **But what Perpich and Dolnick:** The three, to a degree little understood outside the *Times*, continue to see themselves as the institution's long-term stewards, and the true innermost conversation at the news organization takes place in their running lunches and dinners, coffees, and texts.

230   **"The report was just full":** David Barstow, interview with the author, April 2019. He and Sulzberger recall the conversation slightly differently.

Chapter 27—Gawker on Trial

232   **Nick tried to explain himself:** *Nobody Speak: Trials of the Free Press*, directed by Brian Knappenberger (Netflix, 2017), https://www.netflix.com/title/80168227.

233   **But the jury was visibly:** Eriq Gardner, "Gawker Trial: Editor Admits Hulk Hogan's Penis Isn't Newsworthy," *Hollywood Reporter*, March 14, 2016, https://www

.hollywoodreporter.com/business/business-news/gawker-trial-editor-admits-hulk
-875098.

233 **AJ's joke seemed:** Lloyd Grove, "A.J. Daulerio Doesn't Regret Child Sex Quip at
Hogan-Gawker Trial," *Daily Beast*, April 13, 2017, https://www.thedailybeast.com
/aj-daulerio-doesnt-regret-child-sex-quip-at-hogan-gawker-trial?ref=scroll.

234 **Or maybe, Nick thought more:** Nick Denton, "How Things Work," Gawker, August
22, 2016, https://gawker.com/how-things-work-1785604699.

234 **"Denton's unending lust":** Ryan Holiday, *Conspiracy: A True Story of Power, Sex, and
a Billionaire's Secret Plot to Destroy a Media Empire* (New York: Penguin, 2018).

235 **Being left out of that:** A.J. Daulerio, "How Things Work," *Small Bow* 2, no. 46,
https://www.thesmallbow.com/top-newsletters/how-things-work.

235 **AJ was left:** A.J. Daulerio, "Kill the Snakes," *Small Bow* 2 no. 26, https://www.the
smallbow.com/top-newsletters/kill-the-snakes.

235 **In rehab, Daulerio had learned:** Maximillian Potter, "A.J. Daulerio Is Ready to Tell
His (Whole) Gawker Story," *Esquire*, January 5, 2017, https://www.esquire.com
/news-politics/a51625/aj-daulerio-interview.

Chapter 28—Sentiment

238 **Jonah was already raising:** Disney's executives were furious all over again at the
news he'd gone with a rival.

239 **Then on March 2:** Michael S. Schmidt, "Hillary Clinton Used Personal Email
Account at State Dept., Possibly Breaking Rules," *New York Times*, March 2, 2015,
https://www.nytimes.com/2015/03/03/us/politics/hillary-clintons-use-of-private
-email-at-state-department-raises-flags.html.

239 **Facebook lit up:** Katherine Miller, "Facebook Conversation on Hillary Clinton Is
Getting More and More Negative," BuzzFeed News, March 9, 2015, https://www
.buzzfeednews.com/article/katherinemiller/facebook-conversation-on-hillary
-clinton-is-getting-more-and.

240 **BuzzFeed's political editor, Katherine Miller:** Katherine Miller, "Donald Trump
Has Been Dominating the Facebook Conversation, Too," BuzzFeed News, July 13,
2015, https://www.buzzfeednews.com/article/katherinemiller/we-shall-never-be
-again-as-we-were.

241 **And even as American publishers:** Craig Silverman and Lawrence Alexander, "How
Teens in the Balkans Are Duping Trump Supporters with Fake News," BuzzFeed
News, November 3, 2016, https://www.buzzfeednews.com/article/craigsilverman
/how-macedonia-became-a-global-hub-for-pro-trump-misinfo.

242 **Trump's own campaign:** Philip Bump, "All the Ways Trump's Campaign Was Aided
by Facebook, Ranked by Importance," *Washington Post*, March 22, 2018, https://
www.washingtonpost.com/news/politics/wp/2018/03/22/all-the-ways-trumps
-campaign-was-aided-by-facebook-ranked-by-importance.

242 **Still, the explanation that some:** Kevin Roose, Sheera Frankel, and Mike Isaac,
"Don't Tilt Scales against Trump, Facebook Executive Warns," *New York Times*,
January 7, 2020, https://www.nytimes.com/2020/01/07/technology/facebook-trump
-2020.html.

Chapter 29—The Dossier

249   **There, Steele calmly shared:** Barry Meier, *Spooked: The Trump Dossier, Black Cube, and the Secret Rise of Private Spies* (New York: Harper, 2021).

249   **"loved the cloak-and-dagger world":** Meier, *Spooked*.

253   **The *Times* published an article:** Sydney Ember and Michael M. Grynbaum, "Buzz Feed Posts Unverified Claims on Trump, Igniting a Debate," *New York Times*, January 10, 2017, https://www.nytimes.com/2017/01/10/business/buzzfeed-donald -trump-russia.html.

257   **FBI agent who:** Anne Applebaum, "'Who's Putting These Ideas in His Head?,'" *The Atlantic*, September 4, 2020, https://www.theatlantic.com/ideas/archive/2020/09 /anne-applebaum-interviews-peter-strzok/616003.

Chapter 30—Exile

262   **The internet had become:** Rick Webb, "My Internet Mea Culpa," Medium, December 26, 2017, https://medium.com/newco/my-internet-mea-culpa-f3ba77ac3eed.

263   **But, Nick wrote:** Nick Denton (@nicknotned), "Between the Gutenberg Press and the Enlightenment, came 200 years of religious war," Twitter, December 26, 2017, 2:30 p.m., https://twitter.com/nicknotned/status/945738730798829568.

Chapter 31—Down Arrow

264   **He came to be closer:** He sold his house to Sam Dolnick, the *Times* executive and Sulzberger cousin.

265   **white sanitary suits:** Tasneem Nashrulla, "We Blew Up a Watermelon and Everyone Lost Their Freaking Minds," BuzzFeed News, April 8, 2016, https://www.buzzfeed news.com/article/tasneemnashrulla/we-blew-up-a-watermelon-and-everyone-lost -their-freaking-min.

Chapter 32—Meaningful Social Engagement

272   **They had begun to pay:** Sahil Patel, "Inside Disney's troubled $675 Mil. Maker Studios Acquisition," *Digiday*, February 22, 2017, https://digiday.com/future-of-tv/dis ney-maker-studios.

275   **speakers were blasting:** Ishmael N. Daro and Craig Silverman, "How YouTube's 'Super Chat' System Is Pushing Video Creators toward More Extreme Content," BuzzFeed News, May 17, 2018, https://www.buzzfeednews.com/article/ishmaeldaro /youtube-comments-hate-speech-racist-white-nationalists-super.

275   **Facebook employees knew:** Keach Hagey and Jeff Horwitz, "Facebook Tried to Make Its Platform a Healthier Place. It Got Angrier Instead," *Wall Street Journal*, September 15, 2021, https://www.wsj.com/articles/facebook-algorithm-change -zuckerberg-11631654215.

276   **The company did figure:** Evelyn Douek, "The Year That Changed the Internet," *The Atlantic*, December 28, 2020, https://www.theatlantic.com/ideas/archive/2020/12 /how-2020-forced-facebook-and-twitter-step/617493.

Chapter 33—Layoffs

279 **By the time the books:** Financial information can be accessed here: https://www.sec .gov/Archives/edgar/data/1828972/000110465921098380/tm2122219-1_s4.htm.

283 **He'd once told an interviewer:** Ken Lerer, interview by Amy Chozick, "BuzzFeed's Chairman, Ken Lerer, Doesn't Mind Nepotism," *New York Times Magazine,* July 12, 2013, https://www.nytimes.com/2013/07/14/magazine/buzzfeeds-chairman-ken -lerer-doesnt-mind-nepotism.html.

285 **Still, Ozy's slick facade:** Craig Silverman, "A Bunch of Digital Publishers Bought Cheap Traffic and Later Found Out It Was Fraudulent," BuzzFeed News, December 27, 2017, https://www.buzzfeednews.com/article/craigsilverman/these-publishers -bought-millions-of-website-visits-they.

286 **On October 18, 2019:** "Verizon Seeks Buyer for HuffPost Website," *Financial Times,* October 18, 2019, https://www.ft.com/content/6e80c144-f1fb-11e9-ad1e-4367d8 281195.

287 **"Verizon is literally":** Peter Kafka (@pkafka), "Details: All-stock deal *plus* an investment in BuzzFeed from HuffPost owner Verizon. Which means Verizon is literally paying BuzzFeed to take over HuffPost," Twitter, November 19, 2020, 2:15 p.m., https://twitter.com/pkafka/status/1329503476624347136.

Chapter 34—Baked Alaska

291 **"Grizzly Bear Trappin'":** Erika Kelsey," Local Performer Stuffs Rap, Satire and Alas-kana into His Online Music Videos," *Anchorage Daily News,* August 2, 2013, https:// www.adn.com/arts/article/local-performer-stuffs-rap-satire-and-alaskana-his -online-music-videos/2013/08/03.

291 **"I cook moose":** Michelle Theriault Brooks, "He Went from a Childhood in An-chorage to Alt-right Fame. Now, the Social Media Personality Known as Baked Alaska Has Been Arrested for Storming the U.S. Capitol," *Anchorage Daily News,* January 16, 2021, https://www.adn.com/alaska-news/anchorage/2021/01/16/he-went -from-a-childhood-in-anchorage-to-alt-right-fame-now-the-social-media -personality-known-as-baked-alaska-been-arrested-for-storming-the-us-capitol.

294 **"You will not replace us":** "Unite the Right Pre Game Torch March," YouTube, April 17, 2018, video, 8:16, https://www.youtube.com/watch?v=HPPQScy9Z7M.

295 **He'd been deplatformed:** Ignacio Martinez, "The Atonement of an Alt-right Troll," *Daily Dot,* May 22, 2019, https://www.dailydot.com/layer8/baked-alaska-atonement -alt-right-deplatforming.

295 **It was easy to relate:** Tasneem Nashrulla, "We Blew Up a Watermelon and Everyone Lost Their Freaking Minds," BuzzFeed News, April 8, 2016, https://www.buzzfeed news.com/article/tasneemnashrulla/we-blew-up-a-watermelon-and-everyone-lost -their-freaking-min.

295 **His followers excitedly replied:** Hannah Gais (@hannahgais), "users on Tim Gio-net's, aka Baked Alaska, live stream on DLive are calling to give lawmakers the 'rope' and to 'hang all the congressmen' on DLive while he's streaming inside the Capitol building," Twitter, January 6, 2021, 3:15 p.m., https://twitter.com/hannahgais/status /1346913339000156162?lang=en.

296 **The federal court in Washington, DC:** United States District Court for the District of Columbia, Government's Sentencing Memo, July 14, 2021, https://context-cdn .washingtonpost.com/notes/prod/default/documents/b30cc701-33df-4bc8-a99c -0043194d607b/note/9ba32abe-1765-459e-b51f-7aa8b725e7a6.

297 **In January of 2022:** Anne Ryman, "Far-Right Streamer 'Baked Alaska' Found Guilty of Assault, Disorderly Conduct, Criminal Trespass in Scottsdale Case," *Arizona Republic*, November 1, 2021, https://www.azcentral.com/story/news/local/scottsdale /2021/11/01/far-right-streamer-baked-alaska-found-guilty-of-assault-disorderly -conduct-scottsdale/6237640001/.

297 **he appeared in federal court:** Ryan J. Reilly, "Judge Nixes Jan. 6 Plea Deal after Right Wing Streamer 'Baked Alaskas' Declares Himself 'Innocent,'" NBC News, May 11, 2022, https://www.nbcnews.com/politics/justice-department/judge-nixes-jan-6-plea -right-wing-streamer-baked-alaska-declares-innoc-rcna28245.

Chapter 35—Conclusion

302 **Now he'd outmaneuvered rivals:** I didn't have that obstacle and could have sold the options I held—a glaring conflict of interest the *Times* had temporarily tolerated— at once, had there been buyers. Instead I held most of them, selling slowly as the shares fell from ten dollars to four dollars, still amazed that I'd made what seemed like a small fortune from Jonah's dreams.

303 **BuzzFeed dryly disclosed:** SEC filing can be accessed at https://www.sec.gov /Archives/edgar/data/1828972/000110465921098380/tm2122219-1_s4.htm.

Sources

Sections of this book rely on the work of a handful of authors who captured snapshots of the emerging new media world before it faded into memory.

- Brian Abrams's 2015 *Gawker: An Oral History* gave virtually all the people involved in Gawker's founding space the opportunity to reflect candidly on their project before the next year's catastrophe colored their memories, and I've quoted widely from it throughout *Traffic*.

- Matt Lysiak's 2015 *The Drudge Revolution* includes a trove of reporting both on Drudge and on Andrew Breitbart, all the more impressive because Lysiak's subject didn't cooperate with him, and I relied on it heavily for understanding Andrew, Matt, and their relationship.

- Ryan Holiday's 2018 *Conspiracy* supplied both secret narrative and Peter Thiel's motivations in the plot against Gawker (along with a lot of digressions about classicism), and his reporting undergirds parts of chapters 9 and 27.

- David Kirkpatrick's 2010 *The Facebook Effect* offers a rare glimpse at how Facebook saw itself, and how episodes like the One Million Voices Against FARC shaped its own actions and identity.

- Steven Levy's 2020 *Facebook: The Inside Story* helped me understand how the company and our perceptions of it had changed.

- AJ Daulerio's beautiful newsletter on sobriety, *The Small Bow*, offered a glimpse of both his own experience and Aileen Gallagher's, and allowed me to include his perspective though Daulerio didn't cooperate with this book.

- Hannes Grassegger has uncanny instincts for news, and his as yet unpublished account of his time with Nick Denton in Zurich was the basis for much of chapter 30.

- Jill Abramson's 2020 *Merchants of Truth* gave her perspective on the struggles over innovation at *The New York Times*, which forms part of chapter 26.

- Keach Hagey and Jeff Horwitz's 2021 exposé of Facebook's internal debate over "meaningful social engagement" offered the inside story of what Jonah Peretti and I had experienced at BuzzFeed.

- Craig Silverman's reporting on the fake news teens in Veles, Macedonia, was far ahead of its time in understanding the causes of our polluted news ecosystem, and informed that section and much of this book.

This book also relied heavily on interviews with dozens of its participants, named and unnamed in the text, including Cory Arcangel, Scott Baker, Jim Bankoff, David Barstow, Chris Batty, Matthew Bechstein, Ken Bensinger, Kate Bolger, Erin Bried, Nic Carlson, Michael Charles, Jessica Coen, Ana Marie Cox, Jake Dobkin, Sam Dolnick, Miriam Elder, Scott English, Sheera Frenkel, Michael Frumin, David Galbraith, Andrew Gauthier, Jen Gerson, Michael Golden, Emily Gould, Leba Haber, Donna Haraway, Fred Harman, Shani Hilton, Cates Holderness, Anna Holmes, James Hong, Meg Hourihan, Arianna Huffington, Chris Johanesen, Benny Johnson, John Johnson, Saeed Jones, Foster Kamer, Will Kane, Jason Kottke, Sarah Lacy, Scott Lamb, Jonathan Landman, Will Leitch, Jason Leopold, Sam Lessin, Cliff Levy, David Mack, Ornela March, Cameron Marlow, Joel Maske, Ashley McCollum, Bary Meier, Katherine Miller, Matt Mittenthal, Tracie Egan Morrissey, Dao Nguyen, Martin Nisenholtz, Jesse Oxfeld, Eli Pariser, Della Peretti, David Perpich, Will

Porteous, Max Read, Oliver Reichenstein, Carole Robinson, Kevin Roose, Joe Rospars, Joshua Schachter, Vivian Schiller, Mark Schoofs, Ben Shapiro, Doree Shafrir, Jack Shepherd, Tim Shey, Rachel Sklar, Paul Smurl, Elizabeth Spiers, Scott Stanford, Lockhart Steele, Jon Steinberg, Colin Sterling, Dodai Stewart, Lee Stranahan, A. G. Sulzberger, Nabiha Syed, Ryan Tate, Owen Thomas, Katherine Thomson, Maureen Tkacik, Peggy Wang, Duncan Watts, Will Welch, Mark Wilkie, Lizz Winstead, Andy Yaco-Mink, and Katharine Zaleski, as well as many others including current and former executives at Facebook and Disney, current and former employees of BuzzFeed, and former employees of Gawker Media.

Archive.org was indispensable for its role in preserving the eroding history of the internet.

Finally, Jonah Peretti answered endless questions over quick-turn emails and long interviews in Los Angeles. Nick Denton, true to character, participated in this book extensively but only in writing, texting quick answers to questions and responding to others in a Google doc. The experience gave me an idea for a text-based app for collaboration on book projects.

Index